THE DICTIONARY OF
DREAMS
AND THEIR
MEANINGS

THE DICTIONARY OF
Dreams
AND THEIR
MEANINGS

RICHARD CRAZE

HERMES
HOUSE

This edition is published by Hermes House
an imprint of Anness Publishing Ltd
Hermes House, 88–89 Blackfriars Road, London SE1 8HA
tel. 020 7401 2077; fax 020 7633 9499
www.hermeshouse.com; www.annesspublishing.com

Anness Publishing has a new picture agency outlet
for images for publishing, promotions or advertising. Please visit
our website www.practicalpictures.com for more information.

ETHICAL TRADING POLICY
Because of our ongoing ecological investment programme,
you, as our customer, can have the pleasure and reassurance of
knowing that a tree is being cultivated on your behalf to
naturally replace the materials used to make the book you are
holding For further information about this scheme, go to
www.annesspublishing.com/trees

PUBLISHER: Joanna Lorenz
EDITORIAL DIRECTOR: Helen Sudell
SENIOR EDITOR: Joanne Rippin
ADDITIONAL TEXT: Raje Airey and Jenny Barrett
PICTURE RESEARCHER: Frances Vargo
For picture acknowledgements see p252
DESIGNER: Adelle Morris
EDITORIAL READER: Kate Humby
PRODUCTION MANAGER: Steve Lang

A CIP catalogue record for this book is available
from the British Library

CONTENTS

Introduction   6

PART ONE:

ALL ABOUT DREAMING

Why We Dream 10

Dreaming Through History 12

The Nature of Dreams 36

The Sense and Substance of Dreams 54

Working with Dreams 72

PART TWO:

THE DREAM LEXICON

Abstract Qualities 100

Nature Dreams 118

The Cycle of Life 138

Mind, Body and Spirit 152

Engaging with People 172

Living in the World 196

Movement, Machines and Structures 218

Magic and Fantasy 238

Acknowledgements 252

Index 253

INTRODUCTION

In practically every age and culture, dreams have fascinated and puzzled us and we have searched for countless ways to understand their significance and to interpret their meaning. There is a famous story told by the Taoist philosopher Chuang-tzu (399-295 BC). While sleeping he had a dream in which he dreamt he was a butterfly. He could fly and land on flowers, drawing up nectar and feeling the warmth of the sun on his wings. The dream was so vivid that when he woke he couldn't decide who he was: was he a man dreaming he was a butterfly, or could he be a butterfly dreaming he was a man?

When we sleep we drift into another dimension, a dimension that is not bound by space or time. In this magical land the impossible becomes possible, and the nonsensical appears perfectly plausible. This is the land of dreams, a mysterious shape-shifting world where boundaries dissolve and merge, so that when we wake it can take a moment to distinguish between what is a dream and what is not. As Chuang-tzu's story illustrates, our dreams can cause us to question how we see the world and ourselves and how we define what is "real". This is not to say that there is genuine confusion between the outer world in which we live our lives and the world of dreams. Where confusion exists, it is usually labelled insanity. Rather it is an acknowledgement of a different dimension and of a different experience. For dreams are from the inner world, having their own internal logic and subjective meaning and are as valid in their own way as what is happening in the world "out there".

VALUING DREAMS

Among many cultures the dream experience is valued and the mysteries of sleep and dreaming are taken seriously. Whenever this is the case, dream interpretation is also valued. In early cultures for instance, shamans, priests or sages were consulted and their position in society was revered. For a long time in Western society, an interest in dreams went underground. Dreams were variously associated with insanity or were the work of the devil, or were simply written off as meaningless nonsense. These attitudes were revolutionized in the 20th century with fresh insights from science and psychotherapy. Since then our interest in dreams has been growing at a remarkable rate, as more and more of us search for ways to make sense of our lives and to fulfil our potential. We are recognizing that our dreams, far from being nonsense or a sign of mental illness, often contain intriguing and valuable information, which, once decoded, can help us understand our subconscious. We are also learning how to become our own dream interpreters.

ABOUT THIS BOOK

This book is a guide to making sense of dreams. It recognizes that no two people are exactly alike and therefore no two dreams are the same. When interpreting dreams the book takes the view that it is experience rather than theory that counts: you can become your own dream expert. This approach is very different to many dream dictionaries where it is possible to "look up" the meaning of a particular dream symbol or theme and "apply" it to your dream. For instance, you may dream of a tree. Some dream books may say that a tree signifies growth, and if it is bearing fruit, that it prophesies abundance and wealth. What they fail to do is encourage you to look at the tree itself and find out what it means for you. To do this is to approach your dream and yourself with a spirit of enquiry, asking questions about the dream content in order to arrive at your own understanding.

The book is divided into two main sections. The first contains chapters on the history, nature and sense of dreams as well as one on working with dreams. This section is intended to give an overview of dream theories, past and present, and to provide information that can help you recognize different types of dream and dream symbols. It also offers practical suggestions for how to program your dreams and to improve dream recall, as well as techniques to help you unravel the mystery of your dreams.

The second section is the Dream Lexicon. Divided thematically, it begins with an exploration of the world we live in – its abstract qualities and the natural environment. It then looks at our own development through the cycles of life, and aspects of mind, body and spirit. Other people and how we engage with them and with the world at large are discussed in the following chapters, along with a section on motion and mechanics. Lastly we see how magic and fantasy figure in our dreams.

It is hoped that you will find what is here both illuminating and stimulating and can use it as a springboard for further discovery. Remember, dreams come from the dark, the time of the moon, madness and mystery. To understand them, you need to feel your way around, using intuition and instinct rather than reason and logic, and so begin to unlock the secrets of the night.

Trust in dreams, for in them is the hidden gate to eternity.   KAHLIL GIBRAN

ABOVE Artists for centuries have tried to portray their dreams in pictorial representation. What they paint and what we dream may not seem the same but we share the same need to purge the internal demons of dream.

LEFT Images of dreams are but an instant, frozen in time forever, whereas in reality our dreams are flexible, ongoing, and changing rapidly and continuously.

BELOW Surrealist art for most people seems to come closest to how we sense our dreams and may help us to convey the feel of a dream, if not its reality.

ABOVE Sometimes an artist does seem to crystallize a moment in a dream that can haunt us all of our lives.

PART ONE

ALL ABOUT DREAMING

Theories of dreaming have varied widely over time and across cultures. To the ancients, dreams were regarded as messages from the gods or as oracles to predict the future. It was widely believed that dreams had the power to solve problems, heal sickness and bring spiritual revelation. In more recent times, dreams became the subject of psychological and scientific investigation. Widely recognized as the product of the unconscious mind, dream activity is now measured in sleep laboratories.

This section combines the wisdom of the past with contemporary understanding to provide a detailed picture, which tells us all about dreaming. It begins with a historical and cultural overview to the role of dreams. This is followed by an exploration of the nature of dreams, looking at influential ideas from modern times and describing different types of dreams. We then examine the sense and substance of dreams, and finally look at how to work with, and become more aware of, your dream world.

WHY WE DREAM

THERE ARE FEW THINGS WE DO WITH SUCH REGULARITY AND INTENSITY AS SLEEP AND DREAM. WE SPEND ALMOST ONE THIRD OF OUR LIVES SLEEPING AND WE DREAM – ON AVERAGE FOR A TOTAL OF TWO HOURS OR SO – EVERY NIGHT. YET PRECISELY WHY WE DREAM IS STILL UNCERTAIN. MANY THEORIES HAVE BEEN PUT FORWARD: FOR THE SCIENTIST, DREAMS ARE A PRODUCT OF A CERTAIN KIND OF SLEEP AND A WAY FOR THE BRAIN TO PROCESS IMPORTANT DATA; FOR THE MYSTIC, THEY ARE AN OPPORTUNITY FOR THE SOUL TO LEAVE THE BODY AND EXPERIENCE OTHER DIMENSIONS; WHILE FOR THE PSYCHOLOGIST THEY REPRESENT THE WORKINGS OF THE UNCONSCIOUS MIND.

ABOVE Whatever we think we know about dreams is forgotten when we fall asleep and enter the strange reality of the dream world, where physical laws are suspended and a different reality takes place.

SLEEP PATTERNS

Through a night of around seven to eight hours of undisturbed sleep, we experience two alternating types of sleep: orthodox or slow-wave deep sleep, and paradoxical or light sleep. Orthodox sleep lasts for about 90 minutes, and is followed by a shorter period of paradoxical sleep. Paradoxical sleep is marked by rapid eye movements (REM) and it is during this type of sleep that we dream. This alternating cycle goes on through the night, with the REM phase gradually increasing in length with each subsequent cycle, until after about seven or eight hours' sleep it can last for up to half an hour or more. As we get older, the length of time we spend in REM sleep diminishes, while at the other end of the scale, it has been found that young babies spend extended periods of time in REM.

THE ROLE OF DREAMING

Scientific research also indicates that in the later stages of gestation the unborn child exhibits signs of REM activity in the womb. This has led to the

suggestion that dreaming is somehow linked with human growth and development. Similarly, laboratory testing has shown that if you deprive people of REM sleep, the subject becomes unwell very fast. Within a few days, unpleasant symptoms such as depression, anxiety, nausea, irritability and general disorientation are experienced. Irrespective of whether or not we remember them, it seems our dreams play an important part in health and wellbeing. It has even been suggested that we sleep in order to dream.

A LITTLE DEATH

Many believe that our dreams are also linked with spiritual growth. In some esoteric traditions for instance, sleep is regarded as an intermediate stage between life and death. Every night we experience a "little death" as we fall into unconsciousness, and dreams are regarded as gateways into altered states of mind. Learning how to navigate the world of dreams becomes an important preparation for when the soul will eventually leave the body permanently

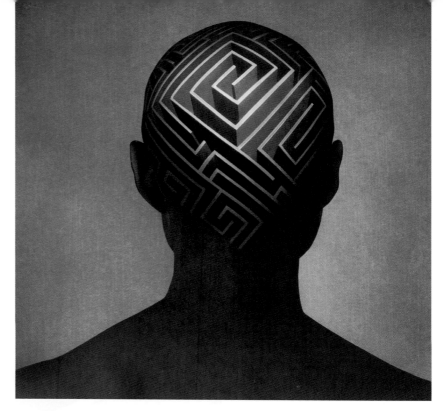

at death. Initiates are taught how to prepare themselves for sleep and dreaming, learning how to influence the dreaming state and to bring back experiences from the dream world.

THE POWER OF THE UNCONSCIOUS

This dream world is not something that exists outside of ourselves but resides deep within. In psychological terms, it is regarded as a product of the unconscious mind.

The unconscious may be described as the deepest level of the psyche in which impulses are held in a dynamic, but repressed state. In contrast to the relatively small proportion of things of which we are aware, the unconscious is a massive storehouse of memories, dreams and reflections, both personal and, some believe, transpersonal. By bringing unconscious material up from the hidden depths of the mind and out into the open, our dreams are a way of gaining greater self-knowledge. They are a way of increasing our conscious awareness and becoming wise. From this perspective, dreams are no longer seen as messages from gods or other independent agents outside of ourselves, but as messages from within.

THE LANGUAGE OF DREAMS

In order to interpret these messages from the unconscious, we need to understand the language of dreams. During the day, the conscious mind is in control and we negotiate the everyday world through reason and logic. At night, the unconscious mind takes over and enters the dream world, using visual imagery, symbols and metaphors. These can elicit a deep emotional response. To understand our dreams we need to listen with the heart rather than the head, developing our intuition while temporarily suspending judgement and disbelief.

LEFT Sometimes we don't remember our dreams but that doesn't mean they aren't continually occurring in our sleeping minds.
BELOW Do babies still in the womb dream? And if they do, where on earth do their dream images and impulses come from?

We are such stuff
As dreams are made on;
and our little life
Is rounded with a sleep.

WILLIAM SHAKESPEARE, THE TEMPEST

ANIMALS' SLEEP

Dreaming does not seem to be confined to human beings. Different animal species also exhibit signs of REM sleep and dreaming. Cats, for instance, enter deep-wave sleep about 30 minutes after sleep onset. In that condition, their neck muscles are fully relaxed and slight twitching of the rest of the body may be observed. Although we do not know what the cat is experiencing, we assume that it is a vivid dream.

DREAMING THROUGH HISTORY

Since time immemorial, our dreams have been a source of awe and wonder. At various points in history, they have been seen as messages from the gods, and supernatural experiences involving visions of the future, as well as indications of the state of our physical and mental health. Dreams have been used to shed light on the past, gain understanding of the present, and even to predict the future. This has not only been true for individuals, but also for whole nations. Some dreams have even changed the course of history.

In this section we will look at how dreams have been regarded through the ages, in the ancient and classical world, in India and the Far East, in Europe and in traditional societies. We will also look at the important role they have played in some of the world's major religions, including Buddhism, Christianity and Islam.

SINCE THE DAWN OF TIME

HOW LONG IS IT SINCE WE BEGAN DREAMING? WE HAVE NO SURE WAY OF KNOWING, BUT STRETCHING BACK INTO THE MISTS OF PREHISTORY, CAVE PAINTINGS IN FRANCE FROM THE NEANDERTHAL PERIOD SEEM TO INDICATE SOME SORT OF DREAM DRAWINGS ABOVE THE HEADS OF THE HUNTERS. THOUSANDS OF YEARS LATER WHEN PEOPLE BEGAN TO DISCOVER WAYS OF WRITING, THEY NOTED DOWN THEIR DREAMS. WE KNOW THAT DREAMING WAS AN IMPORTANT PART OF LIFE IN THE ANCIENT CIVILIZATIONS OF SUMER, ASSYRIA, BABYLONIA AND EGYPT. DREAMS WERE ASSOCIATED WITH DIVINE OR SUPERNATURAL POWERS, AND TEMPLES WERE DEDICATED TO THE GODS OF DREAMS.

THE FIRST DREAM RECORDS

Clay tablets dating back to around 3000 BC provide some of the earliest surviving writings of the human race. These tablets include the dream books of the Assyrians and Babylonians, discovered at Nineveh in the library of Ashurbanipal (c.669-626 BC), an Assyrian king. Other similar tablets were discovered during excavations of a pyramid-type temple at E-zida, in Mesopotamia, on the top of which was a shrine to Nabu, the Sumerian god of wisdom. The tablets' cuneiform script reveals fragments of the Babylonian epic of Gilgamesh, the legendary warrior king of Sumer. They also tell us about Gilgamesh's dreams and how his mother, the goddess Ninsun, interprets them. Her interpretation is often credited with being the first dream analysis, or at least the first for which we have a written record.

THE DREAMS OF GILGAMESH

Night after night, the aggressively powerful warrior king of Sumer, Gilgamesh, was troubled by bad dreams. Disturbed, Gilgamesh takes the dreams to his mother, who tells him that someone as powerful as himself is about to enter his life. She predicted that his struggles to gain supremacy over the newcomer will fail, but that the two men will become close companions and together achieve great feats. Later on in the epic, Ninsun's interpretation proves correct when Gilgamesh meets Enkidu, a "wild man" (an embodiment of an uncivilized, "primordial" human) who does indeed become his friend and helps bring Gilgamesh back down to earth. Further on in the tale, Gilgamesh is warned in another dream of the death of Enkidu, which also comes to pass.

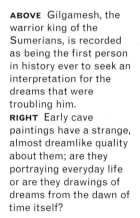

ABOVE Gilgamesh, the warrior king of the Sumerians, is recorded as being the first person in history ever to seek an interpretation for the dreams that were troubling him.
RIGHT Early cave paintings have a strange, almost dreamlike quality about them; are they portraying everyday life or are they drawings of dreams from the dawn of time itself?

PORTENTOUS DREAMS

The primary interest in dreams at this time seems to have been in the salutary warnings they could provide about the future, although dreams were also used as a form of gambling, where the dream symbols were used to predict lucky wins. Furthermore the Assyrian and Babylonian dream books also reveal a concern with the dangerous aspect of dreams, allegedly sent by demons and spirits of the dead. To protect themselves from such harmful influences, people built temples to Mamu, the Babylonian goddess of dreams, and propitiatory rites were practised in her name. An Za Qa, the god of dreams, was recognized and worshipped by the Sumerians, Assyrians and Babylonians.

MYTHOLOGY OF DREAMS

Looking at the mythology of any ancient civilization has been likened to reading a dream. That is because these stories represent what are sometimes referred to as the "cultural pattern dreams" of that civilization. In other words, the gods and goddesses, the heroes and villains, and the shapes and symbols of the stories are the same ones that people would have dreamt of night after night. These characters represent what are known as "archetypal" images, presenting us with the themes and concerns that have always struck a chord deep within the heart and soul of humankind. Irrespective of time or place, these stories are able to teach or remind us of universal truths.

ABOVE In Babylon vast temples were built dedicated to Mamu, the Babylonian goddess of dreams; and dream interpretation was elevated to the status of a religion.

THE GODDESS ISHTAR

Throughout the ancient world, the Moon was worshipped in various forms. The Babylonian goddess Ishtar was known as Ashtarte in Canaan, Isis in ancient Egypt and Artemis in ancient Greece. Like the moon in its waxing aspect, the goddess is a symbol of fertility and all life emanates from her, yet like the waning or dark moon, she is also the destroyer, the one who disappears into the darkness. However, like the crescent moon, the goddess is reborn and appears once again in her beneficent aspect.

The story of Ishtar's descent into the underworld, where she is tortured and bleeds to death before being revived by the twins Plant and Water of Life, is a myth of regeneration, symbolizing the cyclical nature of life and the passage between worlds.

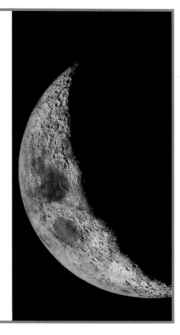

ABOVE Egyptian pharaohs were accorded the status of gods and were therefore linked with dream travel.
ABOVE RIGHT The city of Thebes, source of a papyrus thought to be the first dream record.

ANCIENT EGYPT

Like the Babylonians, the Egyptians also regarded dreams as warnings, although they believed they came from the gods rather than from spirits or demons. The Egyptians viewed dreams as a portal, a gateway to another world which they passed through every night. Here in this other world they could travel in their astral or "dream body", gathering knowledge of far distant places, conversing with the gods and meeting with the spirits of the dead. In general, dreams were regarded as helpful, although they could also be malevolent. In order to avert disaster the gods demanded penance and sacrifices, although they would also answer questions put to them by the dreamer in a practice known as "dream incubation".

DREAM INCUBATION

The practice of dream incubation was widely observed throughout the ancient world, although our first record of it comes from ancient Egypt. Throughout the land, a number of temples, known as "serapeums", were dedicated to Serapis, the god of dreams and dreaming. The most famous of these was at Memphis, dating back to around 3000 BC.

Thebes was another important site. It was in such temples that dream incubation was practised. This was an intensely ritualistic procedure intended to encourage an especially informative dream from the gods. Dream incubation seems to have been very popular and was used for a variety of purposes, including seeking remedies for particular illnesses, obtaining guidance on relationship and/or personal issues and predicting what the future had in store. The practice was often dedicated to Imhotep, the god of healing.

INCUBATION RITUALS

Ritualistic preparations for dream incubation were extremely complex and could last for several days. Typically the incubant (the dreamer) would take part in purification practices, such as fasting, bathing and abstaining from sex, they would also make prayers and offerings to the gods. Sometimes harmless snakes were placed around the dreamer's bed at the serapeum and the dreamer would then go to sleep with his or her request in mind. Through their own rituals, while the dreamer slept, the temple priests often helped to "seed" the dreamer's request. At times a "stand-in" dreamer was used in place of the

THE DREAM OF THOTMES IV

One very early prophetic dream dates back to around 1420 BC. It is recorded on a sheet of granite and held between the paws of the great sphinx at Giza where it can still be seen today (right).

While sleeping next to the sphinx, Thotmes dreamt that he would one day be ruler of Egypt and have a long and prosperous reign. However, for the dream to come true, the gods told Thotmes that he had to clear away the sand from the statue. At that time, the sphinx was neglected and beginning to disappear under the sand.

When Thotmes awoke he did as he had been instructed and then vowed to keep the sphinx clean and well cared for, for the rest of his life. Thotmes later went on to become one of Egypt's pharaohs.

person who was seeking help. The stand-in would be someone who was known to be a gifted dreamer. When the dreamer or the stand-in awoke, the dream would be related to the oracles or priests for their interpretation.

DREAM INTERPRETATIONS

Ancient Egyptian papyri reveal some of the conclusions the Egyptians reached about dream interpretation. One document, dating back to the 13th dynasty (1770 BC), concludes that if a woman dreams of kissing her husband, trouble lies ahead. This is an example of "opposites", in which it is thought that a dream means the reverse of what it appears to suggest.

One of the most famous dream records of the Egyptian era is the "Chester Beatty" papyrus, which was inscribed around 1350 BC. It came from Thebes and contains references to around 200 dreams, many of which date from an earlier period. Particularly interesting are the details of three modes of interpretation, which anticipate principles used by Freud centuries later, these are the detection of hidden associations, the use of opposites, and the use of visual or verbal puns.

DREAM PUNS

Puns in the world of dream interpretation are rather like games of free association, where one thing reminds us of another. Sometimes these "meanings" are catalogued and get handed down in dream dictionaries, where they appear as utter nonsense to later generations, whose cultural references and language are completely different. For instance, the Chester Beatty papyrus reveals that in ancient Egypt to dream about bare buttocks means the dreamer is about to lose his or her parents. This may seem absurd until we realize that the word used for "buttocks" closely resembled the word for "orphan".

DISPOSING OF BAD DREAMS

For dealing with a recurring bad dream, the ancient Egyptians had a curious ritual. On waking after another night of the same dream they would blow out their breath into a special receptacle – usually a wooden cup – which was then thrown into the fire. This symbolic act represented "burning" the dream, its negative power would be destroyed by the fire so that it could never return to haunt the dreamer.

THE CLASSICAL WORLD

ONEIROLOGY IS THE STUDY OF DREAMS. THIS WORD IS DERIVED FROM "ONEIROS", THE WORD FOR DREAMS IN THE ANCIENT GREEK LANGUAGE. LIKE THEIR KNOWLEDGE IN SO MANY AREAS, THE ANCIENT GREEKS' UNDERSTANDING OF DREAMS WAS ESPECIALLY SOPHISTICATED AND SEVERAL WELL-KNOWN THINKERS OF THE DAY DEBATED AND GAVE THEIR INSIGHTS ON THE SUBJECT. THIS INFORMATION WAS LATER EXTENDED AND CLASSIFIED BY THE ROMANS TO GIVE US A WIDE BODY OF KNOWLEDGE FROM THE CLASSICAL WORLD. BOTH CIVILIZATIONS USED DREAMS AS A FORM OF PREDICTION AND AS A WAY OF GAINING INSIGHTS INTO THE MIND OF THE DREAMER.

GATES OF HORN AND IVORY

The earliest mention of dreams in Greek literature is from Homer. We have little information about Homer or his life, but many historians date his era as some time in the 700s BC. We know that at this time there was widespread belief in the divine origin of dreams, which were regarded as messages to humanity from Zeus, communicated by Hypnos, the god of sleep and his son Morpheus, the god of dreams. However, not all dreams were necessarily reliable. Homer distinguishes between true and false dreams, writing that true dreams come through a "gate of horn", and false through an "ivory gate". Such distinctions were not merely of theoretical interest, as to act on a false dream as if it were true could have disastrous consequences. Centuries later

BELOW Homer, seen here being honoured by the gods, made the distinction between true and false dreams, and talked of the danger of being unable to distinguish between the two.

for instance the Persian leader Xerxes' dreams falsely convinced him that an attack on Athens would end victoriously. Acting on this advice Xerxes led his army to destruction in 480 BC.

HOMER'S ODYSSEY

In his epic work *The Odyssey*, Homer enlarges on the idea of true and false dreams through the character of Penelope, who remarks that dreams are awkward and confusing, for what is in them does not necessarily come true. She says: "There are two gates through which these insubstantial visions reach us; one is of horn and the other of ivory. Those that come through the ivory gate cheat us with empty promises that never see fulfilment; while those that issue from the gate of burnished horn inform the dreamer what will really happen".

SIGNIFICANT AND NON-SIGNIFICANT DREAMS

Influenced perhaps by Homer's ideas, the ancient Greeks also distinguished between two types of dream: the significant and the non-significant. Significant dreams were the ones which came from the gods. These were the ones that people wanted to have when they were about to undertake an important project, such as a business venture, a voyage or a new relationship. The non-significant dreams were more personal to the dreamer. The gods played no part in these and the way they are reported makes them sound more like the sort of dream we experience, for the most part, today.

DREAMS AND HEALING

The tradition of healing temples and dream incubation is one that was continued by both the Greeks and Romans, especially for acquiring information to treat disease. In ancient Greece famous sleep temples at Oropos and Epidaurus were

dedicated to Asklepios, the god of medicine, although it is believed that hundreds more temples existed throughout the ancient and classical world. The temples were situated in places of natural beauty, surrounded by fragrant plants and herbs, natural springs or shady forests. Another common feature was the serpent, and today the ruins at Epidaurus show us the pit where snakes were kept for healing and incubation purposes. This association of snakes with healing developed into the familiar symbol of the "caduceus", a healing staff entwined by two serpents. Today this symbol is widely used by many healing professions.

HIPPOCRATES

Known as the father of modern-day medicine, the Greek doctor, Hippocrates (460-377 BC), accepted that some dreams were of divine origin and could prophesy events. He endeavoured to put this capacity to scientific use by using the symbolism of dreams to diagnose the dreamer's state of health, associating the microcosm of the human body with the macrocosm of the universe. In his *Treatise on Dreams*, for instance, Hippocrates asserts that bright

stars in a dream indicate good health, whereas to dream of dim stars precedes illness. Dreaming of flowing rivers, he states, indicates problems with the urinary system, while dreaming of floods points to an excess of blood and the need to "bleed" the patient. Such dreams are referred to by Hippocrates as prodromal, from the Greek word *prodromos*, meaning "running before".

ABOVE Hippocrates, the Greek physician, believed dream interpretation was connected to physical sickness – if you dreamt of a specific sickness or disease it meant that you were suffering from it in real life.

THE DELPHIC ORACLE

The word "oracle" also means "answer" and oracle dreams were incubated at the famous site in Delphi (left), widely believed in ancient times to be the centre of the world. The site was situated on sulphurous hot springs and its entrance bore the inscription "know thyself". Hallucinogenic plants, such as henbane and jimsonweed, were burned to put the seer of the oracle into a trance, and make them ready to receive dreams and visions from the gods.

THE PHILOSOPHERS

It would be wrong to assume that all Greeks subscribed to the mystical significance of dreams. Many famous thinkers challenged this notion and their ideas have been highly influential in the way dreams are regarded by Western society. Heraclitus (450-375 BC) is generally regarded as the first person on record to proffer a purely rational explanation. Far from being a communication from the gods, he asserted, someone's dream world is entirely personal to them. It has nothing to do with anything outside of the dreamer's mind and is simply an ordinary experience, having less significance than anything that happens while in waking consciousness. However, perhaps more than any other thinker, it is Aristotle (384-322 BC) who comes closest to our modern way of looking at the meaning of dreams.

ARISTOTLE'S CONTRIBUTION

From his observations of sleeping animals, Aristotle concludes that it is not only humans who have dreams. He uses this as evidence to counter any theory that dreams have any divine or cosmic pattern or that they have any particular significance. He also notes that since all external sensations are reduced or absent during sleep, subjective sensations must be highlighted. He goes on to assert that dream images can have an influence on subsequent behaviour. In that sense dreams can be prophetic, as our thoughts are influenced by what we have seen during sleep. He also claims that the insights

THE EMPEROR'S DREAMS

After Calpurnia's prophetic dream about her husband, Julius Caesar, Caesar's heir, the emperor Augustus (above) (63 BC-AD 14), made a law declaring that anyone having a dream about the emperor's welfare should announce it in the marketplace. According to another historical text, Tranquillus' *Lives of the Caesars* Augustus set such store by dreams that he made a fool of himself. He went about Rome begging for alms because it had been predicted that he would do so in a dream.

available from dreams are like objects reflected in water: when the water of the mind is calm, the images are easy to see, when the water is troubled, the reflections become distorted. He says that the more the mind can be calmed before sleep, the more the dreamer can learn. Aristotle's theories were outlined in three seminal works: *On Dreams, On Sleep and Waking* and *On Prophecy in Sleep.*

DREAMS AND THE HUMAN PSYCHE

In his theories, Aristotle also links the hallucinations of the mentally ill, the illusions of ordinary people and the content of dreams and fantasies, concluding that they may all share a common origin – an idea which was later developed by the 20th-century psychologist, Carl Jung. Plato (427-347 BC), another of the Greek philosophers, also had ideas about dreams which predate 20th-century psychology. He describes the human psyche as possessing "a lawless, wild beast nature which peers out in sleep". As we

no longer exercise rational control while sleeping, our lust and rage can enjoy free and full expression. Centuries later, such a view would be central to Sigmund Freud's ideas about defining human personality and behaviour.

PROPHETIC DREAMS IN ROME

Accounts of prophetic dreams have occurred throughout history with some of the most well-documented being those foretelling the death of the dreamer or someone close to him or her. The citizens of ancient Rome seemed particularly fascinated by the possibility of this phenomenon and there are several reported instances of such dreams. For instance, the Roman historian Plutarch (AD 45-125) tells us that Calpurnia, the wife of Julius Caesar (100-44 BC), dreamed of Caesar's assassination by Brutus the night before it happened. Similarly the day before Caligula was assassinated, in AD 41, he reputedly dreamed that he was standing beside the heavenly throne of Jupiter, when the god gave him a push with his big toe, causing the emperor to fall to the earth.

DREAM DICTIONARIES

While the Greeks may have brought elements of logic and reason to the world of dreams, it took the orderly Romans to catalogue and classify the information. One of the most outstanding contributions was Artemidorus' five-volume *Oneirocritica* (The Interpretation of Dreams). A Roman soothsayer of the 2nd century AD,

Artemidorus travelled extensively throughout the Roman Empire, researching into dreams and drawing on knowledge from earlier times. His work includes more than 3000 dream reports from his interviewees, and is today acknowledged as the first true dream dictionary ever written.

Artemidorus suggests that dreams are entirely individual and that the contents are relevant only to the dreamer. The dream symbols and imagery that are found in these personal dreams are both cultural and individual, and are influenced by such aspects as the dreamer's health, state of mind and occupation. Artemidorus notes two broad classes of dreams: insomnium are dreams about everyday things and somnium are those that concerned the future. His approach is thorough and systematic and some symbolism is identified. For instance, dreaming of ploughing the earth is regarded as a sexual symbol, while a dream of a mouth represents the dreamer's home. More than a century later, a second *Oneirocriticon* appeared, compiled by Astrampsychus. This one contains such axiomatic statements as "to wear a purple robe threatens a lengthy disease".

ABOVE The assassination of Julius Caesar by Brutus was said to have been foreseen in a dream by his wife, Calpurnia. This detail of the story has survived, and has continued to fascinate people, from ancient Rome to modern times.

She dreamt tonight she saw my statue,
Which like a fountain with an hundred spouts
Did run pure blood; and many lusty Romans
Came smiling, and did bathe their hands in it.

WILLIAM SHAKESPEARE, JULIUS CAESAR

INDIA AND THE FAR EAST

WHILE THE CIVILIZATIONS OF THE NEAR AND MIDDLE EAST ATTRIBUTED DREAMS TO A DIVINE AGENT, IN INDIA AND THE FAR EAST THEY WERE REGARDED AS HAVING AN INNER SOURCE. IN CHINA DREAMS WERE THOUGHT TO EMANATE FROM THE SOUL, WHILE IN INDIA AND TIBET THEY WERE ASSOCIATED WITH A STATE OF MIND. IN ALL THESE CIVILIZATIONS, DREAMS WERE INEXTRICABLY LINKED WITH THE PHILOSOPHY, SPIRITUALITY AND MYTHOLOGY OF THEIR CULTURES. IN THE FAR EAST, IN PARTICULAR, SURVIVING TEXTS REVEAL A SOPHISTICATED UNDERSTANDING OF DREAMS, AN UNDERSTANDING ECHOED IN THE ORAL TRADITIONS OF MANY INDIGENOUS PEOPLES.

THE ATHARVA VEDA

According to legend, the 52 great Rishis (seers) of ancient India travelled to the highest mountains of the Himalayas seeking guidance to help humanity. During their meditations they believed that they discovered how the universe works. This knowledge was eventually transcribed into the Vedas, the sacred books of the Hindus, which scholars date between 1500-1000 BC. One of these texts, the *Atharva Veda*, contains many references to dreams, providing information about how they occur, what purpose they serve and how to interpret them.

LUCKY AND UNLUCKY DREAMS

When trying to make sense of complex information, a first response is often to classify it into opposites. This holds as true for dreams as for anything else. Where other ancient cultures distinguish between good and bad, divine or demonic, and true or false dreams, the Vedas focus on the distinction between "lucky" and "unlucky" dreams, having particular interest in a dream's predictive power. For instance, the *Atharva Veda* comments that showing passivity in a dream is a bad omen, whereas an aggressive dream is favourable. However if the dreamer receives any injury, this is considered an ill omen. The omen is made worse if the injury, such as an amputation of a limb, is something that could occur in waking life. The effects of unlucky dreams can be countered by performing purification rites, such as burning incenses and ritual bathing.

TIMING AND PERSONALITY

For the first time, the personality type of the dreamer is taken into account in dream interpretation. For instance, a depressed person is more likely to have depressing dreams, while a hyperactive sort is more likely to have manic dreams. The *Atharva Veda* also theorizes that a person's dreams occur in cycles throughout the night, with the most important dreams occurring towards the end of the dreaming cycle or later on in

HINDU DEITIES

During the Vedic period a pantheon of Hindu deities developed. A lot of these gods and goddesses have strange, dream-like qualities to them. For instance, Ganesh is the elephant-headed god of wisdom and "remover of obstacles", and the god Shiva has four arms, four faces and three eyes. Shiva wears the skin of a tiger and has a snake entwined around his neck, representing two powerful demons that he has defeated. In his fight against a particularly powerful demon, Shiva calls on the goddess Kali, the "dark side" of his consort Devi, to help him. Kali (shown left) is usually depicted wearing a girdle of severed arms and a necklace of skulls. Her bloodthirsty tongue lolls from her mouth and she carries a sword in her left hand. Intoxicated by her murderous killings, she dances on the bodies of her victims.

the night. In fact the later on in the night a dream occurs, states the Vedas, the more likely, as well as the more quickly, it is to come true.

THE TWO WORLDS

The Vedas also contains texts known as the Upanishads, philosophical works that expose spiritual truths. One of the most elaborate and important of these is known as *Brihadaranyaka*, sometimes described as a "cosmic meditation". This text declares that essentially there are two states, one in this world and one in the other. A third

intermediary state exists: the state of sleep and the land of dreams. It is while we are in the intermediary world that we have the capacity to perceive the real world and the next simultaneously. In this context, the dreaming state is considered to be more important than the waking state because it is then that we have access to realms of knowledge and experience denied to us when we are awake. To this end, techniques such as yoga and meditation were developed to help us "attain" or become more open to this other world, experienced as a place of heavenly bliss.

ABOVE The Hindus believe we can attain enlightenment during our dreams, only for it to evaporate when we wake.

ABOVE To the Buddhists this whole world is a waking dream. Once we perceive this we can really wake up to a new reality. But might not this also be another dream?

THE FAR EAST

It was not only in India that dreams were linked with spirituality and states of mind. An important Chinese Taoist manuscript, known as the *Lie-tsu*, distinguishes between six different types of dreaming: ordinary dreams, day-residue dreams, dreams of waking, dreams of fear, joyful dreams and terror dreams. Taoism, and later, Buddhism, were hugely influential throughout the Far East. Both of these spiritual traditions assert that the worlds we see in our dreams are more or less identical to the worlds we will experience after death.

THE BARDO

The Book of the Dead is an ancient Tibetan Buddhist text. Written to help prepare the soul for death, it describes death as a dream-like condition. When the soul leaves the physical body it must pass through the "Bardo", which has three distinct illusory states.

RIGHT The Tibetan *Book of the Dead* is a very ancient manuscript written on wooden tablets. In it a dialogue with the dead, who are said to have entered the bardo, the dream state between the living and the dead, is carried out.

As we pass through each state we face a multitude of self-created thought forms which may be pleasant or fearful, according to our thoughts and expectations. By becoming aware at any time that what we are experiencing is an illusion, the soul is elevated to a higher plane and avoids the constant cycle of death and rebirth. Consequently, learning to remain conscious while sleeping, being aware that we are dreaming while still in the dream, is seen by Tibetan Buddhists as a vital part of the spiritual preparation for death. Today in the West this state or technique is referred to as "lucid dreaming".

P'O AND HUN

In ancient China, it was believed that we possess two types of soul. The material soul, or "p'o" motivates us in daily life and is implicit in our physical make-up. This soul dies when the body dies. Additionally, we possess an eternal soul, or "hun", which survives us at death, leaving the physical body and the material world for a different plane of existence.

Every night during sleep, the hun temporarily separates from the dreamer's resting body to travel the world of dreams. This concept is similar to the idea many Western esoteric traditions hold today of the dream body and astral travel. As the dreamer sleeps, the hun communicates with spirits, demons and ghosts, bringing back memories of its nightly travels to the dreamer.

THE CITY OF DREAMS

In ancient China, people believed in a divine City of Dreams. Known as Ch'eng Huang, the city was thought to hang halfway between heaven and earth and is the place we go to when asleep. To enter the celestial city the dreamer had to pass through the "moongate", which necessitated being pure in mind and body. Once safely inside the city, the dreamer could leave their body and astral travel anywhere in the world. In this context, it is interesting to note that the Chinese had a god of the South Pole, a geographical region they had not actually discovered. Did the Chinese know of its existence because they had travelled there in their dreams?

BEDROOM RITUALS

To pass through the moongate easily, rituals were practised before going to sleep. These included lighting incense and proceeding around the bedroom in an anti-clockwise direction, beginning in the east and moving through south, west and north before getting into bed. It was also important to make sure the bedroom was decorated in auspicious colours (typically red and gold), and to make sure that nothing hung over the bed which could interfere with the exit of the spirit body. Consequently it was thought inadvisable to sleep under such things as beams, canopies, mirrors or lights. Similarly great care had to be taken to ensure that the spirit body could safely return to the dreamer's physical body. Playing tricks on a sleeping person, such as altering their physical appearance in some way, or else waking someone up too abruptly was believed to be dangerous. The returning soul needed to be able to recognize the sleeping body and it also needed time to re-enter the body. If the soul could not return for some reason, the sleeper would die.

ABOVE The Chinese believe that every part of the natural landscape is ruled by mythical creatures who protect it.
ABOVE LEFT The Chinese landscape has a dreamlike quality.

DREAMS AND ASTROLOGY

Written around AD 640, the earliest Chinese book of dream interpretations is the *Meng Shu*. It suggests that many factors should be taken into account before interpreting a dream. These include the time of year and astrological factors such as the position of the planets. It was also believed that external stimuli could be reflected in dreams. Sleeping on a belt, for instance, might produce dreams of a snake.

MU JEN DOLLS

In ancient China, great faith was placed in Mu Jen, the wooden man, or dream doll. For instance, if a child was suffering nightmares, the parents would "give" the dream to the Mu Jen doll, and he would then be sent away, taking the bad dream with him. Alternatively, if a dreamer wanted to make her wish come true, she would whisper it to the doll and then place him under her pillow as she slept. It was believed that during sleep the Mu Jen would come to life and be a "sacred warrior", capable of granting a person's wishes, protecting them from harm, and generally acting as a friend and helper.

EUROPEAN TRADITIONS

THE CUSTOM OF SLEEPING AT HOLY PLACES TO INCUBATE PARTICULAR DREAMS WAS NOT CONFINED TO THE ANCIENT AND CLASSICAL WORLD. THROUGHOUT EUROPE, THE PAGAN CELTS AND THE EARLY CHRISTIANS ALIKE PRACTISED THE SAME PROCEDURE, SLEEPING AT SHRINES TO ENCOURAGE VISIONS AND DREAMS OF HEALING POWER. FOR THE CELTS, THESE SACRED SPOTS WERE ASSOCIATED WITH NATURE SPIRITS, AND FOR THE CHRISTIANS WITH THE SAINTS AND MARTYRS OF THE EARLY CHURCH. AS THE INFLUENCE OF THE CHURCH BECAME MORE WIDESPREAD HOWEVER, DREAMS WERE REGARDED WITH INCREASED SUSPICION UNTIL, BY THE MIDDLE AGES, THEY WERE LARGELY SEEN AS THE DEVIL'S WORK.

CELTIC WISDOM

The Celts believed that all things possess an immortal soul, which exists through many lifetimes, learning from its experiences on the earthly plane in its journey towards perfection. To ascertain the will of the gods and help the soul along its way, many methods of prophecy and divination were used. The natural world was believed to be an infinite source of magic and spiritual wisdom, and symbolic significance was given to such things as the shape of clouds, a particular animal or plant species, as well as the portents of dreams. Dreams were interpreted by the druid, which literally means the "oak seer", or "one who sees with the aid of the oak". In fact, trees were especially important, and specific qualities were attributed to each species. Dreams were incubated in sacred groves, where the dreamer could ask the spirit of the trees for healing and assistance.

THE EARLY CHURCH

Traditional Celtic lore was frowned upon by Catholic doctrine, but theologians of the early Church also began to comment on their dreams. In his treatise *On the Making of Man* (380 AD), Gregory

BELOW RIGHT Dreams were part of the religious and artistic world of the Celts and artefacts from this era reflect this.
BELOW Dreams to early cultures were powerful messages from the gods, from nature, and from deep within. They were never to be ignored.

THE SALMON OF WISDOM

Stories about the source of all knowledge are practically universal. These symbolic tales have a rich, dream-like quality to them.

In the Irish Celtic tradition, the well of Nine Hazels is the dwelling place of the Salmon of Wisdom. The Salmon became wise when he imbibed the hazel nuts that fell into the well from the nine hazel trees. It is said that whoever catches and eats the salmon, will be imbued with its wisdom and filled with "imbas", or inspiration. Finn Eces, an elderly druid, captures the salmon and asks his young apprentice, Fionn mac Cumhail, to cook it for him. While it is cooking, some liquor from the fish splashes on to Fionn's thumb, and it is he and not Finn who gains the inspiration from the well.

of Nyssa asserts that dreams occur when the intellect and senses are at rest during sleep. The actual dream content is determined by the dreamer's memories of activities during waking life and his or her physical state. In other words, an individual's nature is revealed in his or her dreams. In Nyssa's view, dreams are most commonly motivated by the

passions, expressions of our "brute" nature which should be rigorously held in check by the intellect if we are to remain pure. Because the intellect is "off guard" during sleep, our passions can be given unbridled expression in our dreams. A little later, St Augustine (354-430 AD) noted that certain aspects of his mind were beyond his control, and he worried that God might hold him responsible for his dreams.

THE MIDDLE AGES

It was not long before the Christian Church associated human passions, especially sexual desires, with the devil or Satan. In their dreams, people were vulnerable to the temptations of the flesh: they could sin while asleep and not even know it, risking their souls to eternal damnation and the terrors of Hell. They therefore should practise great vigilance against the devil and all his works, as he was believed to intervene in human affairs in order to possess people's souls. A regime of devout prayer and austerity was recommended and any who continued to "sup with the devil" were branded as witches, facing persecution, torture and a terrible

death. Consequently the capacity to have vivid dreams was greatly feared and dream divination became linked with sorcery. It was at this point that dream divination in the West became anathema and consequently went underground, until its secular revival centuries later.

ABOVE Dreams are mysterious markers of landscapes that affect us very deeply – archetypes aren't just people but also symbolize aspects of ancient cultures.

TREE LORE

The Celts ascribed a symbolic meaning to trees. The oak, or "godhead" tree, held divine power and significance. Sleeping next to an oak tree could inspire prophetic dreams. Other important trees were the hazel, used as the druid's staff; holly, its red berries symbolizing the food of the gods; and ash, denoting health and immortal life.

THE DEVIL'S HELPERS

One of the dangers facing the dreamer was a nightly visitation from one of the devil's helpers. A succubus is a demon who assumes a female form and has sex with sleeping men. She then collects the semen, using it in magical rites to produce an "incubus", a male demon, satyr, faun or devil. Any man unfortunate, or some would say, wicked, enough to attract the attentions of a succubus was destined to follow the ways of the witch forever. By this means, Satan was said to "increase his horde, his progeny and to spread the diabolical craft of the witch".

ABOVE Today we are much more forgiving of people who suffer or enjoy sexual excitement while asleep but to the ancient Church such people were very wicked indeed, and were inevitably accused of Devilish practices.

Witches, it was claimed, had sexual intercourse with incubi in order that they could give birth to the children of demons.

NOCTURNAL INTERCOURSE

The word "incubus" means "to lie on", and it was believed that any heavy feeling in bed, such as a weight pressing down on your chest, especially if accompanied by nightmares, was a sure sign that an incubus (or succubus) had attempted to have nocturnal intercourse with you. Today we know that dreaming affects the body as well as the brain. For both men and women, the body regularly shows signs of sexual arousal (sometimes to the point of orgasm) during sleep, even when erotic dream content is absent. Given the religious fervour of the Middle Ages, it is not altogether surprising that the idea of a demon lover was believed to account for this phenomenon.

THE SHEPHERD AND THE SUCCUBUS

The 16th-century author, Nicolas Remy, reports that a young shepherd who was found guilty of witchcraft began his evil ways by being seduced by a succubus while attending his flocks. It was said that whenever he fell asleep in the warm afternoon sunshine, he would dream of his demon lover, who took the form of a dairymaid with whom he was in love. She would allow the shepherd to fulfil his sexual desires with her provided that "he acknowledged her as his Mistress and behaved to her as though she were God Himself". The shepherd claimed that "she so possessed me that from that time I have been subject to no will but hers".

FORERUNNERS OF THE MODERN AGE

Although St Augustine was concerned about his inability to control his dreams, it was hundreds of years later before the idea that something goes on inside us that we know nothing about was clearly formulated. Von Leibniz (1646-1716) compared the workings of the soul to the circulation of blood through the body: it is something that happens even though we are unaware of it. A little later, a German physicist, G.C. Lichtenberg (1742-99) made the first link between unconscious mental activity and dreaming.

At the beginning of the 19th century, signs of a renewed interest in dreams began to gather momentum. Robert Cross Smith from England became very successful as an astrologer, practising under the pseudonym of "Raphael". In 1830, he published *The Royal Book of Dreams,* which gave the reader interpretations of particular kinds of dream. However, it is through the work of a French doctor, Alfred Maury (1817-1892), that we begin to enter a new age of dream interpretation. From his study of more than 3000 dreams, Maury concludes that external stimuli are often responsible for what we dream about. Recent memories appearing in dreams, especially of the day before, are referred to as "day residues", and Maury discovered that stimuli such as noises and smells often register as we sleep and become included in our dreams.

ABOVE RIGHT Much of the accusations levelled against so called witches by the Church involved detailed, nightmarish descriptions of the devilish creatures the women were said to have under their control.
RIGHT The only way to redeem a witch or possessed person was to exorcise the malignant spirit and extract a confession from the accused.

MAURY'S DREAM

In one of his dreams, Maury dreamt he had been condemned to death by the guillotine. As the blade was falling, he woke up to find the top of the bed had fallen and hit him on the back of the neck at the exact time the guillotine would have struck him. This gave weight to Maury's theory that dreams happen so quickly that they are almost concurrent with the external stimulus that produces them.

THE DREAM DEMON OF MORAY FIRTH

Legend has it that in the 16th century, a demon lover lived near the banks of the Moray Firth River in Scotland. The lover seduces a young girl, but the lovers are caught when the girl's parents overhear sounds of lovemaking coming from her bedchamber. The parents call the priest and together break down the bedchamber door to find the girl fast asleep in the embrace of a "monster horrible beyond description". The priest recites from the gospels, whereupon the evil demon gives a terrible cry, setting fire to the furniture in the room and vanishing upwards, carrying the roof of the bedchamber with him.

INDIGENOUS PEOPLES

TRADITIONAL SOCIETIES ACROSS THE GLOBE HAVE DREAMING TRADITIONS THAT STRETCH BACK INTO THE MISTS OF TIME. IT SEEMS THAT DREAMS HAVE ALWAYS BEEN PART OF THE FABRIC OF LIFE FOR PEOPLES AS DIVERSE AS THE AUSTRALIAN ABORIGINES, THE INUIT FROM THE ARCTIC REGIONS AND THE PEOPLES OF AFRICA, AS WELL AS THE NATIVE AMERICAN INDIANS. EACH CULTURE HAS ITS OWN THEORY OF DREAMING AND PARTICULAR TECHNIQUES FOR INTERPRETING DREAMS. THEIR DREAMS AND SYMBOLS RELATE TO A PARTICULAR WAY OF LIFE, YET THEY ALL HAVE SOMETHING IN COMMON. THEIR DREAMS ARE RESPECTED AS COMING FROM A REVERED SOURCE AND ARE SEEN TO CONTAIN IMPORTANT INFORMATION.

ABOVE To the Aborigines of Australasia nothing is more sacred, more important, or more meaningful than the dreamtime, when the world was first created out of the seeds of the spirit ancestors.

THE DREAMTIME

Hundreds of thousands of years ago, the Aborigines travelled from Asia to the northern shores of Australia. Here they split into groups and moved around the land in search of water. They travelled great distances, and their legends say that as they did so they deposited the spirits of those yet to be born along the way, leaving marks on the landscape, on the rocks, mountains and other geographical features, to signpost the places they had been. According to legend, these ancestors were mythical figures, spirit beings who emerged from the earth, sea and sky and who took on various forms, particularly of animals. They were given symbolic names such as Red Kangaroo, the Blue Lizard or the Bell Bird Brothers. This era is known as the "dreamtime", when the ancestors created the landscape and set the pattern for the future. For centuries the Australian Aborigines have followed in the footsteps of their ancestors, tracing the paths trodden by these giant beings and marking their sacred sites with ritual, song and legend.

Those who lose dreaming are lost.

AUSTRALIAN ABORIGINAL PROVERB

The dreamtime is like a "cosmic dreaming energy" which can be set free if the ground is rubbed or stroked at the exact spot where the ancestor left the world at death and went into the ground. In ritual dances, these sacred sites on the landscape are struck and the power of the ancestors is brought back to life from the sleep of death. If no-one remembers or honours the dreamtime, the stories say, we shall remain trapped in the earth when we die and will cease to be.

THE DREAM IS LIFE

The dreamtime of the Aborigines is a complex concept: it is at once a creation myth, a whole series of fables and an entire spiritual philosophy. For the native Australians, the whole of life had its evolution in the dreamtime, and for them everything around us is brought to life by the dream. They do not perceive time as a linear process but rather see humans as existing in an eternal "now", where past, present and future exist simultaneously. The world as they see it is a magical place imbued with

supernatural forces, and we are at all times "dreaming the dream" so that it can become impossible to differentiate between the waking and the dreaming state.

AFRICAN SOCIETIES

The Bushmen of the Kalahari hold a similar viewpoint, seeing the whole of life as a dream and believing that they are the ones being "dreamed". Similarly, the Pagiboti people of Zaire consider that dreams are sent from their ancestors and believe that the spirits of the past have access to wisdom that can help with daily life. For instance, hunting is important to the survival of the Pagiboti and they believe their dreams can give them important information that can help them be successful: to dream of encountering an animal in the forest is regarded as a good sign. Many other African societies set great store by dreams, believing that they are linked to destiny. All aspects of life, from cures for sickness to political decisions, can be based on dream advice.

ABOVE According to the Aborigine creation myths we are all holders of the dreamtime.
ABOVE LEFT The Aborigines' sacred art consists of pictorial representations of the dreamtime and how the world was created.

THE DREAM SMOKE OF ULURU

The two Bell Bird Brothers were hunting emu at the rock pool near Uluru, the most sacred of all Australian Aboriginal sites (right), when their prey was disturbed by a young girl eating grubs. On her head she carried a sacred bundle which fell to the ground – the indentation is still to be seen at the base of the rock – but the brothers managed to catch the emu. They killed it and cooked it but Blue Lizard came and stole it. In punishment the Bell Bird Brothers set fire to Blue Lizard's hut and he was burned alive. The smoke from the fire can still be seen across the face of Uluru, and it is the smoke from this fire that sets us dreaming.

This story indicates one of the reasons why Uluru is so important to the Australian Aborigines. Take the rock out of their control and they lose their power of dreaming, and by implication, the power to live.

NORTH AMERICAN INDIAN TRADITIONS

Like other traditional societies, Native American cultures find it difficult to define the border between the waking and the dreaming state, and the ability to dream is highly valued. Each of the great tribes has its own understanding of dreams and a complex dream culture exists. Iroquois traditionalists, for instance, have a strong belief in dream precognition and respect the ability of a gifted dreamer to provide information vital to the survival of the people. Because Iroquois culture is built on warrior values, any sign of being taken care of in a dream is greatly feared, as it is believed that it will undermine

ABOVE LEFT Through dream journeys the shaman is able to connect with the animal world.
ABOVE RIGHT The shaman is the guide through the dream. Without the shaman our dreams are dangerous places to go.

bravery. Where a dream indicates trouble or disaster, it is believed to be possible to change its outcome by playacting the event that the community wishes to avert. In fact drama and ritual play an important part in Iroquois dream culture. Each year people travel great distances to attend a festival where dreams are acted out in a theatrical performance known as the *Ondinnonk*. According to the Iroquois, big dreams occur either because we have an out-of-body experience during sleep or because we receive an interesting "dream visitor". These are the dreams that put us in touch with our deepest spiritual source and contain vital information for health and wellbeing.

The Navajo pay particular attention to the diagnostic aspect of dreams, seeing them as tools to pinpoint illness, particular mental states and emotional disturbances. Dreams can also reveal a ritual cure for what is wrong, and if this is carried out in waking life the dreamer will return to health. For instance, there is a story of a sick girl

LEFT Ritual dances can be followed to interpret the dream in song and music. This is a valuable tool in dream interpretation but one that is specific to a culture, to those who understand the steps.

THE FOUR DIRECTIONS

Each of the four directions is associated with a particular element and quality. The element of the North is air. North is associated with the power of the mind and clear-thinking. Water belongs to the South and is associated with feelings and intuition, while the power of the West revitalizes and renews the physical body. Its element is earth. The power of the East triggers enlightenment and spiritual realization and its element is fire. This Navajo sand painting uses the four elements in its symbolic representation of abundant crops.

It is believed that positioning the bed in a particular direction allows the dreamer to "work" with the qualities of its associated element.

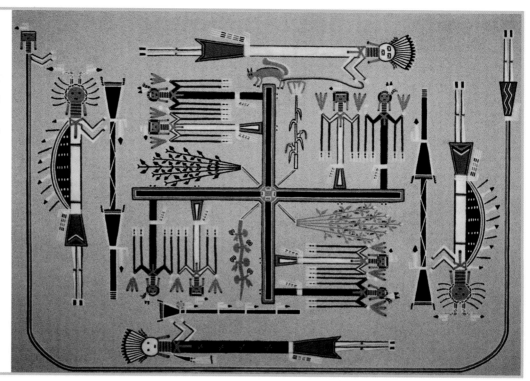

dreaming of nine feasts and being persuaded by the medicine man that if she has these feasts in reality, she would recover from her illness.

HOPI DREAM PROMPTERS

For the Hopi, a dream is viewed as a message from spirit guides who can appear in the form of an animal or other guises. Waking up and not remembering a dream is seen as losing something essential and people go to great lengths to ensure that this does not happen.

A commonly used dream prompter is a squared circle, a symbolic device used to aid dream recall. A circle is drawn on a square piece of cloth or leather. The circle is then divided into four quarters to represent each of the four directions: North, South, West and East. The square is then placed by the side of the bed. An item of symbolic value is placed in each of the four quarters – for instance, a tiny pot of water, a bunch of fresh grass, a lit candle and some burning incense – these items represent each of the four elements of water, earth, fire and air. Sleeping next to a dream prompter is believed to enhance dream recall.

THE INUIT SHAMAN

The Canadian Inuit culture is similar to those found in other northern regions, such as in Russia and the northern Scandinavian countries, where survival is challenged by the extreme climate. The Inuit believe that *anua* (souls) exist in all people and animals. Individuals, families and the tribe follow a system of taboos to ensure that animals will continue to make themselves available to the hunters, and rituals and ceremonies are performed before and after hunting expeditions to encourage success.

The shaman is the spiritual leader of each tribe. He is able to interpret causes of sickness or lack of success in hunting. In a manner similar to shamans or medicine-men in other cultures, he enters a trance-like state with the aid of drum beating and chanting. This allows him to travel out of his body, traversing great distances to determine the causes of sickness and other community problems, and to bring back solutions. In this dream-like state the shaman is imbued with magical powers and can move about outside of the dream.

CULTURAL PATTERN DREAMS

Anthropologists have suggested that the dreams of traditional societies can be broken down into four types: "big" dreams are those that possess cultural significance; prophetic dreams predict or give advance warning of events; medical dreams promote diagnosis and healing; and "little" dreams are purely personal to the dreamer. Although all dreams are valued, the ones held to be the most significant are the big dreams. These powerful dreams are also known as "cultural pattern dreams" or "official dreams".

The dream world is the real world.   SENECA INDIAN HEALER

SACRED DREAMING

THROUGHOUT THE ANCIENT WORLD, THE CONNECTION BETWEEN DREAMS AND SPIRITUAL BELIEF WAS CLOSELY INTERWOVEN. DREAMS SEEM TO HAVE PLAYED A SIGNIFICANT ROLE IN THE SHAPING OF MANY OF THE WORLD'S MAJOR RELIGIONS, APPEARING AS PART OF THEIR HISTORY AND IN THEIR HOLY TEXTS. MANY OF THESE DREAMS HAVE A REVELATORY OR VISIONARY QUALITY TO THEM, WITH RICH SYMBOLIC IMAGERY AND METAPHOR. THESE EXPERIENCES ARE NOT THE SAME AS THE ORDINARY DREAMS MOST OF US HAVE MUCH OF THE TIME — ALTHOUGH IT IS POSSIBLE TO EXPERIENCE A DREAM OF SUCH PROFOUND SIGNIFICANCE THAT LIFE CAN NEVER BE THE SAME AGAIN.

BUDDHIST ENLIGHTENMENT

For a long time before the birth of Gautama Buddha (c.563-c.483 BC), many predictions had been made that a "chosen one" would arrive. While she was pregnant, Gautama's mother dreamt that she was carrying a shining, silvery white elephant with six tusks. Interpreters regarded the dream as an announcement of the chosen one's arrival. Elephants had holy status in India: the Hindu god, Ganesh, remover of obstacles, is depicted with an elephant's head, while the unusual colour and appearance of the elephant in the dream was also seen as significant. Later on in the Buddha's life, his father, a nobleman, had a dream in which his son left the family to become a monk. This came to pass when Gautama was 30 years old, when he left his family, renouncing his worldly status to seek enlightenment.

BIBLICAL VISIONS

Dreams also figure largely in both the Old and New Testaments. In the Old Testament, important dreams often coincide with critical times in the development of Judaism. For instance, while in exile in Egypt Joseph interprets the Pharaoh's dreams. The Pharaoh

BELOW Gabriel, a universal archetype who appears in several different traditions, played a significant part in the dreams of Mohammed, who dreamt that they journeyed together to the seven levels of heaven.

HINDU BELIEFS

The Hindu religion has its own interpretation of what dreams are all about and believes that some dreams come from the dreamer's own emotional nature, some from hidden fears, and some from playing back experiences in daily life. Certain dreams, however, come from the gods. These dreams only appear to very religious people, such as this sadhu (right), who live a disciplined life, or sadhana, getting up before sunrise and practising austerities.

And He said, 'Hear now my words: If there be a prophet among you, I the Lord will make myself known unto him in a vision and will speak to him in a dream'.   OLD TESTAMENT, NUMBERS 12:6

RIGHT Joseph became a dream interpreter to the Pharaoh, and in this role became one of the most important people in the land. The Egyptians believed that dreams were messages from the gods.

dreams that seven fat cattle are eaten by seven lean ones, and then that seven ripe ears of corn are destroyed by seven blighted ones. Joseph realizes that both dreams mean the same thing: they predict seven years of plentiful harvest followed by seven years of scarcity, which will destroy the bounty of the previous seven years. The Pharaoh acts on Joseph's interpretation and during the bounteous years builds up large stores of grain. The interpretation not only saves the populace and the ruling system, but Joseph is promoted to a position of great political influence.

In the New Testament, divine messages are often relayed in dreams. The angel Gabriel appears in a vision to the pregnant Mary, announcing that she will give birth to a child of the Holy Spirit. The angel also visits Joseph in a dream, telling him to accept Mary's pregnancy and to name the baby Jesus, because he will save his people from their sins. Dreams also contain warnings. For instance, Joseph is told to take his family to Egypt in order to escape Herod's jurisdiction that all newborn male infants should be slain. Later the same angel returns to Joseph, informing him that it is safe to return after Herod is dead.

ISLAMIC DREAMS

Dreams also seem to have played an important part in the building of Islam. It is said that Mohammed (c.570-632 AD) had visions of the archangel Gabriel, who appeared to him when he was alone at night, praying and meditating. During one such

THE TALMUD

The body of Jewish civil and ceremonial law, the Talmud, divides dreams into three types: dreams of prophecy, dreams of nonsense, and dreams that originate from a person's thoughts and experience during the day. The way a dream is interpreted helps determine its outcome, and actions such as fasting or reciting special prayers are recommended as atonement for a bad dream.

visitation, the angel dictated the first chapter, or Sura, of the Koran, the holy book of Islam. The Arabic root for the word *Koran* means "address" or "recitation". According to tradition, Mohammed could neither read nor write, but the Koran was recited word by word by him just as he had received it from Gabriel. Later Mohammed had a dream or vision that he journeyed in the company of Gabriel and other angels. He was taken to holy places and to the seven levels of heaven and hell, meeting important religious leaders and prophets from the past. This experience, referred to as the Night Journey, has inspired many writers and artists.

ABOVE Angels have appeared to many in dreams – are these dreams or visions? Moments of madness or divine communications? One of the most well known angelic dreams is Mary's, as she is told of the coming of Jesus.

THE NATURE OF DREAMS

A dream is a series of pictures or events that occur in the mind. Generally dreams are experienced as we sleep, although it is possible to enter a dream-like state while awake. These images seem to be based on the dreamer's thoughts or experiences although certain dreams seem to bear little or no relation to the dreamer's normal life. Precisely how and why these images occur and what relevance they may have is a subject that has inspired a great deal of research and provokes much debate.

In this section we shall explore the nature of dreams, looking at some of the most influential ideas from science and psychology, drawing particularly on the work of Freud and Jung. Some modern approaches to dreaming are discussed before going on to investigate paranormal phenomena, dream travel and out-of-body experiences. Other dream states in the "twilight zone" are examined before finishing with a look at lucid dreaming. Although we may not have one single, comprehensive theory about dreaming, there can be few who would deny it is a fascinating subject.

SCIENTIFIC RESEARCH

THE RELATIONSHIP BETWEEN THE BODY AND MIND, THE BRAIN AND SLEEP HAS ALWAYS BEEN A PUZZLE, YET SCIENTIFIC RESEARCH INTO DREAMS IS A RELATIVELY RECENT PHENOMENON. EARLY RESEARCH IN THE 19TH CENTURY SUGGESTED THAT EXTERNAL STIMULI, SUCH AS NOISES AND SMELLS, CAN INFLUENCE DREAM CONTENT AND CERTAIN DREAM EXPERIENCES WERE GIVEN A PHYSIOLOGICAL EXPLANATION. HOWEVER IT WAS NOT UNTIL THE PHYSICS OF ELECTRICITY WAS UNDERSTOOD AND EEG (ELECTROENCEPHALOGRAM) INSTRUMENTS WERE INVENTED THAT SCIENTISTS BEGAN TO DISCOVER HOW THE BRAIN WORKS, TRANSFORMING OUR KNOWLEDGE OF SLEEP AND DREAMS.

EEG INVESTIGATIONS

In the early 1950s at the University of Chicago, Kleitman and Aserinsky made a breakthrough in sleep research using EEGs. They found that when a person was asleep the brain had periods of intense activity, demolishing the widespread idea that during sleep the brain was resting. They also found out that blind people have vivid dreams in colour.

Another important dream researcher was Kleitman's pupil, William Dement, to whom we owe the term "REM (rapid eye movement) sleep". REM occurs after periods of slow-wave or deep sleep, at regular intervals throughout the night. REM is characterized by visibly detectable movements of the eye behind closed eyelids together with a change in brainwave frequency. It is during REM sleep that we experience dreams.

Dement's research team found that if someone is woken in or immediately after REM sleep they usually have good recall of their dreams. On the other hand, if even as little as five minutes has elapsed before they wake, they usually have little or no memory of their dreams.

PHASIC AND TONIC DREAMS

We now know that REM sleep falls into two types, generating two different types of dreams. Firstly there is the phasic component. This is characterized by jerky eye movements, spasmodic limb and facial twitching and sudden breathing changes. When volunteers are woken from this sort of REM sleep, they typically describe their dreams as being strongly visual, active and "real". Phasic REM and its accompanying dreams tend to occur later on in the sleeping period. Nightmares are associated with this type of sleep.

The second type of REM sleep is known as tonic and is accompanied by muscle relaxation and

PHASIC AND TONIC DREAMS

REM sleep has two components, each having its own dream characteristics.

phasic dream I was running down a metal tunnel. It was very cold and hard and my feet made a noise on the floor as I ran. There were vibrant colours inside the tunnel and I felt I could reach out and touch them. Behind me I could hear the echoing roar of rushing water and it made me tremble. I wasn't afraid but I did feel very anxious – you know the sort of feeling, where you think the worst is going to happen at any minute. It was pretty overpowering.

tonic dream I was sitting in a temple meditating. There was a monk beside me and I could sense what he was thinking. There was a feeling of calm and peace all around and I drifted away in the swirling incense smoke. I felt weightless and insubstantial.

sometimes sexual arousal. Tonic REM takes place earlier on in the sleeping cycle. It is calmer and more restful, and tonic dreams are more passive and "feely". When woken, the dreamer typically reports such things as "I was feeling floaty" or "there was a feeling of peace".

DATA THEORIES

Although we now know much more about the brain, scientists remain divided as to the exact purpose that dreaming serves. In the 1960s, some dream researchers thought that while we are asleep the brain, like a computer, is "off-line". This does not mean it has shut down, but is that is going through a process of reassessing, filing and updating data from the day's activities. Many dreams certainly seem to fall into this category.

Some researchers took the analogy even further by suggesting that the brain, like the computer, discards redundant information through the process of dreaming. In the 1980s, Crick and Mitchison called this process "reverse learning". Dreams, they reasoned, help the mind to jettison an overload of data which could otherwise cause confusion. Dreams are like a rubbish-bin of the mind and have no particular meaning. From this perspective, we dream in order to forget.

UNDERSTANDING THE BRAIN

The brain has two hemispheres: the left side is associated with logic and language, while the right is more connected with intuition and creativity. It seems that dreaming is associated with right brain activity. Scientists have also discovered that dreams flow along visual and verbal "pathways" or nerve channels to the brain. We also know that the brain emits different types of electrical signals or waves. Of these, the following four types are of interest to sleep researchers. Beta waves (30-13 hertz) are associated with normal waking activity, with waves near the top end of the scale (30) signalling states of extreme agitation. Alpha waves (12-8 hertz) are produced during rest, while theta waves (7-5 hertz) are produced on the point of sleep. Delta waves are the longest and slowest (4-1 hertz) and are produced during deep sleep or in the womb. It is usually when alpha moves into theta that dreaming begins.

ABOVE The more we understand the function of the brain the better able we are to understand our dreams and thus not only our emotional impulses but also, perhaps, our spiritual function.

BELOW LEFT Our dreams may be a simple way of us downloading all the data we have picked up during the day and may have no meaning at all.
BELOW On the other hand dreams may be imbued with mystical importance and we would be lost without them – lesser beings indeed.

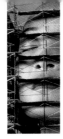

FREUDIAN PSYCHOLOGY

WHILE PEOPLE HAVE ALWAYS BEEN INTERESTED IN THE WAY THE MIND WORKS, IT WAS NOT UNTIL THE 20TH CENTURY THAT OUR UNDERSTANDING WAS REVOLUTIONIZED. THIS BREAKTHROUGH CAN BE ATTRIBUTED TO THE WORK OF SIGMUND FREUD (1856-1939), AN AUSTRIAN NEUROLOGIST AND THE FOUNDER OF PSYCHOANALYSIS. FREUD "DISCOVERED" THE UNCONSCIOUS AND DESCRIBED DREAMS AS THE "ROYAL ROAD" TO ITS UNDERSTANDING. WHEN HIS *INTERPRETATION OF DREAMS* WAS PUBLISHED IN 1900 IT WAS HIGHLY CONTROVERSIAL, YET HIS IDEAS PERMEATED ALMOST EVERY ASPECT OF WESTERN CULTURE. BECAUSE OF FREUD, DREAMS WERE ONCE AGAIN TAKEN SERIOUSLY.

THE CONSCIOUS AND THE UNCONSCIOUS MIND

According to Sigmund Freud, the conscious part of the mind represents a small fraction of the whole. It is like the tip of the iceberg, with the unconscious lying below the surface of the water. Like the iceberg, part of the unconscious is near the water's surface. Freud refers to this level as the "pre-conscious" and it is relatively easy to get in touch with. The deeper levels, however, are more difficult to access. It is a journey into the dark.

The unconscious is not static but dynamic. Freud believed that underneath our social exterior, the tip of the iceberg, at rock bottom we are a seething mass of instincts and unspeakable desires, most of which relate to sexuality and aggression, or our biological drives. He refers to this part of the psyche as the "id". Any experiences, thoughts or desires that are either too painful to allow, or that will contradict our self-image are either denied by the rational, conscious part of the personality (referred to as the "ego"), or repressed by an internal "censor" (also known as the "superego"). The unconscious is a bubbling cauldron of our personal and social taboos, yet it also provides the underlying motivations for our behaviour, of which we are largely unaware.

THE ROLE OF DREAMS

Freud believed that the unconscious cannot be studied directly but can only be inferred from clues in a person's behaviour, speech patterns and also their dreams. Dreams are symbolic representations of our unconscious needs, wishes and conflicts. Freud describes them as being in essence "the hallucinatory fulfilment of a forbidden wish". He asserts that dreams not only represent current wishes but are also the irrational expressions of infantile wishes, usually of either a sexual or an aggressive nature, that are left over in our subconscious from early childhood.

Because the wish is perceived as dangerous by the censor, it is expressed in the dream in a disguised or symbolic form. Freud believed dreams have two aspects: a latent content (the repressed desire) and a manifest content (the dream itself). So, for instance, repression of sexual desires (latent content) leads us to dream in metaphors of sexual imagery (manifest content): to dream of a chimney is to dream of an erect penis, to dream of a cave is to dream of a vagina. In other words, dream symbols are coded

BELOW Sigmund Freud was the first modern Western scientist to make a detailed attempt to understand and interpret dreams, and his legacy continues to this day.

Anyone who behaved while awake in the way the situations in the dream present him would be regarded as insane.

SIGMUND FREUD

RIGHT Freud believed that dreams mask what is really going on in our subconscious, and we have to strip away the scaffolding to discover the true, to him invariably sexual, meaning of the dream.

messages, having sufficient ingenuity to slip through the tight webbing of the censor's net. Freud believed that this subversive activity was necessary because it allowed the sleeper to go on sleeping. Without such disguise techniques, the content would be so disturbing that the dreamer would be woken from sleep. This leads to Freud's description of dreams as "the guardians of sleep and not its disturbers".

APPROACH TO INTERPRETATION

Freud's approach to dream interpretation is to look for the underlying meaning, or the latent content, behind the dream. To help his patients identify the latent content of their dreams, Freud developed the technique of word association, known as "free association", where words and ideas derived from the dream are freely associated without being censored. This technique forms the basic method of psychoanalysis.

DREAM DISGUISES

Central to Freud's theory is that dreams use "disguise" techniques to hide the latent content from the internal censor. This is how he accounts for the peculiar and irrational nature of the manifest dream. These are the different disguise techniques that Freud identifies:

Condensation dreams use a kind of shorthand, coalescing or "condensing" different ideas together into a single image which is often unusual or bizarre.

Displacement dreams are when a potentially disturbing idea is redirected or "displaced" on to another person or object so that it becomes less disturbing. For instance, a young man harbours feelings of murderous rage towards his father. In his dream, he sees his father being killed by a stranger, whereby his aggressive desires are displaced on to the stranger.

Symbolization dreams are where a neutral image is used to represent a potentially disturbing, usually sexual, idea. For instance, putting a key into a keyhole is interpreted as a penis entering a vagina.

Representation dreams are when thoughts are converted into visual imagery.

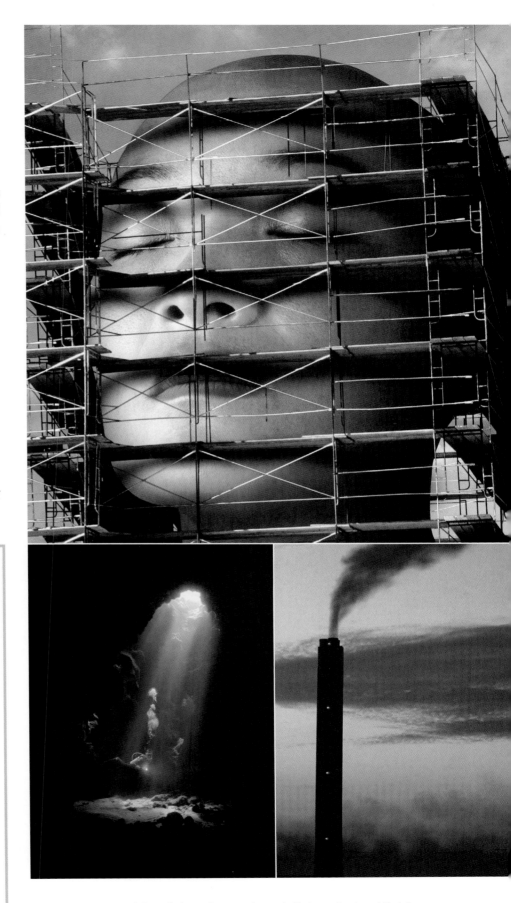

ABOVE Freud believed that all dream imagery is symbolic in content, and that the symbolism is universal rather than personal. For example if you dream of holes in the ground, tunnels or caves (above left) you are dreaming about the vagina. Similarly, if you dream of chimneys or towers (right) you are dreaming of the penis.

PSYCHOLOGY AND JUNG

For our contemporary understanding of dream interpretation we are indebted to the work of Carl Gustav Jung (1875-1961), a Swiss psychiatrist and founder of "analytical psychology", who made the study of dreams and the unconscious his lifework. Jung was a one-time pupil of Freud, and was in agreement about the importance of unconscious processes in the cause and treatment of mental illness and in the production of dreams. Gradually however, Jung became dissatisfied with Freud's theories and proposed that dreams played an important part in the healthy functioning of the psyche.

JUNG'S BASIC PHILOSOPHY

It was Freud's emphasis on sexuality and the overly biological orientation of his theories that gradually alienated his pupil, Jung. Freud's is a deterministic, and some would say, pessimistic, view of human behaviour. In a sense, he argues, we are little more than machines, driven by blind forces arising from our biological inheritance, over which we have little or no control. In contrast, Jung believed that human beings possess the capacity for growth and fulfilment and regarded sexual energy as part of a much more general, innate drive towards psychic health and wholeness. Jung calls this process individuation and describes it as the most important task any person can undertake in life – the attainment of harmony between all the aspects of the psyche, which makes us one and whole.

Essentially Jung saw life in terms of a spiritual journey and, far from being a dangerous melting pot of repressed and forbidden wishes, he saw the unconscious as a friend and guide to help us on our way. Jung applied these principles to his own life and used his dreams to help him make decisions, resolve uncertainties and move him along his path to self-realization.

THE PURPOSE OF DREAMS

Jung saw the psyche as self-adjusting, helping us to reconcile opposing parts of our nature and restore inner balance, and believed that dreams had an important part to play in this process. Dreams have a compensatory function, alerting us to imbalances in our personality and allowing us to change. They also have a teaching function, where certain aspects of the personality that need revising can be given attention. Jung believed that dreams are a way of communicating, of bringing levels of unconscious information into conscious awareness. They express the current state of the dreamer's unconscious and, Jung believed, they also provide clues as to future potential – a view that contrasts with Freud's more backward-looking perspective.

APPROACH TO INTERPRETATION

Unlike Freud, Jung never published a systematic theory of dream analysis because he believed that every dream carried its own meaning and must be interpreted individually. For Jung, the dream itself is the content and its symbols are subject to subjective interpretation. Rather than leading the person away from the dream by free association, Jung's method is to stay focused on the content of the dream itself. Through amplification or "direct association" he

BELOW During his life, Jung estimated that he interpreted around 80,000 dreams. He found that the details of a dream were not only relevant to the dreamer, but were sometimes part of a bigger picture relating to the world we live in.

JUNG'S DREAM OF HIS FATHER

Following a dream of his dead father, Jung became interested in the spiritual dimension to life.

"Six weeks after his death, my father appeared to me in a dream. Suddenly he stood before me and said that he was coming back from his holiday. He had made a good recovery and was now coming home. I thought he would be annoyed with me for having moved into his room. But not a bit of it! Nevertheless, I felt ashamed because I had imagined he was dead. Two days later the dream was repeated. My father had recovered and was coming home, and again I reproached myself because I had thought he was dead. Later I kept asking myself: 'What does it mean that my father returns in dreams and that he seems so real?' It was an unforgettable experience and it forced me for the first time to think about life after death."

The general function of dreams is to restore our psychological balance.   CARL JUNG

encourages the dreamer to explore all their associations with a particular image, returning to the image itself again and again.

THE COLLECTIVE UNCONSCIOUS

The other important area where Jung diverges from Freud is in the way he conceptualised the unconscious. Although many dreams are expressions of a personal unconscious and related to the individual psyche of the dreamer, Jung noticed that there were other dreams that do not fit into this category. These make use of symbols which have no particular personal significance for the dreamer, but have a "universal" quality about them. Through his studies of religion, art, anthropology and mythology, he concludes that many of these symbols stem from some common source – the "collective unconscious" the largest and deepest area of the psyche. He refers to these universal symbols as "archetypes" and argues that their meaning transcends the personal.

ABOVE To understand our personal archetypes is to unlock the power of our dreams and to be truly released.
ABOVE LEFT Jung encourages the dreamer to explore their own dream, and discover its meaning for themselves.

LEFT Archetypes can be traced back thousands of generations, and traces may even be seen in the landscape, where the first human cultures in our history drew the creatures of their imaginations.

DREAMS AND PREMONITIONS

TALES OF PROPHECY AND FORESEEING THE FUTURE ARE AS OLD AND DIVERSE AS HUMANITY ITSELF. WHILE ORTHODOX SCIENCE INSISTS THAT PSYCHIC PHENOMENA DO NOT EXIST, DREAMS CONTAINING INFORMATION FROM OTHER PEOPLE OR NEWS FROM THE FUTURE AS WELL AS DREAMS OF PROPHECY AND WARNING HAVE ALL BEEN RECORDED AT VARIOUS TIMES. SIMILARLY THERE HAVE BEEN MANY INSTANCES OF DREAMS BEING USED AS A DIAGNOSTIC TOOL FOR HEALING PURPOSES. HOWEVER WE ACCOUNT FOR SUCH PHENOMENA, THERE IS A BODY OF EXPERIENCE WHICH CANNOT SIMPLY BE DISCOUNTED OR READILY BE ABSORBED BY OUR RATIONAL, SCIENTIFIC WORLD VIEW.

PRECOGNITIVE DREAMS

An estimated 40 per cent of reported psychic experiences concern knowing the future in some way, with dreams being the most common way for premonitions (precognitions) to appear. Precognitive dreams are ones where the dreamer somehow receives information about the future which subsequently turns out to be verified by events. This information could not have been obtained or inferred by any other means.

Traditional societies typically take precognitive dreams seriously, believing that they may contain information that could be vital to the survival and wellbeing of the community. In modern society, many precognitive dreams have been linked with major disasters, including the sinking of the *Titanic*

BELOW Are we to take notice of precognitive dreams? There have been cases where the veracity of such dreams is utterly convincing to the dreamer, but does that mean it is really possible to dream the future?

in 1912 and the Japanese attack on Pearl Harbor in 1941. Dreams of earthquakes, volcanic eruptions, and transport disasters on land, sea and air, as well as the assassinations of public figures have all been foretold in dreams. There are also instances of particularly gifted dreamers using knowledge gleaned in their dreams or in a dream-like state to help the police solve crimes.

Significant historical figures have also dreamt of their own destiny. For instance, Ghengis Khan, Oliver Cromwell, Napoleon Bonaparte and Adolf Hitler all had prophetic dreams of their success in battle, while the US president Abraham Lincoln saw his dead body laid out in a coffin two weeks before he was assassinated. Although Lincoln took the dream seriously he was unable to avoid its fulfilment. On a lighter note, there are also many instances of people dreaming racehorse winners or lottery numbers, sometimes on a sufficiently regular basis to make money from it.

C. J. ASHFORD

THE SLEEPING PROPHET

Perhaps one of the most spectacular revelatory dreamers of recent times was Edgar Cayce (1877-1945). Known as the "sleeping prophet", Cayce was able to diagnose illness, prescribe treatments, and correctly describe people he had never seen while in a sleep or trance-like state.

Cayce practised clairvoyance for 43 years and by the time he died, he had gathered together around 30,000 diagnostic reports and case studies containing testimonies from his patients and doctors that vouched for the accuracy of his diagnosis and treatments. Cayce also used his psychic abilities to help the police identify and track down criminals.

Dreams must be heeded and accepted, for a great many of them come true. PARACELSUS

LEFT Did Napoleon really dream of his battle triumphs? Or was it another way for him to justify his imperial ambitions? The trouble with precognitive dreams is that they are unverifiable.

OTHER TYPES OF PSYCHIC DREAMS

These are also relatively common types of psychic dream phenomena.

dreams of apparitions These dreams involve the deceased, whether you know the person or not. The theory suggests that the person appears in the dream in order to convey a personal message. This message is not necessarily for the dreamer. For instance, it is common for apparitions to appear to people who didn't know them very well, giving them a message to pass on to the loved ones of the deceased.

clairaudient dreams These dreams involve sounds in which you can clearly hear information.

empathic dreams These dreams involve clear and sympathetic feelings or sensations about an event that is occurring as you dream it.

clairvoyant dreams Events occur at the same time as a dream experience of the same event. There is absolutely nothing you can do about changing or preventing anything you see in a clairvoyant dream, although the information can be used to help people.

telepathic dreams Communication is made directly from one energy source to another without any mechanical assistance of any kind. These dreams tend to show us people and events not in our immediate environment. Such dreams sometimes occur when someone is either in danger or in an unusual predicament.

SCIENTIFIC RESEARCH

The problem with premonitions is that the knowledge of the event appears to precede the cause, which in conventional science is impossible. It also raises the principle of free will. Arguments are put forward that the events could be inferred, that the dream was not specific enough, or that they are just coincidences. However research suggests that there is some evidence for foreknowledge. Tests have been conducted where participants guess which card will be shown next, or which light on a panel will come on next, and correct predictions happened surprisingly often.

RIGHT Perhaps dreams are a way for our subconscious to experiment with our hidden fears, rather than any kind of premonition of oncoming disaster that might be creeping up behind us.

NIGHT TRAVELLERS

THE QUESTION ABOUT WHAT HAPPENS TO US WHEN WE ARE ASLEEP IS ONE THAT CONTINUES TO PUZZLE US. SCIENTISTS ARE NOW ABLE TO EXPLAIN THE PHYSIOLOGICAL CHANGES THAT TAKE PLACE IN THE BODY AND ALSO TO MONITOR BRAIN WAVE PATTERNS TO INDICATE STAGES OF SLEEP. PSYCHOLOGISTS CAN EXPLAIN SLEEP AND DREAMING IN TERMS OF UNCONSCIOUS PROCESSES AND RECOGNIZE ARCHETYPAL DREAM SYMBOLS AND PATTERNS. YET NEITHER SCIENCE NOR PSYCHOLOGY CAN ACCOUNT FOR OUT-OF-BODY EXPERIENCES (OBE), WHERE A DREAMER LEAVES THEIR PHYSICAL BODY YET STILL RETAINS CONSCIOUS AWARENESS.

ASTRAL PLANES

Some people believe that dreams are our jumbled and distorted memories of our experiences in the astral kingdom, in which we have wandered while our physical body was sleeping. The astral planes are the supposed non-physical worlds that exist beyond time and space as we know it. Almost all esoteric traditions believe in the astral world in some form or another and that adepts can learn how to "astral travel", or journey into this realm at will.

The astral world is not regarded as an "imaginary" world in contrast to the physical reality of this one, but one that exists in parallel. In fact many spiritual traditions turn the argument on its head, saying that it is our present world that is illusory, and the astral world that is our spiritual home.

BELOW Many cultures believe we leave our body at night and go travelling on the astral plane – in some societies it is the job of the shaman to guide the dreamer and bring them safely back to their body.

THE ASTRAL OR DREAM BODY

In the West, the concept of astral bodies largely originated with Paracelsus, the 16th-century alchemist and healer. Paracelsus was convinced that we are influenced by the sun and moon and planetary constellations, but was not sure how. He came to the conclusion that stellar influences were exerted through what he called the "astral" or invisible energy body that surrounds the physical body. The astral body is roughly the same size and shape as the earthly one, but can detach from it and move about independently.

Psychics who are able to see the astral body maintain that it is connected to the physical body via a "silver cord". When we die, this cord is finally broken and the dream body no longer unites with the physical body.

FLYING DREAMS

During sleep, the astral or dream body lifts away from the physical body to explore other dimensions, but remains connected by the cord. The astral body can travel vast distances, but if the dream body strays too far, the physical body jerks it back again, which may register in sleep as a sense of falling, the sleeper sometimes abruptly waking from the "jolt" with feelings of disorientation and even physical symptoms, such as headaches and nausea. Some commentators believe that dreams of flying are related to psychic out-of-body experiences, the dream body floating weightless into the air, defying the laws of gravity. Such dreams are usually marked by a sense of euphoria and are rarely forgotten by those who have experienced them.

A man dreamt that he slipped out of his flesh just as a snake sheds its old skin. He died the following day. For his soul, which was about to depart from his body, provided him with these images.

ARTEMIDORUS

OUT-OF-BODY EXPERIENCES

The concept of the dream body may help to explain what is happening in an out-of-body experience (OBE). There are many well-documented instances where people have described not being "in" their bodies, but outside them, having no physical sensation but otherwise being able to see and hear what is going on. Some people have reported these experiences at the edge of falling into or out of sleep, describing themselves as "floating" near the ceiling while seeing themselves in bed. There are also many instances where people have reported OBEs while under anaesthesia. As they "float" above their physical body on the operating table, they are able to watch the proceedings and later are able to recount accurate details of what took place.

Many other people have experienced OBEs as a result of a near-death experience or shock. Such experiences are generally life transforming and seem to indicate that we have a level of consciousness that exists independently from our physical condition.

SCIENTIFIC STUDIES

Volunteers who have claimed to be able to generate out-of-body experience at will have been clinically tested. During a reported OBE, EEG readings reveal a change in brain wave patterns from a relaxed alpha rhythm to beta. Beta waves are the ones produced during normal waking activity. Similarly the breathing and heart rate both showed signs of increase, suggesting that some activity or stimulus, similar to a waking condition, was going on in the body. REM was absent, although there were more eye movements than in the usual non-dreaming (orthodox) sleep.

These findings seem to indicate that the sleeping subject was in a relaxed state but with a considerable degree of alertness. They were not, in fact, asleep. Physiological changes and changes in brain wave patterns indicate that something is happening, but more research and validated evidence is needed before science can describe something that "proves" an OBE.

ABOVE Are our dreams a tunnel from this world to the next? Or are our minds perhaps simply experimenting with fears that we avoid when we are awake but still need to confront?

ABOVE LEFT Do dreams give us a little taste of what it is like to be dead? Many claim they do and until it actually happens to us there is no way of being sure.

THE TWILIGHT ZONE

A DREAM IS AN ALTERED STATE OF CONSCIOUSNESS THAT WE FALL INTO DURING SLEEP. HOWEVER THERE ARE OTHER DREAM-LIKE STATES EXPERIENCED WHILE AWAKE OR ON THE BORDERS BETWEEN SLEEP AND WAKING. THESE INCLUDE DAYDREAMS AND HALLUCINATIONS, AS WELL AS HYPNOGOGIC STATES (OCCURRING AT THE EDGE OF SLEEP). ALL ARE CHARACTERIZED BY VIVID IMAGERY AND HEIGHTENED SENSITIVITY. THROUGH TRAINING AND DISCIPLINE, SOME PEOPLE ARE ABLE TO ENTER THESE STATES AT WILL, AND CERTAIN PLANTS AND HERBS HAVE BEEN USED TO ASSIST THE DREAMER'S ENTRY INTO A TRANCE-LIKE STATE. OTHER PEOPLE MAY EXPERIENCE THEM THROUGH MEDITATION.

HYPNOGOGIA

As we relax and drift into sleep, our brain wave pattern lengthens and slows down, changing from beta to alpha, and finally to theta. During this nodding-off stage, we can experience what is known as "hypnogogic" imagery, a series of vivid pictures or surreal imagery that bears little or no relation to waking memories. The imagery doesn't have the narrative quality of most sleeping dreams, but consists of a series of shifting and seemingly unconnected pictures that appear as if from nowhere: an animal, a face or a figure, an eye, a swirling rainbow of colours – the variety is infinite. The same process can also happen in reverse, emerging from sleep into drowsy wakefulness, where the fleeting visions may be referred to as "hypnopompic" imagery. Sometimes these persist into full consciousness when we are fully awake.

This state, also known as hypnogogia, is not only associated with sleep, but may occur in other situations where the brain wave pattern slows down sufficiently and we "switch off", such as during meditation, or even through boredom – as on a long stretch of motorway driving for instance.

HALLUCINATION

The Latin root for the word "hallucination" means "to wander in the mind", while the word "sleep" is derived from the Old English meaning "a vision". While visions, hallucinations and trance-like states are not the same as a sleep-induced dream, they nevertheless represent a dream-like experience where the boundaries between normal waking life and another dimension dissolve and merge. Within these blurred boundaries, there is a fine line between sanity and madness. For instance, people

BELOW As we begin to fall asleep, or sometimes during deep meditation, where the brain slows down, we go through a hypnogogic stage, where our mind tries to make sense of all the images in our head.

> But the dreamers of the day are dangerous people, for they dream their dreams with open eyes and make them come true.
>
> T. E. LAWRENCE

who suffer extreme states of mental illness, or who have misused certain drugs can become overpowered by hallucinations to such an extent that their grip on conventional reality breaks down, and is never really recovered.

SHAMANIC DREAMING

In many traditional cultures, the ability to enter a trance consciously and safely is a skill that is cultivated for the good of the wider community. The role of the dreamer, typically filled by the shaman or priest, is to travel "between the worlds", in search of a vision that can assist or advise his or her people. In fact the word "shaman" may be translated to mean "one who is exalted or lifted up". The shaman has the ability to step outside of their being in ecstatic trance, and is able to enter the dream world at will. While present in the other world they will be able to communicate with the "dream guides" and to bring back gifts of wisdom and healing.

BELOW LEFT Is sleep the same as an hallucination? Research on the brain suggests that the two states are very different although they share similar language, imagery and themes.
BELOW RIGHT The shaman needs to know how to explore the world of the dreamer, and this requires a rigorous and lengthy training.

SACRED HERBS

There are many plants and herbs that are known for their mind-altering effect. Some, such as fly agaric (*Amanita muscaria*) stimulate hallucinations, others such as peyote (*Lophophora williamsii*) produce out-of-body experiences, while cannabis (*C. indica*, *C. sativa*) and morning glory (*Ipomoea*) produce euphoria. Dramatic and vivid dreams can be induced by the infamous opium poppy, shown right, (*Papaver somniferum*). It was while under the influence of opium that Coleridge is alleged to have "visioned" his Kubla Khan poem. In many cultures, including our own, these plant substances have degenerated from their traditional sacred use by initiates in search of higher states of consciousness, into drugs used to escape the realities of everyday life. Most of these drugs are highly addictive and their use is illicit.

To become a shaman involves years of arduous training that typically involves lengthy periods of solitude, fasting and other "tests" designed to build inner strength and preserve sanity in preparation for when the ego's defences are dropped. Certain plants and herbs, as well as incense, talismans and objects of "power", are used to assist the dreamer in entering a trance-like state.

LUCID DREAMING

IN 1913, FREDERICK VAN EEDEN, A DUTCH PSYCHIATRIST, COINED THE TERM "LUCID DREAMS" TO DESCRIBE THE STATE OF BEING AWARE THAT YOU ARE DREAMING, WHILE IN THE DREAM STATE. HE BASED THIS ON HIS EXPERIENCE OF HIS OWN NUMEROUS LUCID DREAMS. CENTURIES EARLIER IN ANCIENT GREECE, ARISTOTLE HAD ALSO CONCLUDED THAT DURING SLEEP "THERE IS SOMETHING IN CONSCIOUSNESS WHICH DECLARES THAT WHAT THEN PRESENTS ITSELF IS BUT A DREAM". WHAT HAPPENS IN THE CONSCIOUSNESS OF THE DREAMER IS SOMETHING WE BARELY UNDERSTAND, BUT IT SEEMS THAT LUCID DREAMS INTRODUCE US TO THE PART OF OURSELVES THAT CREATES OUR DREAMS.

ABOVE A lucid dream is one in which we know we are dreaming. They can be very terrifying and unsettling, but if controlled can become liberating and empowering.

DIRECTING A DREAM

Frederick Van Eeden describes a lucid dream he experienced on the night of 9th September 1904. His experience indicates that not only did he retain a level of conscious awareness in the dream, but also that he was able to direct the dream's content and action to some extent.

"I dreamt that I stood at a table before a window. On the table were different objects. I was perfectly aware that I was dreaming and I considered what sorts of experiments I could make ... I took a fine claret glass from the table and struck it with my fist, with all my might, at the same time reflecting how dangerous it would be to do this in waking life; yet the glass remained whole. But lo! When I looked at it again after some time, it was broken. It broke all right, but a little too late, like an actor who misses

ABOVE There will always be clues in a lucid dream that will give the game away and become the trigger that lets us know we are in a dream – minor or major things that are utterly impossible in waking life.

his cue. This gave me a very curious impression of being in a fake world cleverly imitated but with small failures."

SPONTANEOUS LUCIDITY

In general, people who have good recall of their dreams report at least one experience of being in a lucid dream, while for those who regularly record and work with their dreams the experience seems more familiar and frequent. However, we are not really sure what it is that turns a normal dream into a lucid experience. The most common trigger seems to be that the dreamer recognizes a dream-like

For lucid dreamers nothing is impossible!   STEPHEN LABERGE

quality to the events taking place. Sometimes this is when the dreamer becomes aware of a fantastic element, such as a talking dog or being able to fly, while others come to recognize the sensation of the dream state and seem to "just know" they are dreaming. People who record their dreams regularly appear to actually incorporate their recognition of dreaming into the dialogue and action of the dream.

VIRTUAL REALITY

Many people are attracted by the notion of lucid dreams because the idea strikes us as a kind of virtual reality. Once you know that you are in a dream, perhaps you can control the action and influence the course of events – go places, do things, meet people and generally have the kind of experience you want. Because the dream world is not bound by logic or the rules of physics, it is possible to do or be anything that you desire. You can travel through the universe, turn yourself into an alligator, meet a long-lost lover or enjoy an extravagant luxury. This creates an exhilarating sense of freedom and expansion beyond everyday life.

PERSONAL DEVELOPMENT

Many Western therapists regard lucid dreaming as an essential skill on the path to inner development. Charles Tart, an American psychologist, suggests that we use the freedom in lucid dreams to seek or create a wise guide whom we can call upon for advice relating to our spiritual and psychological growth. Lucid dreams can also provide an opportunity to try out new strategies that are different to our habitual responses. By seeing all aspects of the dream as part of yourself, it is possible to stand outside of the role you are playing in the dream, analyse it and change it if you so wish. For instance, instead of fleeing in the face of a tiger, you can try turning around and facing it head on. A recent study indicates that lucid dreamers may have a stronger sense of their individuality and personal power, and may be less likely to succumb to group pressure or conform to society's expectations.

LEARNING TO LUCID DREAM

The most important key to learning how to generate lucid dreams is your level of motivation. The second is being adept at recalling your dreams, something which comes through practice. However, the following techniques may also be used to encourage lucidity:

pre-sleep suggestion As you drift to sleep, repeat a request or statement in your mind about becoming lucid in your dreams.

periodic questioning Develop a "critical-reflective attitude" to your state of consciousness while awake, asking yourself "could I be dreaming now?" at regular intervals throughout the day.

rehearse dreaming Sit down and pretend that you are dreaming. Use your imagination to create a dream.

if this were a dream Several times a day, stop and ask yourself "if this experience were a dream, what would it mean?"

meditation People who regularly practise meditation techniques seem to have more lucid dreams.

dream groups It is possible to join up with other people who are interested in exploring their dreams. People with an established forum in which to discuss their dreams tend to become regular lucid dreamers.

THE SENSE AND SUBSTANCE OF DREAMS

Every night we all dream. What we dream about can be hard to remember, or when we do remember, may be difficult to comprehend. During sleep the brain is active and our dreams are perceived through the deeper layers of the unconscious mind. The unconscious does not communicate in words or through reason, but uses visual images to stimulate intuition and feeling. When we wake we are left with a residual "sense of" something that stays with us through the day, an imprint in our memory like a footstep in the snow.

This chapter looks at some of the characteristics of dreams, the importance of archetype and symbol, and the logic and landscape of the dreaming world. This information will help you start to make sense of your dreams and of what they are about.

ARCHETYPES

In art or literature, a recurrent symbol or motif may be described as an archetype. In Jungian psychology it is the term used to describe the basic building blocks of the human psyche, which reside in the collective unconscious. According to Jung, the collective unconscious contains our inherited cultural, ancestral and historic memories. These elements are derived from the universal human experience and transcend the purely personal. Archetypes are the "original patterns", the deepest part of the human soul that feature in our enduring folklore and art and, now and again, in our dreams.

CULTURAL PATTERNS

The collective unconscious may be universal but the form its archetypes take are culture-specific. We see what we have been conditioned to see. For instance in Western culture, angels are celestial beings that mediate between humans and higher powers. In both the Old and New Testaments they appear in dreams and visions, bringing messages from God to the dreamer. Yet in other cultures the concept of the angel is unknown. Among the Sioux Indians of North America it is the full moon that is the heavenly messenger, holding out choices to the dreamer in its hands.

Our dreams therefore are patterned according to our culture, giving us roots deep into our ancestral and historic past. It is these "cultural pattern" or archetypal dreams that seem to be some form of communication from the beyond, from something bigger and outside of our "little selves". They are the ones that wake us up with a start.

DREAMS BIG AND SMALL

Malinowski, a contemporary of Jung's, distinguished between two types of dream. Cultural pattern or archetypal dreams he calls "official" dreams, while "free" dreams are those that are entirely of our own making. Jung refers to these official dreams as the big or meaningful dreams as opposed to the little or everyday dreams. The little dreams are the ones where we seem to be doing our mental filing, sorting and processing all the information we receive while awake. They are the ones where we can easily identify the imagery and symbolism: "Oh, yes, I dreamed of that because I had watched a particular film just before going to bed", or "Ah, I know why I dreamed of that, it was because we were talking about it earlier in the day". The big dreams on the other hand are the ones that seem to mean something profound and defy rational explanation.

From the collective unconscious we draw images (archetypes) of extraordinary potential and power. These images present themselves to us in our big dreams. The big dreams are the ones we remember, that haunt us. They are packed with vivid imagery, symbolism and metaphor that are too powerful to be held in our mental grasp. These images are sometimes disturbing, frequently new and very often wonderful. They seem larger than life and to come from another dimension, and can provoke the question: "Am I dreaming, or being dreamed?"

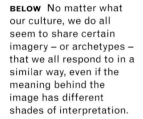

BELOW No matter what our culture, we do all seem to share certain imagery – or archetypes – that we all respond to in a similar way, even if the meaning behind the image has different shades of interpretation.

We may expect to find in dreams everything that has ever been of significance in the life of humanity.

CARL JUNG

THE POWER OF ARCHETYPES

Examining these archetypes is essential if we are to understand our dreams and the personal messages they hold for us. The archetypes are there to challenge us, to stretch us, to take us out of our normal everyday life and throw us back into the mysterious world of myths and magic. They are there to remind us that we are more than going to work, watching TV or eating out at the latest restaurants. At rock bottom, we are creatures of spirit and imagination, intuition and mystery. No matter how "civilized" we become, like a tidal wave an archetypal dream will suddenly appear, a shocking reminder that we are more than the little selves of our everyday life.

THE TIMING OF BIG DREAMS

Times of change and transition are generally recognized as "stress points". This is because there is a wealth of new material for us to process and integrate into the psyche and our normal ego defences are weakened. This may help to explain why a powerful dream is more likely to get through to us at such times.

Archetypal dreams often occur when we are undergoing major life events. Typical instances include puberty, marriage, pregnancy, death or divorce as well as children leaving home, taking up a new job or moving house. Major events do not have to be personal to trigger an archetypal dream. Dramatic global news can also affect us at a deep soul level and there are typically many reported incidences of big dreams after major world events, such as the unexpected death of a public figure or outbreaks of war and violence.

ABOVE Archetypal dreams often occur when we are going through life's rites of passage – as if they are needed most then.
ABOVE LEFT Most archetypes are instantly recognizable and we would probably associate this character with ancient wisdom and nobility.

LEFT Perhaps your dreams contain images that your mind has taken with it from your day's activities. If you watch television in bed it seems logical that visual elements from that will be revisited in a dream.

JUNGIAN ARCHETYPES

In his investigations into the collective unconscious, Jung formulated several archetypal forces or principles. These may not be definitive, but they nevertheless remain a handy and convenient tool for making sense of our dreams.

THE PERSONA

The conscious personality, the Persona, is akin to Freud's concept of the ego. It is the person we present to the outside world, the mask we wear in order to protect our most real and vulnerable self. To find the Persona in our dreams is to look for a symbolic representation of "me".

We have many guises and wear many masks depending on the social role we are playing. Responsible parent, respected professional and rebellious teenager are just a few examples. Appearing naked in a dream is an indicator that the mask has slipped, our Persona is absent and we are literally naked before others, physically, emotionally and even spiritually. If we feel the mask is tarnished we may appear as a scarecrow, a tramp, or a degenerate. If we feel the mask is too firmly in place we may wear armour or a visor.

THE SHADOW

Jung described the Shadow as a "splinter personality". Anything that does not fit with how we like to see ourselves is pushed into the background, repressed into the unconscious. Yet no matter how hard we try to keep it under control, every now and again it erupts, like a wilful and disobedient child. The Shadow is our dark side, our "sinful" nature that we judge and condemn as wrong and bad. It is our temper tantrums, black moods, anger, violence, lust, greed and unspeakable desires. It is the things we fear and hate the most.

We are very afraid of the Shadow, for it has the power to rip away the mask and reveal our true face. In our dreams it may appear as a shadowy figure, a cloaked evil-doer, a malignant force threatening to overpower us. Yet Jung did not perceive the Shadow as inherently evil, merely "somewhat inferior, primitive, unadapted and awkward". It does things in the old way, as Jung put it, and its messages are often actually for our own good.

THE ANIMA AND ANIMUS

We each wear the mask of our gender. Yet within every man and woman resides the seed of the opposite sex. "Anima" and "Animus" were the terms coined by Jung to personify the "inner woman" and the "inner man", or the feminine part of a man's personality and the masculine part of a woman's.

Both the Anima and Animus are shaped by the child's experience of his or her mother and father. Broadly speaking however, the Animus is the hero within, practical, adventurous, independent and self-assured. The Anima is the heroine, both goddess and seductress. She is sensitive, compassionate, sensual and instinctive. It must be remembered that these are psychological attributes rather than characteristics of men and women as such. When these qualities are not integrated into the psyche, we project them on to other people, particularly our partners, in our desire for that perfect person who, we believe, will make our dreams come true.

THE TRICKSTER

Hard to define because he is always one step ahead, the Trickster leads us a merry dance as we follow pipe dreams. He is the shape shifter, the joker in the pack and the jester or clown. His is the leering, jeering face in the carnival, painted and seductive. He is the Pied Piper, the Lord of the Dance who offers us delight and pleasure, but if we follow his call we will end up a laughing stock, with dust in our mouths.

Although a mischievous fraudster and saboteur, the Trickster's antics can also be corrective. With great skill he pricks the balloon of our inflated sense of self, mocking our vanities and self-obsessions, ridiculing our ambitions and desires. Not of this world, the Trickster is also the shaman, the one who can enter the realm of magic and interpret our dreams. He represents our intuitive side.

THE DIVINE CHILD

A symbol of innocence and purity, the Divine Child embodies birth and growth, potential and latent energy. The Divine Child is a link between past, present and future, a mediator who brings healing and wholeness, and possesses enormous transforming power. Symbols for the Divine Child include the changeling, the jewel, the flower and the chalice. By becoming the Divine Child ourselves we strip away all our preconceptions and judgements, as well as our ideas and goals. The Divine Child is a return to innocence, a readiness to be reborn without the mask.

THE LITTLE PRINCE

The following extract is from Antoine de Saint-Exupéry's novel *The Little Prince* in which he describes a dream-like landscape and an archetypal Divine Child figure.

"Look very carefully at the landscape so as to be sure to recognize it ... And if you should happen to come upon this spot, please do not hurry on. Wait a little, exactly under the star. Then, if a child comes towards you, if he laughs, if he has golden locks and if he refuses to answer questions, you will surely guess who he is."

ABOVE The image of the Divine Child is a very powerful one and it has inspired painters and poets for centuries. Here it is contrasted with the archetype of the hero, the youthful aspect of the Father.

THE GREAT MOTHER

From the Great Mother's loins springs all of humanity, created and birthed from her womb and her fruitfulness. This archetype has three aspects: virgin, mother and crone, each of these having a positive and a negative face. The virgin is a young bare-breasted girl garlanded with spring flowers. She dances, sings, and plays music, she is a creature of the meadows and fields. In her negative aspect she is a seductress, purposely attracting and then spurning her suitors. The round-bellied "earth" mother is the healer and nurturer, caring for the physical and emotional needs of her family. She inhabits the kitchen and bake house, the summer lodges, the woods and the glades. Or else she is the "terrible mother", possessive, demanding and devouring. The crone is the wise woman and priestess. She is intuitive and free thinking, living life according to her own rules. She possesses psychic, magical powers. Her other side is the ugly hag, a nightmare creature of the forests and caves, the underground, the underworlds. She is the evil sorceress and harpy.

THE GREAT FATHER

Parallel to the Great Mother is the Great Father. His aspects complement those of the Mother: prince, father and hermit, each with a positive and a negative side. The prince is the young man with high ideals, setting out on the quest of life. He is the dreamer and poet and is capable of greatness. In his negative aspect he is a vagabond and wastrel, the lazy lout who thinks the world owes him a living. He uses women to gratify his sexual desires.

The father is the hunter and provider. He procreates and preserves the race and represents standards and ideals to live up to. He is an authority figure and we seek his approval, but his judgements are fair. On the negative side he is the despot and ogre, an authoritarian figure who is sadistic and uncaring. The hermit excludes himself from society to nurture his soul in prayer and meditation. He is the "wise ancient", the guru, priest and spirit guide, who can help us find our inner light. He brings

---

FINDING YOUR ARCHETYPES

Some archetypes will have more meaning for you than others. These are the ones most likely to appear in your dreams. Draw up a list of archetypes that have the most meaning for you. This could contain characters and personalities, as well as objects and situations. Use the list to help you, adding or deleting any as appropriate.

archetypal characters

king/queen	alchemist	mythical beast	traveller
prince/princess	artist	(sphinx, unicorn,	skeleton
baby/child	monk/nun	dragon)	criminal
messenger	priest/priestess	jester	prisoner
angel	any animal	pregnant woman	ghost
devil	crows/other birds	lovers	

archetypal objects and locations

sun	rainbow	graveyard	chalice
moon	temple/church	landscape	jewels or money
stars	battlefield	sailing boat	
the four elements	clouds	cave	
lightning	maze	sword	

practical understanding to our problems and dilemmas and a sense of personal power. In his dark aspect he is the black magician who misuses his powers for personal gain.

OTHER ARCHETYPES

Archetypal themes and patterns can also appear in many other forms. For instance the journey, the eternal triangle, temptation and redemption, birth, death and disaster are all common themes that appear in myth and religion as well as in our dreams. The four elements (fire, water, earth and air) are archetypal energies, representing the natural forces of the universe that shape and sustain our lives. Animals too can be archetypal symbols. For instance, a dog may characterize loyalty, a hawk clear vision and a cat freedom and independence. Esoteric arts, such as astrology and the tarot, as well as the world's greatest myths are also based on archetypal symbols, which may help to explain their enduring fascination. Defying rational explanation they strike a chord deep within us, speaking the eternal language of the soul.

UNDERSTANDING ARCHETYPES

Archetypes permeate every facet of our lives. To begin to understand how they work and how they relate to your life, try the following questionnaire for fun. Don't think about the answers but go for the one that first comes to mind, elaborating on it as much as possible. You might be surprised at the results!

1 Choose a flower to represent yourself. What does it say about you that is hard to express in words alone?

2 What is your favourite colour and why do you like it?

3 Which is your favourite domestic animal? What qualities does it have that resonate with you?

4 Describe your favourite foods. How do you feel when you eat these foods?

5 What is your favourite tree? What is it about the tree that you especially like?

6 What kind of water do you like best: rivers, streams, lakes or the sea? Do you know what this kind of water says to you?

7 If you could shape shift, which animal would you like to become? Can you say what it is about this animal that you find so inspiring?

explanation

1 The flower represents your attitude to your soul.

2 The colour represents your emotional attitude.

3 The domestic animal represents the qualities you look for in your friends.

4 The food represents how you feel

about your body and sex as a physical activity.

5 The tree represents your attitude towards life in general.

6 The water you have chosen represents your sexuality.

7 The wild animal represents the hidden you beneath the mask.

FAR LEFT AND LEFT
Archetypes help us understand ourselves and our partners, friends and family. By identifying different archetypes, such as the hero (far left) and the unicorn (left) and how they affect us, we can learn a lot about ourselves.

LEVELS OF DREAMING

THE UNCONSCIOUS IS MADE UP OF DIFFERENT LAYERS, REPRESENTING SUCCESSIVELY DEEPER STRATA OF THE MIND. FREUD CONCEPTUALIZED THESE LAYERS AT TWO LEVELS: THE PRECONSCIOUS AND THE PERSONAL UNCONSCIOUS. TO THESE JUNG ADDED A THIRD LEVEL, WHICH HE REFERRED TO AS THE COLLECTIVE UNCONSCIOUS. THERE MAY ALSO BE A DIMENSION OF THE MIND THAT CAN PRODUCE VISION-LIKE DREAMS OF EXTRAORDINARY POWER AND SIGNIFICANCE. OUR DREAMS ARISE FROM THESE DIFFERENT LEVELS, AND ALTHOUGH ANY DREAM CAN CONTAIN MATERIAL FROM MORE THAN ONE LEVEL, USUALLY ONE OR OTHER LEVEL PREDOMINATES.

BELOW Level one dreams are most often associated with the preconscious; the most accessible part of our mind. The elements within these dreams may be random mental images with no meaning.

LEVEL ONE DREAMS

These dreams are associated with the preconscious, the most accessible part of the mind. Level one dreams contain material that can be easily linked to waking life. These dreams tend to revolve around the events of the day, and opinion is divided as to whether or not they are particularly meaningful.

Some would say that these dreams represent random, jumbled nonsense. They are a way of the mind unburdening itself and have no particular significance. Others suggest that trivial events should not necessarily be automatically dismissed: they may be used as a "way in" to deeper levels of the mind which are more difficult to access directly.

LEVEL TWO DREAMS

Dreams at this level are capable of giving us insights which we could not achieve during normal waking life. These dreams, from the personal unconscious, can include forgotten memories, repressed wishes and fears, and unacknowledged emotions and expectations. The symbolism of these dreams is uniquely personal to the dreamer and the dream scenario is usually quite different to anything in waking life. Such dreams usually have an intriguing quality to them and are not easily forgotten.

LEVEL THREE DREAMS

The collective unconscious is a storehouse of archetypal themes and symbols, forming the raw material for the deepest longings and aspirations of the human race. This level transcends the purely personal. Dreams from this level are concerned with profound issues such as life and death, love, transformation and spirituality. Dreams in this category are much less common, although people engaged in self-exploration practices such as psychotherapy or meditation, or who consciously choose to work with their dreams in some way, often report an increase in level three dreams.

COSMIC DREAMS

On very rare occasions, maybe once in a lifetime only, you may encounter an extremely important and extraordinary dream that is truly awe-inspiring. Cosmic dreams go even further than level-three type

Sometimes dreams alter the course of an entire life.

JUDITH DUERK

dreams. They are ones in which the qualities of the universe itself are the major themes. They are made up of formless shapes and colours, a swirling mass of light and dark and shade with no recognizable objects or identifiable substance. Cosmic dreams are an attempt by the unconscious to make sense of the vastness of the universe and our place within it. The Moscow-born writer and mystic, P.D. Ouspensky (1878-1947) said such dreams "disclose to us the mysteries of being, show the governing laws of life, and bring us into contact with higher forces". These dreams have the capacity to change our life.

THE TUNNEL OF LIGHT

A man had the following cosmic dream when he was 41 years old, and finds that it has stayed with him through the following years:

I was rushing down this incredible tunnel of light – but it was a dark light. I had no body and was pure spirit, pure energy. There was a sound, a voice which was saying something like, "You are entering sector 16". At the end of the tunnel I came to a sudden stop and was aware that I had arrived at a sort of hole in a cliff face, but this was a cliff face a million miles high. The hole was halfway up and I was looking out over a wide plain that was completely occupied by some divine being. It was a sort of giant eye but there wasn't a physical eye – only a divine way of seeing everything. As I stood there I was aware that this eye was turning towards me, was going to look at me. I felt I wasn't worthy. This wasn't my time. I was frightened and was immediately whisked back up the tunnel. I woke up sweating and very shaken.

I have thought about this dream almost every day since having it seventeen years ago. I am determined to be "worthy" next time I go back. I think the next time will be when I die. I believe that what I was given a glimpse of was my own mortality, my own death. This dream has had a huge impact on me. Everything I do is judged against that worthiness. I can't explain what it is that would make something I do worthy, but I just know instinctively what is right and wrong."

ABOVE Each of the images in our dreams has been carefully chosen so that it means something to us, the dreamer.

LEFT Into our dream worlds we take with us the images we have accumulated through our lives.

DREAM LOGIC

LOGIC IS NOT THE FORTE OF THE DREAMING MIND. IN OUR DREAMS THE IMPOSSIBLE BECOMES POSSIBLE AND THE NONSENSICAL APPEARS PERFECTLY NORMAL, AS PEOPLE, ANIMALS, OBJECTS AND PLACES BEHAVE IN BIZARRE AND UNACCOUNTABLE WAYS. FREUD ONCE REMARKED THAT ANYONE WHO BEHAVED WHILE AWAKE AS THEY DO IN THEIR DREAMS WOULD BE REGARDED AS INSANE. IN THE WORLD OF DREAMS, THE NORMAL RULES OF LOGIC, REASON AND "COMMON SENSE" ARE THROWN TO THE WINDS AS EVENTS APPEAR TO KALEIDOSCOPE INTO A THEATRE OF THE ABSURD. YET STRANGE THOUGH IT MAY SEEM, OUR DREAMS DO IN FACT HAVE A CURIOUS LOGIC OF THEIR OWN.

ABOVE All our dreams have their own curious dream logic, stemming from our own personal logic. Once we crack the code all our dreams can be understood.
ABOVE RIGHT It is useful to look at other people's dream logic but bear in mind they might only match yours slightly, more likely they will bear no resemblance at all.

FREUD'S DREAM LOGIC

Intrigued by the absurdity of dreams, Freud began his investigation into how dreams work. His work claims that dreams express an element of logical connection in four different ways: simultaneity, contiguity, transformation and similarity.

When two elements in a dream are presented close together, simultaneity suggests that an intimate relationship exists between the two. Dream combinations are not randomly formed but have meaning within the dream. Contiguity is when dream elements occur sequentially, and transformation is when one thing turns into another. Similarity is the direct or indirect association between things in the dream.

The work of American psychologists Hall and Nordby adds the idea of "relative consistency" to Freud's ideas, noticing that dream motifs have a certain frequency and uniformity about them.

YOUR DREAM LOGIC

Other people's ideas may be helpful when practising dream interpretation, but they will not necessarily fit with everyone's dreams all of the time. We all have our own unique dream logic which may be completely different from anyone else's. If you are keeping a dream record, see if you can find a consistency of pattern to your dreams. It may be that you always appear as yourself or always as someone else. Your dream logic is a bit like Woody Allen films. You may see a different film each time but the style is consistent and recognizable. You get to know your way round as you study the subject.

MICE AND SPIDERS

Your unique dream logic invariably extends to your dream symbolism and will most likely influence the type of archetypes you are working with. These represent what you need to "bring to the surface"

What is life? An illusion, a shadow, a story. And the greatest good is little enough: for all life is a dream and dreams themselves are only dreams.   PEDRO CALDERON DE LA BARCA

emotionally and indicate the sort of imagery you feel more or less comfortable with. For even in the depths of the most awful nightmare, you will find yourself being terrorized by the sort of thing that you already know you find scary. In a sense this is a comforting thought, because you will not frighten yourself in your dreams with an image that is totally alien. If it is mice and spiders that scare you in waking life, then they are the most likely creatures to pop up and scare you in your dreams. Conversely if it is the Bogey Man, ghosts or monsters that terrify you, then that is what will stalk the nightmare corridors of your dreaming mind.

BLOOD IN THE TAPS

Your own curious dream logic is likely to remain fairly constant over the years and you will gradually come to know your dreams, and yourself, pretty well. Once you know your own dream logic you can to a certain extent ignore what is following those predictable patterns. For instance, if someone dreams that water comes out of the taps, then their logic is following a natural course. If, however, they

ABOVE Whatever scares or disturbs you in your waking life is likely to scare you just as much in your dreams. The nightmares that frighten you will carry images that you have an instant fearful reaction to.

always dream that blood comes out of the taps then that is their unique dream logic. Neither dream is good or bad, right or wrong. They are merely the unique expressions of two different dreamers whose minds are processing their unconscious material while they are asleep.

DREAMS AND EVERYDAY LIFE

There does seem to be a close relationship between what happens in our "real" lives and what happens in our dreams. The situations may change but the rules governing them tend to be the same as in everyday life. For instance if you are always concerned with what people wear, then it is likely that clothes and the way they are worn will be just as important in your dreams. If, on the other hand, you are more interested in what people say, then it is likely your dreams will follow a similar pattern.

DREAM SCENERY

DREAMS HAVE TO BE SET SOMEWHERE, TO HAVE A PHYSICAL SITUATION THAT THEY TAKE PLACE IN. THIS IS THE DREAM SCENERY, SIMILAR TO THE BACKDROP OF A THEATRE STAGE. THE LOCATION AND PROPS PROVIDE A CONTEXT FOR THE DREAM AND GIVE CLUES ABOUT THE ACTION THAT IS TAKING PLACE. FOR MOST OF US MOST OF THE TIME, THE CHARACTERISTICS OF THIS BACKDROP REMAIN MUCH THE SAME AS IN EVERYDAY LIFE. IT IS UNUSUAL FOR DREAMS TO BE SET IN A LANDSCAPE WHERE, FOR EXAMPLE, EVERYTHING IS PERMANENTLY UPSIDE DOWN. IT IS MUCH MORE LIKELY THAT THE SCENERY WILL BE THE RIGHT WAY UP AND THE DREAM ACTORS AND PROPS BEHAVE ACCORDING TO THE NATURAL LAWS OF PHYSICS.

THE SENSE AND SUBSTANCE OF DREAMS

BELOW RIGHT Once we are immersed in the dream the landscape will appear real; it is only when we wake that it seems odd. It may be a symbolic or real place, or even both.
BELOW Interpreting the landscapes in your dreams will depend on what significance they have to you in real life. Tall buildings would have suggested the phallus to Freud, but to you they might represent anything from soaring ambition to intimidation.

SURREAL LANDSCAPES

Now and again of course, dream settings and characters do not obey natural laws. Trees may appear upside down, the sky may be green, the sea a brilliant shade of yellow, cats may swim and people may fly weightless above the ground. Within the context of the dream, all of these things appear perfectly normal. It is only when we wake that they strike us as odd, as the rational mind tries to make sense of the illogical and therefore impossible.

These surreal dreams are often the ones that stick in the memory and usually have particular significance for the dreamer. The landscape is what we would focus on when trying to interpret the dream, although the conclusions we reach will depend on each individual.

According to Freud, the landscape of our dreams can be interpreted, and represents the uncharted territory of the unconscious mind and our repressed sexual longings.

Then suddenly I ... fly slowly over the lane, over the houses, and then over the Golden Horn in the direction of Stamboul. I smell the sea, feel the wind, the warm sun. This flying gives me a wonderfully pleasant sensation... P. D. OUSPENSKY

INTERPRETING THE LANDSCAPE

In a Freudian world, soft round or curvy shapes and narrow indentations represent the female form. For instance, hills represent a woman's breasts, belly or womb, and a dark doorway or passageway, her vagina. Alternatively, hard, upright or elongated shapes represent the male form. Mountain peaks, tall buildings, a train and an aeroplane are all phallic symbols. Only you can decide if these ideas have meaning for you in the context of your dreams.

Jung did not interpret the dream landscape in the same way as Freud, yet he nevertheless believed that the place where the dream is staged makes a tremendous difference to the way the dream is interpreted. A dream that is set in a wood or forest has quite a different feel about it to one that is set in a living room or office. Some dream experts believe that dreams staged in a man-made setting are more based on the concerns of the personality, while those dreams that are set in nature come from the deeper reaches of the soul.

MOODS AND FEELINGS

It is not only the physical nature of the dream setting that is important, but the mood or atmosphere it inspires. The dream landscape has the power to provoke feelings and emotions in the dreamer. Although the scenery may look the same as it does in ordinary life, it may take on a curious surreal quality, appearing melting and hypnotic, as deeply experienced and more real than real. People in a state of hallucination have reported similar occurrences, experiencing a world where walls are sad or happy, trees can sing and dance, and crockery can throw itself at you in a fit of angry pique.

Yet dream scenery does not need to take on a life of its own for it to inspire mood and feelings. Some of the most lasting impressions of our dreams

LEFT Dream landscape not only refers to natural scenery, but to any context in which your dream takes place, inside or out. You might dream about your own living room – it would still be your dream landscape.

COMMON DREAM SETTINGS

Research indicates that the most frequent dream setting is a building, usually a domestic residence, with the living room, bedroom or kitchen being the most common place. The average number of characters in a dream is three, with strangers appearing slightly more often than friends or family members. Predominant dream activities are action-based, such as walking or running, followed by talking, sitting, socializing and playing. The most common emotions are apprehension and anger, followed by happiness and excitement.

are fragments of a landscape dimly remembered. Beautiful, awe-inspiring, tantalizing or downright peculiar, the dream setting is not only a backdrop for the action to take place, but is an integral part of the dream's content and the message it is trying to convey to the dreamer.

BELOW The dream setting allows us the freedom to imagine that anything can take place; that anything is possible, it doesn't have to be real or feasible, and it is important to examine why you have dreamt it like this.

NIGHTMARES

ALMOST EVERYONE KNOWS WHAT IT'S LIKE TO HAVE A NIGHTMARE. THE CHINESE DESCRIBE THEM AS DREAMS OF TERROR
AND DREAD, WITH THE POWER TO JOLT US OUT OF SLEEP. WITNESSING ACTS OF HORROR OR BEING IN SOME KIND OF
DANGER ARE THE MOST FREQUENT NIGHTMARE SCENARIOS. THESE ARE USUALLY ACCOMPANIED BY FEELINGS OF
HELPLESSNESS AND PARALYSIS, OF BEING LOST OR OUT OF CONTROL AND AT THE MERCY OF AN EXTERNAL AGENT OR EVENT.
FOR THOSE WHO SUFFER FROM FREQUENT NIGHTMARES GOING TO BED IS FILLED WITH FEAR. SLEEP IS NOT RENEWING AND
REFRESHING, BUT IS MORE LIKE GOING INTO A STRESSFUL SITUATION, NIGHT AFTER NIGHT.

THE SUBJECTIVITY OF NIGHTMARES

Although we share a broad consensus about what is
frightening, the content of our nightmares is always
subjective. What is frightening in one person's
dream world may seem innocuous in someone else's.
What makes a nightmare upsetting is how it feels,
the emotional experience, rather than the symbols or
events in themselves. Consequently people who are
emotionally sensitive seem to be more likely to
experience nightmares than those who can shrug
unwanted thoughts and feelings away. This may help
explain why people with a creative bent, as well as
young children, seem to suffer more frequent
nightmares than other people.

WHY WE HAVE NIGHTMARES

Although nightmares are unpleasant, they may have
a positive intention. They can be a message from the
unconscious mind, a way of alerting us to something
that is going on in our waking life that we need to
become more aware of. When this is the case, the
nightmare may recur, growing progressively more
frightening until we understand what it is about and
can root out the cause. Sometimes nightmares may
be signs of illness and/or drug reactions, so do check
with your doctor to eliminate this possibility.

CREATIVE VISUALIZATION

When nightmares become a real problem, and begin
to disturb your waking life too, there are self-help
measures you can take to reduce their frequency and
intensity. The following suggestions are based on the
techniques of creative visualization. Use them to
begin to learn how to tap into the powers of your
imagination in order to create change.

LEFT The more sensitive we are, the more artistic and
creative, the more likely it is we are going to have
nightmares. If you suffer from them, you might take
some comfort from that fact.

> To sleep: perchance to dream: ay,
> there's the rub:
> For in that sleep of death what
> dreams may come...
>
> WILLIAM SHAKESPEARE, HAMLET

CREATING AN IMAGINARY SCENE

Some people are able to visualize very easily; for others it might take some practice. You are trying to develop your ability to experience a mental escape from the scenes of your nightmares. Aim to make your imaginary scene such a strong image in your mind that it travels with you into your dream, and becomes your refuge over which you have control.

1 Sit in a quiet place where you feel safe and won't be disturbed. Close your eyes, breathe gently and allow yourself to relax.

2 Now imagine yourself in a beautiful place. This may be outside in nature, or indoors. It can be a real or an imaginary place. Visualize the scene as fully as possible, noticing the objects or scenery that surround you, any sounds or smells, whether it is warm or cool. Notice how you feel and what you are wearing. If you find yourself stopping at various points as you go through your imaginary scene, take notice of where you stop and then start again. It may take a few stops and starts to develop the scene in your mind's eye, but with time and regular practice it will come.

3 When you are comfortable with your scene, experiment by making small changes in it. For instance, you could change the colour of the walls, or add an animal that you like, or maybe a doorway or pathway. Continue to practise until you feel confident that the power of your own imagination has been added to your collection of skills. If at any time you start experiencing a negative reaction to what you are imagining, stop the scene and start again.

WORKING WITH NIGHTMARES

When you are able to create an imaginary scene and play about with it at will you are ready to use the technique with your nightmares. For some people, nightmares arise as a result of an actual trauma. Traumatic events can be too much for us to deal with at the time, so for the sake of preserving our sanity, they get pushed into the basement of the unconscious. Later the unexplored material may resurface in our dreams, perhaps so that any leftover memories and feelings associated with the event can be worked through and healed in relative safety. You may need to seek professional help when dealing with these sorts of nightmares.

1 Write down a recent nightmare. After you have written it down, allow yourself to change the nightmare in any way you wish, writing out a new and less threatening scenario.

2 Using your creative imagination, visualize the new dream you have written. See the scene in as much detail as possible. Let it play through your mind for 5-10 minutes, as if it is a new dream that you are actually experiencing.

3 Imagine this new dream at least once a day for a week, preferably before going to sleep. It is best to work with one dream at a time and not more than three a week.

After three months you should see some improvement in your nightmares. If no change is happening, change the dream again, creating a different scenario.

ABOVE The beautiful imaginary place that you create in your mind can take many forms. If you always return to the same place it can become more and more real, with a potency that can overcome the nightmare.

WORKING WITH DREAMS

There are many different kinds of dream. Some are at a relatively superficial level. These are largely concerned with daily trivia and seem to represent a cataloguing of the day's events. Others seem to bubble up from the deepest, darkest corners of the psyche and are not so easily understood. These are the ones that usually strike us as important in some way, even if we cannot be sure why. Learning to capture these "dreams from the deep" and finding ways to decode their meaning is what the following pages are all about.

Keeping a dream diary, working with dream tools and using your dreams for problem-solving as well as learning how to control your dreams are some of the different ways you can work with your dreams. With these keys you will be able to unlock the secrets of your dreams. This will bring a greater understanding of yourself and your relationships and increase your capacity to live life to the full.

DREAM RECALL

Many people claim that they do not dream. It is much more likely that they are unable to remember their dreams. Our dreams tend to slip away, like a thief in the night, before we have chance to apprehend them. Yet our dreams are the one place where we can relax, where we can be ourselves. Our dreams are ripples in the pool of our unconscious, the place where the worries and anxieties that we so successfully hide from the world may surface in safety. Dreams can give us valuable insights into our lives, and to get the most out of them, we need to train ourselves in the art of dream recall.

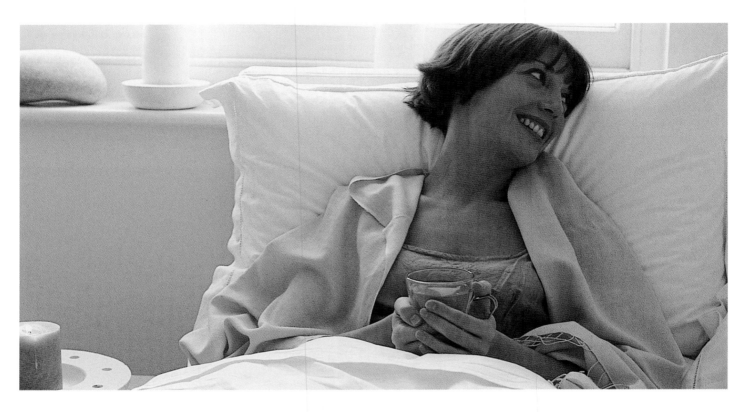

ABOVE Talking about dreams is a good way to defuse them, but also to begin to understand them. Women tend to talk about their dreams more than men, and express more of an interest in others' dreams.

DREAM JOURNALS

One of the best and easiest ways for remembering dreams is to keep a dream journal. It's worth keeping a special book or note pad and using it only for recording your dreams. Keep the book and a pen by your pillow and write in it as soon as you wake each morning. When you wake up, make as little physical movement as possible – even turning over can be enough for the memories to evaporate before you have had chance to record them. Lying still, in the same position as when you woke up, often increases dream recall. Keep your eyes closed. Not only will there be less distraction this way, but many people are often able to see the dream again.

If you can't remember any dreams, then just jot down feelings or thoughts that spring to mind. These may well be echoes of your last dream, a sort of dream vapour trail, and may be enough to trigger further memories of your dreams. If you wake up from a vivid dream in the middle of the night, it is a good idea to record it straightaway before going back to sleep. Some people keep a torch by the bed to save putting the bedside light on.

RECORDING DREAMS

There is no single, right way to record your dreams. You may want to jot down key words or feelings, or make a note of the people or events. Some people prefer to write a narrative of their dream while others like to include pictures or sketches. If you can't remember the start of your dream, don't give up. Don't worry about sequence; working backwards or from the middle can lead you to remember more details. Sometimes you'll be halfway through

RIGHT The more we keep a journal the more likely it is to actually influence our dreams – we begin to dream the journal. This makes analyzing and understanding our dreams much easier.

remembering a dream when you'll remember something from dreams you had previously forgotten. Even fragments of dreams are valuable and can contain useful information. Writing in the present rather than the past tense can help you re-live the dream as you record it.

You might want to record your dream on one side of the page and leave the other side blank for comments and interpretation later on. It is, however, a good idea to record the date and the place where you had the dream and to generally include as much detail as possible; some people like to include the phase of the moon for instance. If you can't write the dream in your journal immediately you wake up, then make a note of the things you remember the most. These will jog your memory later on when you do have time to continue your journal.

THEMES AND PATTERNS

As you keep your journal, images, incidents and even emotions will slowly build over time to create a picture of your unique psychic identity, but you should keep the journal for at least a month before you try to make any sense of it. When you look, you may notice recurring themes or patterns in your

dreams. Perhaps a recurring vision of being chased, or falling from a high place, or being confined in a small place for instance. Or it might be a symbol, such as a flower, a road, a boat, or a particular animal that keeps cropping up. Recurring themes often indicate there is something in your life that needs your attention, perhaps a part of you that wants expression. You could also look for links between your dreams and events that happened recently. Identifying a pattern can make us better equipped to deal with life.

LEFT Dreaming of a particular symbol and seeing it crop up repeatedly might indicate an important theme that you need to work on.

ABOVE Recurring themes often indicate recurring worries. By paying attention to what the dream is trying to say to us we can help alleviate the stress.

A dream is an answer to a question we haven't yet learned how to ask.　　FOX MULDER, THE X-FILES

PREPARE TO DREAM

PEOPLE HAVE ALWAYS SUSPECTED THAT THE INNER UNIVERSE OF OUR DREAMS IS A SOURCE OF WISDOM. THROUGHOUT HISTORY, DREAMS HAVE BEEN USED FOR HEALING, TO STIMULATE INVENTION AND DISCOVERY, AS WELL AS INSPIRE GREAT LITERATURE AND WORKS OF ART. THEY HAVE ALSO BEEN USED TO PREDICT THE FUTURE AND BRING SPIRITUAL REVELATION. FOR MOST OF US, MOST OF THE TIME, OUR DREAMS ARE NOT ON SUCH AN EPIC SCALE, BUT THEY ARE A VALUABLE SOURCE OF SELF-KNOWLEDGE. ONCE WE HAVE ACCEPTED THAT DREAMS ARE AN IMPORTANT PART OF OUR LIFE, WE WILL FIND THAT THEY BECOME MORE POTENT AND REVEALING. WE NEED, THEREFORE, TO FIND WAYS TO DREAM THE BEST POSSIBLE DREAMS.

A SHRINE FOR SLEEP

In the ancient world, dreams were "incubated" in sacred or lonely places, such as a temple or the wilderness, in order to create an ideal birth place for them. Take this principle into your own sleeping habits and transform your bedroom into a "shrine for sleep". Make sure the room is as comfortable and relaxing as possible. The temperature should be not too hot and not too cold, and there should be sufficient ventilation. Keep the space clear and free from clutter, and surround yourself with colours and objects that gently stimulate your senses in a positive way rather than depress you. Relaxing colours are lilacs, neutrals and pinks, although any shade that appeals to you is fine. Tidy away any objects that are associated with the outside world, such as shoes and clothes, and use soft lighting. Any kind of electrical equipment is best kept to a minimum in the bedroom.

BEDTIME RITUALS

In the past, societies who recognized the importance of dreaming created elaborate rituals to prepare body, mind and soul for the journey. To get the most from our dreams, we need to be in a relaxed, receptive state and approach going to sleep in a spirit of openness and enquiry. If we go to bed stressed or completely exhausted then we are unlikely to get the most from our dreams.

To get ourselves into the right frame of mind, we can create our own modern-day rituals to prepare for sleep and dreaming. One simple way of doing this is by listening to music. A little gentle classical music is a good choice, although you could experiment with other types of music to see if they have any effect on your sleep and dreaming patterns. Alternatively you could try burning incense or vaporizing essential oils in the evening. Useful scents include sandalwood as an aid to meditation and to

MEDITATION FOR DREAMS

When we meditate, we enter a state of altered consciousness. As body and mind unwind, our brain rhythms slow down to produce a relaxed alpha wave pattern, similar, yet of greater intensity, to that produced during deep sleep. In such a state, we become quiet and receptive. Try this meditation every night for a week and make a note in your dream journal of any changes to your sleep or dreams.

1 Sit in a relaxed position, close your eyes and focus on your breathing. As you breathe in, imagine a stream of golden light entering through the crown of your head.
2 Hold your breath for a few seconds, or as long as is comfortable and visualize the light circulating around your body.
3 Now breathe out, imagining the light leaving your body through the soles of your feet, taking away all the cares of the day.
4 Repeat the sequence several times.

You may want to experiment with breathing in different colours, depending on your changing needs. Pink is good for emotional healing, blue for calm, lavender for spiritual awareness, and green for fresh and original thinking.

ABOVE Creating a bedroom that is a shrine to sleep will help you to incubate dreams.
FAR LEFT Essential oils and scents can also help to create the right atmosphere for dreams and trouble-free sleep.
LEFT Bedroom rituals, such as taking a warm candlelit bath, are a good way to wind down for bed, free the mind from the day's troubles and make us more receptive to dreams.

connect with your higher self; lavender to encourage relaxation and calm; frankincense to open up to the angelic realm; and myrrh to connect with mysterious, archetypal energies. Experiment with other aromas, but make sure you choose scents that relax and soothe rather than ones that stimulate. A herb sachet placed under your pillow can also induce soothing sleep. Suitable fillers include dried hops, lavender, marjoram and passion flower.

Taking a warm, candlelit bath before bedtime is also a good way of letting go of the cares of the day in preparation for sleep. A couple of drops of essential oil can be swished into the water if you wish. Try practising a meditation technique last thing at night. It is a good way of switching off from your worldly concerns and creating a space for your unconscious to "come through" in the night without any worries and problems getting in the way.

Reach high, for stars lie hidden in your soul. Dream deep, for every dream precedes the goal.

PAMELA VAULL STARR

Dream Tools

In many parts of the world, great store is set by dreams, for instance many African societies believe that dreams are linked to destiny. Dreams are seen as a vehicle for the spirit world to communicate with the dreamer, giving important information relating to health, enemies or the future. Among Native Americans there is a widespread belief that a "sacred power" speaks to you in your dreams. This power will often appear as an animal. In such societies dreams are taken seriously and dream tools are used to assist the dreamer in a variety of ways, especially for protection from bad dreams and to assist in dream programming and recall.

ABOVE We have access to a wide range of tools to help us interpret our dreams, including those used by other cultures.

DREAM WISDOM

People have always suspected that the inner universe of our dreams is a source of infinite wisdom. Throughout history, dreams have been used for healing, to stimulate invention and discovery, as well as inspiring great literature and works of art. They have also been used to predict the future and bring spiritual revelation. For most of us most of the time, our dreams do not fall into these epic categories, yet increasingly we are recognizing them as a valuable source of self-knowledge. Once we have accepted that dreams are an important part of our life, we will find that they become more potent and revealing. This means that we should prepare ourselves for the best possible dreams that we can have.

THE DREAM DOCTOR

The Cuna Indians of Central America see dreams as having an identity or power, with bad dreams signifying an impending disaster or illness. A disturbing dream would be taken to the "dream doctor" or medicine man for interpretation and a "prescription" to make it better.

Typically the prescription is an object into which special "power" or spells have been worked. The dream tool is then taken to bed by the dreamer to work its magic through the night and nullify the bad effects of the dream. Dream dolls and spearheads are the Cuna's most common dream tools, but stones, pegs, crosses and miniature weapons, such as axes or knives, are also used.

RIGHT A Cuna Native American woman, with a young girl beside her, takes care of a dream doll. As a potent dream tool the doll will be an integral part of the owner's daily life, linking the waking and dream worlds.

The dream doctor may also make up a powder containing a special wood mixed with black date palm and rub it over the dreamer's eyes to protect them from the effects of the bad dream. Through these actions it is believed that the dream's power is negated or "earthed".

SKY AXES

The Cuna Indians live on the islands off the Atlantic coast of Panama, and their lives are very much influenced by the weather and the natural elements. Violent storms during the night frequently disturb their sleep, and a favourite dream-doctor cure is to sleep with a "sky axe". Sky axes are real axe heads that have been found at the old burial ground sites of the Cuna people. The Cuna Indians believe that these axe heads help protect their dream spirit guides from the power of thunder by making the spirit guides invisible.

As we would expect, the dream tools used by the Cuna Indians and other indigenous peoples are intimately related to a specific culture and lifestyle. However, we can adapt the principle of dream tools to suit our particular circumstances and create our own tools to assist our dreaming.

YOUR OWN DREAM TOOLS

If you want to create your own dream tools, you need to choose objects that have special meaning for you. This could be an item that has special significance in your everyday life, or a childhood toy, a memento from a lover, a gift from a friend, or a treasured photo. If it is nature that inspires you, look for natural objects such as a piece of driftwood, a pebble from a favourite beach, a piece of tree bark or a fragrant flower. Dream tools can also be chosen to tie-in with the kind of dream you are trying to have or recall, maybe in answer to a particular question or on an important theme in your life. For instance, if work is an issue, then choose an object to symbolize what it is that you do: a tool for an engineer, a mixing spoon for a chef, a pen for a writer, or a thermometer for a nurse for instance.

ABOVE Like other Native American traditions, the Fox and Sauk tribe uses costume and ritual to help people recall and interpret their dreams.

EMPOWERING YOUR DREAM TOOL

Before a dream tool can work its magic, traditionally it is "empowered" by the dream doctor with special spells. You can do this yourself using colour and visualization. Use red for dreams of passion and adventure, blue or lilac for healing, green to be shown new pathways in life, and orange when looking at relationships. If you are working on communication issues, choose deep blue; for power and authority use purple; or work with yellow when seeking an answer to a health question. You could also use any other colours that intuitively spring to mind as being the ones that are most appropriate for you at the time.

To work with the colour, visualize your dream tool surrounded in coloured light, wrap the tool in a piece of the right coloured fabric or tie coloured ribbons on to the object. As you do so, spend some time visualizing the colour in your head, and mentally surround the item with it. When it is ready, take your dream object and put it under your pillow. It may help you have the sort of dream you want or else help protect you from bad dreams.

DREAM CATCHING

In Native American culture, dreams are seen as messages from sacred spirits in the night sky. Certain tribes also believe in the idea of the Great Dream. In the womb, everyone has their own great dream but this gets forgotten at birth. This dream bestows gifts such as courage, creativity, humour or empathy upon the individual and gives a vision for the best pathway through life. From a young age, children are encouraged to "catch" and explore their dreams and young men will fast until they have a vision of their "song of life". Dream catching plays an important part in initiation ceremonies, where the initiate makes a magical or sacred circle around himself to "capture" the messages from the dream spirits in the space inside the circle. The dream catcher tool is a symbolic representation of this magical or sacred circle.

CATCH YOUR DREAMS

Dream catchers not only capture the good spirits, but also filter out any negative or unwanted powers. They consist of a cobweb-like structure on a circular frame, usually with beads or feathers attached to it. This structure symbolizes the "web of life"; in other words, it shows how all aspects of life are not separate but are intimately connected to one another. At the centre of the web sits Iktome, the spider, and keeper of dreams. Iktome is often represented by a coloured bead or shell. The dream catcher is hung near the sleeper's bed. The good dreams pass to Iktome, who holds them for the dreamer. The bad dreams are ensnared in her web and can be emptied away in the morning.

Dream catchers can be made in many shapes and sizes. They are not only useful but are also bright and colourful and make an interesting decoration in a bedroom. Children find them especially appealing and many parents have experienced positive results with children who suffer nightmares or who are afraid of the dark. Remember to empty the dream catcher each morning by tapping any unwanted dreams into the waste bin. Do this with the child, or encourage them to do it for him or herself.

MAKING A DREAM CATCHER

A good way of protecting yourself from disturbing dreams is to make your own dream catcher. It may also help you gain more insight into where you should be going in life and show you the best choices to help you achieve your ends. A dream catcher is a very personal thing and there is plenty of scope to make it in a way that appeals to you.

YOU WILL NEED

- a thin and bendy piece of wood about 60cm (2ft) long. A freshly cut piece of bamboo or hazel is ideal.
- a length of twine, such as fishing line or strong cotton thread
- feathers, a few beads and some coloured ribbons for decoration

1 Curl the bamboo or hazel into a circle and fasten it with twine wrapped around. Some people like to cover the whole of the wood in ribbon before they start, but it is up to you.

2 Cut off any sharp ends of wood at the join and wrap some ribbon around it.

3 Tie one end of the twine onto any point on the circle and tie it to the opposite point of the circle. Cut off the long end of twine.

4 Tie another piece of twine across the middle of the circle, at right angles to the first piece.

5 Attach four shorter pieces of twine between the four tying-on points to form a square. From the middle of one of the shorter lengths, attach a piece of twine to the two tying-on-points on the other side of the circle. Repeat for the other short lengths. This gives you a sort of "cat's cradle" effect. Experiment until you have a pleasing criss-cross of lines resembling a spider's web.

6 Add a bead in the centre to represent the spider.

7 Finish by decorating the dream catcher with some ribbons hanging from the bottom of the circle. Add some feathers and beads to these downward-hanging ribbons.

When your dream catcher is finished you can empower it in the same way as with a dream tool. Hang your dream catcher at the window of your bedroom, or above the bed.

ABOVE The dream catcher is a Native American device that filters your dreams so that only the pleasant ones get through.

DREAM GUIDES

Sometimes an ally or guide will appear in our dreams. In Native American culture, animals often symbolise these guides or helpers, with each person having their own totem or "power" animal. To find your totem animal, ask to be shown in a dream, or devise a dream journey to find it. This involves a visualization in which you see in your mind a path that you begin to walk down. As you walk, take notice of the scenery and the details around you, then open your mind and call for your power animal. The animal could be anything, from a wolf to a beetle, when it arrives greet it warmly, touch it and give it love. Be aware of what it feels like and feel the love it has for you. Remember, the greater the detail the more real it will be. Your dream guide might be an animal that you feel an affinity with in real life, you might love horses, for example, or feel inspired by the traditional north American wolf or bison, but don't try and manipulate the choice, let the animal make itself known to you.

CONTROLLING DREAMS

ALTHOUGH OUR DREAMS APPEAR TO BE OUT OF OUR CONTROL, WE CAN IN FACT TAKE A MORE ACTIVE ROLE AND LEARN HOW TO INFLUENCE OR PLAN THEM. THIS MAY NOT BE SOMETHING THAT YOU THINK IS POSSIBLE, BUT IF YOU ARE WILLING TO GIVE IT A TRY YOU MAY BE SURPRISED. WE CAN ASK OUR DREAMS TO PROVIDE US WITH ADVENTURES OR SELF-KNOWLEDGE OR SHOW US CREATIVE SOLUTIONS TO OUR PROBLEMS. WHEN WE ARE FEELING LOST WE CAN ASK OUR DREAMS FOR CLARITY AND GUIDANCE, INSPIRATION AND INFORMATION. WHAT WE ARE DOING IS ASKING FOR A MESSAGE FROM DEEP WITHIN OURSELVES, CONVEYED TO US BY WAY OF METAPHOR, MOOD AND SYMBOLS, VIA OUR DREAMS.

DEVELOPING DREAM SKILLS

Dreams speak in a language of pictures and feelings rather than thoughts and words. The greater our ability to sense and visualize, the more we are able to take control of our dreams. A good place to start is in everyday life. We can begin by really starting to notice the visual impact of the world around us, observing the colours, shapes and textures more profoundly. Spend some time soaking up visual imagery that you find interesting. For instance this could include looking at paintings and works of art, tarot cards, mandalas or any other pictures that appeal to your senses. At the same time, pay more attention to your feeling state. Be aware of those things that alter your mood, noticing not only what you see, but also what you hear and maybe smell. Listening to music and reading is another way of developing your imagination and sensitivity.

BELOW To help increase your sensitivity to images, try really looking at the images on post-cards or tarot cards, and concentrate on absorbing every detail. This skill of recording visual imagery will transfer to your dream world.

CLEAR INTENTION

In the first instance, to plan a dream means having a good idea of why you want it and what it is exactly that you expect from it. The more sincere you are, the more likely is the chance that your unconscious mind will co-operate with you. Perhaps you need to work out some aspect of a relationship, or maybe you are trying to make an important decision and are not quite sure which way to go. Drawing on information from our dreams can give us a very clear idea of where we really want to be rather than where we think we ought to be.

SETTING THE SCENE

If you want to generate a particular type of dream, first you need to be in a relaxed and open frame of mind. Next you need to focus on what it is you want to dream about. This could mean writing it out

Don't be afraid of the space between your dreams and reality. If you can dream it, you can make it so.

BELVA DAVIS

LIFE DIRECTION

A young man is unsure about his direction in life so he asks for guidance in his dream.

"I really wanted to know where I was going, what I was supposed to be doing. I played some soothing music as I went to bed and let my mind go blank. I was asking for guidance as I fell asleep. I had an amazing dream in which I was riding a camel across the desert. All I really remember was the utter silence, the loneliness and isolation, but also a real feeling of peacefulness.

The message of the dream seemed very clear to me. 'Go alone and with nothing until you are ready to be with people again.' It all made perfect sense to me, and helped me a great deal."

LEFT Dreaming Bread – an old recipe for making your dreams come true. Perhaps an old wives' tale, but perhaps also a method of triggering a dream event, the act of performing any kind of ritual has its own potency.

on a piece of paper and tucking it under your pillow. You could also write in your dream journal. If you have any questions, make sure they are as open-ended as possible. Repeat your requests to yourself just before going to sleep. Sometimes holding an object that is connected with the situation is helpful. Reviewing the events of the day last thing at night may also help you relate your dream to what is happening in everyday life. A good way of training your mind in this way is to add an element of ritual to your bedtime routine.

DREAMING BREAD

You might like to try this traditional ritual for generating dreams. It involves making a "dreaming bread". You can use an ordinary bread recipe but bake a round loaf. As you knead the dough concentrate on what sort of dream you want to have. When baked cut the bread into three and take a bite out of each piece. Put the remaining pieces under your pillow and that night it is said that you will dream your requested dream, as long as you don't speak between eating the bread and sleeping.

BELOW LEFT Listening to music can also help you to develop your imagination and sensitivity. But make sure you really listen, use your mind to process the sounds rather than just letting it wash over you.
BELOW By creating the right atmosphere, and performing simple rituals, our dream work can become more connected.

PROBLEMS AND INSPIRATION

THERE IS A TENDENCY TO SEE PROBLEMS AS A SERIES OF HAZARDS TO BE AVOIDED, OR ELSE HINDRANCES TO BE SKILFULLY NEGOTIATED. WHEN WE HAVE A PROBLEM, MOST OF US WANT TO SOLVE IT AS QUICKLY AS POSSIBLE. HOWEVER, IT IS ALSO POSSIBLE TO SEE PROBLEMS AS CHALLENGES. PROBLEMS PRESENT AN OPPORTUNITY TO LEARN AND GROW, TO CHANGE AND IMPROVE. SOMETIMES A PROBLEM IS A GATEWAY TO A BETTER FUTURE. IF WE RUSH AT SOLVING OUR PROBLEMS INSTEAD OF TRYING TO LEARN FROM THEM WE RISK NOT GROWING, NOT LEARNING. WE CAN ALSO USE OUR DREAMS TO HELP US. IF WE ARE PERCEPTIVE ENOUGH THE SOLUTION MAY BE SOMETHING WE WOULD NEVER HAVE THOUGHT OF.

SLEEP ON IT

Some of the most creative solutions to problems have not come through logic or reasoning but through dreams. For instance, in the 19th century, Dmitri Mendeleyev, a Russian chemist, was having a problem about how to organize chemical elements. Deciding to "sleep on it" he had a dream in which he saw the elements falling in the correct order. Using the information from his dream, he went on to devise the periodic table of elements, a central concept of modern inorganic chemistry.

Creative solutions do not arrive out of the blue however. They are usually preceded by plenty of "spade work", which may have taken days, weeks, months or even years before the final flash of genius. A shift in perception seems to happen more easily when the logical mind has given up on the problem. When we relax and stop trying, our innate, inner intelligence can take over and put the pieces of the puzzle together while we sleep.

DECODING THE MESSAGE

It can sometimes be the smallest detail in a dream that can provide the clue to help us solve the problem or dilemma we are working on. It might be a visual image or symbol, a smell or a sound, a mood or a feeling. It is a question of being alert and allowing intuition, rather than the conscious mind, to help us solve the riddle.

While we sleep, the mind continues to work. Freed from the restraints of logic and convention, the unconscious is free to take an unorthodox

LEFT Our dreams can expose what lies beneath the surface, thoughts or emotions that were hidden. In the same way they can help with problem solving, bringing a solution up to the surface of our consciousness.

All this inventing, this producing, takes place in a pleasing lively dream. WOLFGANG AMADEUS MOZART

RIGHT Our mind doesn't go to sleep when our body does; it begins its most creative work. When we are awake it is to our benefit to try and decode that work, to access the creative part of ourselves.

approach to the problem and come up with a solution. It is not even necessary to be able to remember our dreams for this process to work. Most of us will have experienced being unable to solve a problem one day, but the next, after a good night's sleep, suddenly finding that either a new way of looking at the problem has appeared, or the problem itself has vanished. If you enjoy completing crossword puzzles, you could test this theory on a superficial level. Find a clue that you're unable to crack, and just before you go to sleep run it through your mind. The next day, revisit the clue and see if the answer comes to you.

DREAMS TO INSPIRE

Many writers, artists and musicians have literally "dreamed up" stories, poems, melodies and other works of art. For instance, Robert Louis Stevenson, the 19th-century Scottish writer, spent days

wracking his brains for a suitable plot to explore the idea that we all have our good and bad sides. He claimed that the storyline for his novel *The Strange Case of Dr Jekyll and Mr Hyde* came to him in a dream. More recently, the famous surrealist paintings of 20th-century artists such as Salvador Dalí or René Magritte are set in dream-like landscapes, while singer-songwriter Paul McCartney says the Beatles' hit-song "Yesterday" was in his head when he woke up one morning.

BELOW Dreams have always inspired writers and artists and painters – they can still inspire us, motivate us, stimulate and encourage us. Will your dreams help to complete the jigsaw of your waking life?

DREAM DECISION

A young man is having trouble making a decision about a job offer. After a day thinking out the pros and cons, he decides to sleep on the problem, and before he falls asleep deliberately places in his mind the problem that is preoccupying him.

"I couldn't work out whether I should take the job I was being offered. On paper it seemed to be just what I was looking for, but something was holding me back. I couldn't make a decision. I went to sleep wondering about this and had a dream where I saw myself smoking a cigar. That was all. I couldn't remember anything else but the dream struck me as very evocative, very symbolic.

The cigar seemed to represent everything that was holding me back about taking that job. It represented success, winning and achievement and being like my father. I could almost smell myself in a city suit, all aftershave and cigar smoke, like a banker or a tycoon. It wasn't an image I liked and I realized it wasn't a job I really wanted, so I turned it down. The cigar made me realize that I was thinking about taking the job because it was what my father would have wanted, but it wasn't me."

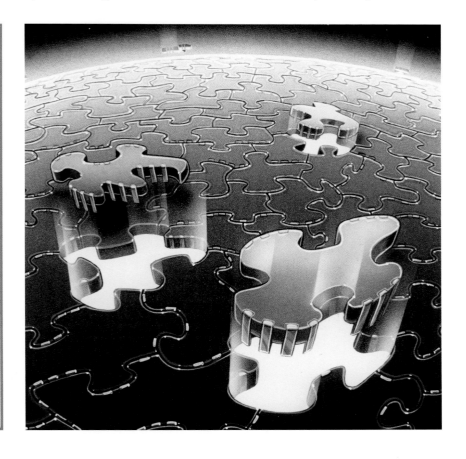

DREAMS AND RELATIONSHIPS

WE ARE SOCIAL BEINGS AND OUR INTERACTIONS WITH ONE ANOTHER AFFECT US DEEPLY. RELATIONSHIPS OF ONE KIND OR ANOTHER WEAVE THE FABRIC OF LIFE, FORMING A RICH TAPESTRY. SOME OF THESE RELATIONSHIPS ARE RELATIVELY SUPERFICIAL, WHILE OTHERS HAVE THE POWER TO AFFECT US AT A DEEP EMOTIONAL LEVEL — FOR GOOD OR BAD. OUR DREAMS CAN GIVE US GREAT INSIGHT INTO OUR RELATIONSHIPS WITH LOVERS, FRIENDS, FAMILY OR COLLEAGUES. THEY CAN HIGHLIGHT AREAS OF TENSION, REVEAL THINGS, ANSWER OUR QUESTIONS AND HELP US COME TO TERMS WITH OUR FEELINGS. WE CAN USE OUR DREAMS AS A "WAY IN" TO HELPING IMPROVE THE RELATIONSHIPS THAT MATTER TO US MOST.

ABOVE Dreams about relationships can act as a way in to understanding them more. Don't dismiss even the most banal ones, as they still could be a way of accessing how you really feel about people close to you.

MAKING SENSE OF IT ALL

Sometimes it is tricky to disentangle the messages carried in a dream. Another person appearing in a dream may be representing an aspect of the dreamer's own psyche rather than themselves. Other people may also appear in disguise as an animal or an inanimate object for instance. We also have to remember that our dreams are not our everyday lives being acted out. They are an attempt by the unconscious to comment on and try and make some sense of what is going on for us. They can reveal what is frightening or worrying us, what is making us happy or sad, jealous or angry, and what we need to further growth and development.

When using your dreams to work on relationships, avoid the temptation to come up with a quick and easy interpretation. You need to tread

carefully and keep asking yourself "have I got this right?" It may also be helpful for close friends or partners to work on their dreams together, checking the meaning of the dream with one another. This can be an exciting journey of discovery and strengthen the bond that is between you.

Of course it isn't just our lover that we might dream about. All sorts of other relationships are reflected in our dreaming – children, friends, colleagues, even enemies or mere acquaintances. How we view our relationships in our dreams can indicate how we really view them on a waking level – without the need for any social niceties. We may find that the relationships no longer sustain or support us, or that they need some care and attention. What our dreams can tell us is dependent on how honest we are with ourselves.

Personal relations are the important thing for ever and ever.

E M FORSTER

DREAM DETECTION

A good place to start doing some relationship work is to play "dream detective" and begin by asking some basic questions about the dream. By working through them, you will gain a lot of insight into what the dream is trying to tell you, which is very different from interpretation. The questions can be used to investigate any type of relationship that you wish to explore, not only sexual partnerships.

DREAM QUESTIONNAIRE

Asking the following questions may help to unlock the symbolism of your relationship dreams.

1 What exactly are you doing in the dream? How are you doing it? Describe your thoughts and feelings as you do it.

2 What aren't you doing in the dream? Is there anything specifically missing from the dream that is important, anything that you feel you should or want to be doing?

3 Imagine the dream is a play being acted out and you can rewrite any section of it. Which bits would you re-script and why? With regard to what you are doing, how would you replay the action of the dream differently?

4 Is there anything in the dream that remains unfinished or that you would like to know more about? Is there anything in the dream that brings up conflicts that you feel have not been dealt with in the dream?

5 How do your actions (and those of anyone else in the dream) parallel your actions in daily life? How far are they similar and how far are they different? If they are different, can you think of any reasons why this might be so?

6 If this dream were a film or play, what sort of film or play would it suggest to you? For instance, would it be a romance, a thriller, a comedy, a farce or an adventure story? How does this correspond with daily life? How is it different?

7 If this dream were an educational device for relationship training, what message would it be teaching? What are you learning from the dream? Does it provide any useful insights into the relationship?

8 How will you apply these insights from the dream to your everyday life? What will you do with the information you have gained from the dream?

ABOVE The relationships we have with peers are often some of the most formative and influential of our lives.
LEFT Once we become parents our emotional lives take on a whole new depth. This could well be reflected in our dreams.
BELOW Close friendships can be sustaining and supportive, but can also create angst and turmoil in our lives. Examine your dreams for clues to how you really feel about those who are closest to you.

ABOVE Acting out a dream might be impossible, and certainly impracticable. But if there is a possibility of at least recreating some part or proportion of a significant dream you are exploring, then why not try it?

WORKING WITH THE RELATIONSHIP QUESTIONNAIRE

To understand how the relationship questionnaire might be used, we can use the example of a dream had by a young man named Billy. In the dream, Billy and his girlfriend are at a railway station standing on opposite sides of the track when an express train whooshes into the station. The train doesn't stop, but when it leaves, Billy's girlfriend has disappeared.

A classic Freudian interpretation of the dream would be that the express train is a phallic symbol. It represents Billy's fear of losing his sexual prowess and the sadness he feels when his girlfriend leaves him as a result. However when Billy worked through the dream relationship questionnaire, he arrived at very different conclusions, none of which related to his sexuality. He saw the dream as a message that life was passing him by and he needed to take more risks rather than being a bystander.

WORKING WITH THE DREAM

This is how Billy works through the dream that he feels is about his relationship with his girlfriend.

"My girlfriend and I are standing on opposite sides of the railway tracks at the station. We are waving to each other. An express train comes between us and when it is going she has disappeared. I remember feeling very sad and wondering how she had got on the express train when it hadn't stopped."

Billy's answers and insights

1   I am waving at my girlfriend and I feel sad when she disappears. I am thinking about the mechanics of her disappearance as if it is a magic show at a theatre.

2   I am not going anywhere. I realize the reason I came to the station was to see her off. She was going away somewhere, not me. I am staying.

3   If I could rewrite the dream I wouldn't change anything except I wouldn't feel sad about her leaving. Now I realize that the sadness isn't about her going away but is about me not understanding how the trick was done.

4   The dream didn't bring up any conflict but it did make me realize that my girlfriend going away wasn't such a bad idea. In fact I feel our relationship isn't going anywhere but I have no idea what to do about it.

5   I think my actions in the dream are pretty similar to those in real life. I didn't behave any differently in the dream.

6   I think this would be a spy story, some sort of mystery or thriller. I guess I would like my life to be a bit more exciting and I think I'm actually a bit bored with my relationship.

7   To me the message is loud and clear. The dream teaches me that this relationship isn't going anywhere and I really ought to do something about it. It also makes me realize that it isn't just the relationship that is wrong, but my whole life is somehow over-ripe. I'm getting lazy and stuck in my ways. Deep down I think I'd like to go travelling or take up a dangerous sport or do something to wake myself up a bit.

8   The dream is trying to tell me that I have to take some action. I need to get off my backside and achieve more instead of watching other people have all the fun. I need to take some risks, make my life more exciting and enjoy being alive more.

FREE ASSOCIATION TECHNIQUE

You can take any element from a dream and use it as a starting point for free association. This means you can work with feelings as well as objects, people or places. Billy also used this technique with his express train dream, starting from the word "train". Interestingly, he arrived at a similar understanding as when he completed the dream relationship questionnaire: that he needed to take more control of his life.

TRIGGERING DREAM RECALL

Sometimes the more we look for meaning in our dreams the more such a meaning seems to elude us, or slip away. We can use techniques used in business to improve creativity and see if they might not also work with dream interpretation. For instance opening a book at random and seeing if any words that catch our eye there might trigger a memory or meaning. You could also try combining odd

sequences in the dream and trying to tell a story using them. Or how about sleeping on it – using the next dream to see if it will make sense of the dream we are worrying about. It doesn't have to be a full night's sleep; try just having a quick nap and nod off thinking about your dream.

ACTING IT OUT

If you are feeling adventurous, you could try acting your dream out. This could literally mean going to a place that resembles your dream location and imagining yourself back in the dream. Alternatively, you could act it out at home, setting up a "stage" with the relevant props and characters. This exercise can be very effective when you do it with someone else. It may not always be appropriate to act out relationship dreams with the person you are dreaming about. Sometimes someone who is neutral in the relationship makes a better sounding board.

ABOVE Working with your dreams can take place at any time and in any place, all you need are a few quiet moments when you can focus your mind on your dream. Relax and allow your mind to drift.

BELOW LEFT Sitting quietly in a meditative state can often help us unlock the key to a dream's meaning.
BELOW Sometimes we need to turn our attention elsewhere and stop thinking about a dream. Try to do something completely different, and see if it rises to the surface of your mind.

USING GESTALT

A good way of understanding our dreams is to assume that everything in the dream is an aspect of ourselves. Gestalt techniques are based on this principle. Applying them to his dream, first Billy "became" the train. He discovered that this part of him moves very fast, is forging full steam ahead and has no time to stop for anything or anyone. Next he was the rail track. He thought that this showed him that the fast part of him is "on track", moving ahead to a goal. To be on this track means leaving behind a part of himself, the onlooker who is waving "goodbye". The tracks are also what keep him separate from his girlfriend. When he thought about the dream some more, he realized that his girlfriend represented the part of himself that wants to move forwards, that wants to jump on the train and go off and have adventures, but there is another part holding him back, keeping him at the station. This brought him to the wave goodbye. At first when he had the dream, he thought the wave meant he was saying "goodbye" to his girlfriend and was feeling sad because of the separation from her. Now he wondered if the sadness was because he was separated from that vital, exciting part of himself that is prepared to jump on moving trains while he stays stuck at the station. It was like waving goodbye to his freedom and sense of adventure.

OPPOSITES

Another interesting way of working on relationship issues is to turn the Gestalt technique on its head and assume everything in the dream is the other person. In Billy's dream for instance, his girlfriend becomes the train. Looking at it like this, Billy thought it meant that she is moving too fast for him, and needed a more committed relationship than he felt he was ready for. Thinking about her as the station, he saw that she represented a stopping off point in his life. She is not the partner with whom he wants to journey through life with.

HIDDEN MESSAGES IN DREAMS

Sometimes it is not so obvious that a dream is about a relationship. However, we can rest assured that whenever we have a relationship issue, it will surface

BELOW RIGHT Our dreaming isolates us and makes us aware of the fragile and vulnerable parts of ourselves. This is nature's way of making us turn inwards and begin to question what our dreams mean.
BELOW While we sleep, doorways open in our mind, and our dreaming self takes wings and becomes capable of anything. In the world of dreams the impossible becomes achievable.

in our dreams in one guise or another. We can assume that the dream is about the problem that is worrying us, and we can try to understand it in this light. This happened to a young woman called Sandra. She was worried that her partner didn't care for her, despite the fact that he told her he loved her. She thought he wanted to leave the relationship. She then had a mysterious dream about a sailing boat with a red sail going round in circles on a lake. The person sailing the boat was a stranger, not her boyfriend. In the dream she felt worried the boat was going to capsize and there would be no one to rescue the sailor.

Using the Gestalt technique with her dream, Sandra concluded that her sense of impending disaster had nothing to do with her boyfriend but was being generated from within herself. The boat represented the relationship, and she and not her boyfriend was the one who was "rocking" it. It was as though a part of her wanted to sabotage the relationship, the part that feels claustrophobic and uneasy. She realized that in some ways she felt trapped in the relationship, that it was not going anywhere, but "round in circles". The red sail spelled danger to her, a signal to look where she was going and keep out of dangerous waters.

ABOVE In our dreams we may be faced with decisions that need to be made, choices that are reflected in our waking life. These choices may be represented by doorways or paths. Your dream is reminding you to act, not avoid.

USING MYTHS AND LEGENDS

If you enjoy and are familiar with myths and legends, you could also use these to gain insight into your relationship dreams. For instance, you could use the Arthurian legends as archetypes for dream understanding. They are a rich picking ground for all sorts of relationships, ranging from the fairly commonplace to the bizarre. You could imagine yourself in the same situation as one of the characters and notice how the story turns out. Alternatively you could consider what "message" the legend has for you.

In the Arthurian legends there are many archetypes and relationship situations that you can work with. The main characters are as follows: Arthur, a king who stands for many different aspects of the Great Father, is married to Guinevere. She meanwhile is in love with Lancelot, Arthur's closest friend. Their affair causes Lancelot to betray Arthur. Morgan le Fay, Arthur's half-sister and a powerful sorceress, has a supposedly incestuous relationship with him. Merlin, the archetypal wise old man is obsessed with a young girl, while the archetypal hero, Sir Galahad, is celibate and devoted to purity.

PART TWO

THE DREAM LEXICON

There is nothing in our dreams that we cannot conceive of, or even that we haven't already experienced in some form or another. Our dream images and feelings are generated by our unconscious, for our own benefit. In our dreams, our unconscious talks to us directly, one to one. We are the dreamer and the dream – the playwright, director, actors and audience, rolled into one.

The lexicon that follows is different from a traditional dream dictionary in which individual elements are listed alphabetically with a set meaning attributed to each. Rather, it aims to provide a vocabulary that will enable you, the dreamer, to start interpreting the key symbols and metaphors of your dreams in a way that makes sense to you. To tease out the meaning of your dreams, you need to understand the simple relationship between the feelings and issues your unconscious is working with, and what is being shown to you symbolically. We know better than anyone else what our own dreams mean, and how to respond to the subtle nuances and quirky associations that our dreams carry.

HOW TO USE THE LEXICON

Every dream has one or more major themes or individual elements that seem to hold particular significance in the context of that dream. Often there will be several themes running concurrently, or a handful of elements or qualities that seem important, and each should be investigated and seen in relation to the others.

So for instance, if you dreamt about being chased across a mountain top by a dark man on a wet night, some themes you can look up would be pursuit, mountain, man, stranger, darkness, night, rain, danger, see how you feel – afraid, excited, confused or whatever. Because there are several elements working together in this example, a dream like this may take quite a lot of work to understand fully, or it may all fall into place quite simply if the dream points up major issues in your life that you are struggling with or if the symbols have strong, clear meanings to you.

ASSOCIATIONS

It is useful to start by noting whether any of the themes or elements have any obvious personal associations or connotations. Often these may have been formed by significant events or situations in your past, but sometimes they may be somewhat random – for instance if the lyrics in some music you were

listening to before you went to bed made you think of someone you know or sparked off a memory of some period in your life.

If you have any pressing preoccupations or are undergoing important changes in your life – such as moving house or beginning a new job – you can use these as your starting point and see if the symbolism or story in your dream seems pertinent.

CONTEXT

The significance of something that appears in a dream can be quite varied, even contradictory, and the conventional dream dictionary approach does not take into account personal meanings, or the fact that the context of the dream elements and the relationship between them is essential to the meaning of each element and the dream as a whole.

For example, in its basic interpretation a feast may signify wealth and abundance to you, but whether you are the host, a guest at a king's banquet, or serving others, whether the food and wine are unlimited or in short supply, and whether the food is delicious or inedible, normal or bizarre, all provide essential information regarding how you regard wealth and abundance, and how they are relevant in your life. It is much more effective and rewarding to try to understand the dream from your own point of view rather than have meanings assigned without any reference to the dream or the dreamer. In the lexicon meanings are suggested for many elements that you may encounter in your dreams, but you are encouraged to work with these creatively to generate your own understanding of your dreams, rather than accept them as simple truths with only one interpretation.

FRAGMENTS

Not all parts of the dream will be accessible to you – some symbolism may remain hidden, or you will simply forget parts of the dream. If these memories don't return, you may be trying to see the big picture when half of it is missing. You may well remember enough of the dream to get the gist of it and work out its meaning, but what has been lost may have been the greater part, the importance of the dream, and what you remember of the dream could be a mere snippet, a fragment.

If whatever the dream was trying to draw your attention to is lost in this way, you can be sure that your unconscious will try again another time. The images next time round may be similar or quite different, but the meaning or the message will stay the same.

Trust in dreams, for in them is the hidden gate to eternity.   KAHLIL GIBRAN

ABOVE The landscape of your dream is one of the most important aspects of dream analysis.

LEFT Dreams allow you to travel through time and space, and visit realms that only exist inside your imagination.

RIGHT Aspects of the divine can also be a part of your dreams, and can help you to make contact with your subconscious in a profound and remarkable way.

ABOVE Travelling into your own dream world can be one of the most amazing journeys you will ever undertake, and one that you can repeat every night of your life.

LEFT Are dreams tunnels or stairways into other worlds? There are no limits in your dream world, anything and everything is possible.

RIGHT The shapes and textures that appear in your dream can have as profound a message as the characters and feelings, the trick is to remember the detail so that you can analyse the meanings when you awake.

ABSTRACT QUALITIES

The properties of the countless people, objects and ideas that we encounter in our dreams can be highly significant when we are trying to work out what our dreams mean. We may focus on particular qualities because they are so dominant, or because they are distorted or unusual. Abstract concepts such as time and space, power or number, may hold a particular relevance in your dream, either pointing to a literal preoccupation or working symbolically.

When properties that we would take for granted are changed it is almost certainly significant. To work with these elements you need to note what it is that has changed and consider the qualities and meaning of that object as it is in real life as well as how it is in your dream. Occasionally in our dreams abstract concepts are so important that we divest them of all associations, then we can focus on the feelings that such dreams generate.

TIME AND SPACE

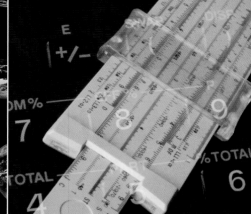

WE LIVE AS PHYSICAL BEINGS IN A PHYSICAL WORLD AND OUR LIVES UNFOLD OVER TIME. THESE TWO VERY OBVIOUS FACTS PROFOUNDLY AFFECT HOW WE LIVE OUR LIVES — AND THOSE WHO LEAD A MODERN, URBAN LIFESTYLE, WITH ITS CONSTANT ACTIVITY, RUSHING AND LIMITED SPACE, WILL BE ESPECIALLY AWARE OF THEM. DREAMS THAT FEATURE TIME AND SPACE — OUR RELATIONSHIP TO THEM, WHETHER THERE IS TOO MUCH OR TOO LITTLE OF EACH — CAN TELL US MUCH ABOUT THE QUALITY OF OUR LIVES.

SCALE AND DISTANCE

We are affected by the amount of space we have around us and by how near to or how far we are from other people and objects. A small room may feel cosy and intimate or frustratingly restrictive. Cathedrals are built on a massive scale not only to accommodate large congregations but also to represent the power of God and to inspire awe, and perhaps feelings of insignificance.

It can be useful to look at how we feel in relationship to the spaces in which we find ourselves in our dreams, as this can point to how comfortable we are as physical beings, whether we are feeling protected or exposed, and how isolated or crowded out we are feeling. The extreme of this is found in outer space, where we are truly unconstrained by the bounds of our earthly lives or physicality.

POSITION

Where we are in relation to other objects in our dreams may also be worth noting. Being above or in front of something could indicate that we are asserting ourselves in relation to what the object is representing symbolically, feeling self-confident or dominant. Conversely, being below or behind something could point to feelings of inferiority or subservience, an urge to hide or be protected – or it could be that we are being invisible or "not seeing" something important.

MEASUREMENT

Rulers, weighing scales and other instruments of measurement show a particular focus on size, distance, scale or space – how near or far, how tall or long or short something is. We are

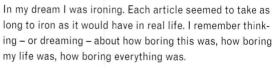

NEVER-ENDING DREAM

In my dream I was ironing. Each article seemed to take as long to iron as it would have in real life. I remember thinking – or dreaming – about how boring this was, how boring my life was, how boring everything was.

When I woke up after what seemed to be hours of ironing I was almost screaming with boredom. I realized that my life was really tedious and I worried that I was a bore. I felt that I had to do something about it, and changed a lot after that.

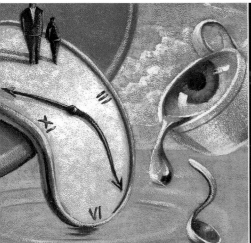  

subconsciously measuring ourselves against the world we live in, especially in relation to social expectations. It may also be that we are trying to establish some kind of control over our environments, or using objective means to measure ourselves.

Dreaming of clocks may indicate a preoccupation with time, how it is regulating our lives, perhaps preventing us from having enough time to do the things we want, or having too much time on our hands. In a broader sense timepieces may be reminding us of our mortality.

ELASTICITY OF TIME AND SPACE

Time in dreams is very flexible, becoming distorted, elongated or slowed down. First there is the fact that dreams that seem to last an age might have occurred in only a second. Within the dream itself, distortions of time may relate to feeling out of control – perhaps everything is happening faster than you can cope with, or you are trying to get somewhere fast but don't seem to be moving.

As time can be stretched out or compressed in our dreams, so too can space. In a flash we can travel from one end of the universe to another, between worlds, between states of consciousness. Space can become condensed and compressed, or we become expanded, to such an extent that we can actually fill the universe. In such cosmic dreams we address our beliefs in the nature of the universe, and how we feel about our place within it.

In a dream your attention may be drawn to a preoccupation with space or time by the fact that it is distorted. *Alice in Wonderland* is a story about a dream in which the bewildered and frustrated heroine finds herself too big or small for what she wants to do or for the space in which she finds herself.

ABOVE Crowded areas full of people and activity might give you a feeling of unease, or even terror, or you might find them the most reassuring and natural places to be.
ABOVE LEFT Cosmic dreams about how planet Earth is positioned might be a way of establishing your own position in your personal universe.
ABOVE FAR LEFT Do you feel that time is slipping away from you in your waking life? Perhaps this feeling will be reflected in your dreams.
LEFT In our dreams, the boundaries between time and space can become blurred and we discover new dimensions. In dream time vast epics are played out in what seems an age but is, in real time, only seconds.

SIGNS AND SYMBOLS

FREUD WROTE AT LENGTH ABOUT SEXUAL SYMBOLS, OF THE MULTITUDE OF OBJECTS IN OUR ORDINARY ENVIRONMENT THAT COULD BE USED TO REPRESENT OR ATTRACT OUR ATTENTION TO SEXUALITY. JUNG EXPLORED SYMBOLIC ARCHETYPES, SUCH AS THE MASK, THE MAGICAL JOURNEY OR THE RITUAL BAPTISM, IN WHICH A PERSON, PLACE OR EVENT COMES TO REPRESENT A SHARED HUMAN EXPERIENCE. IN A SENSE, EVERYTHING DISCUSSED IN THE LEXICON FUNCTIONS AS A SYMBOL IN THE CONTEXT OF OUR DREAMS, BUT WHEN WE TALK ABOUT SIGNS AND CULTURAL OR PERSONAL SYMBOLS WE ARE TALKING ABOUT ACTUAL ICONIC OBJECTS THAT CARRY CERTAIN SIGNIFYING FACTORS.

THE COMPLEXITY OF SYMBOLS

In this context, the word "symbols" denotes icons that we use to signify allegiance, power, authority, status, belief systems and so on – such as the cross or swastika or a country's flag. It also covers alphabets and hieroglyphs – symbolic systems that have arisen in cultures around the world to

BELOW In our dreams we will seize on any symbol and put it to virtually any use. Flags, for example, can signify a range of emotions – pride, aggression, power, belonging and alienation, to name a few.

communicate efficiently with others across time and distance.

The difference between these and the other symbols that we discuss in the Lexicon is that these have all been generated consciously by people to represent certain things, as a shortcut to communicating a raft of meanings, rather than evolving in a more organic way through human experience. Each of these symbols provides a complexity of meanings, which are reinforced every time we see them, much the same way that corporate or product logos are used to reinforce an image that an organization wants to project.

RELIGIOUS SYMBOLS

Our relationship with religion and spirituality in general, and with particular religions, is addressed by the manifestation of religious symbols in our dreams. These symbols evoke a highly personal response, which depends on our attitude, our own beliefs, any religious experiences we might have had, and so on. The cross, for example, is for many a revered symbol of Christ's love, but it could also be a symbol of suffering (we speak of "having a cross to bear" meaning a burden of responsibility) or even bring to mind the cruelty of religious

persecution and conquest. The Star of David is a common symbol of Judaism, but it may bring associations of oppression and discrimination because of how it was used to mark out Jews in Nazi Germany.

SYMBOLS OF POWER AND AUTHORITY

National flags are associated with particular countries and their assumed or stated cultures and value systems, and so as symbols can be highly emotionally charged – think of how often the flags of certain countries are ceremonially burnt, for instance. In a general sense, they also signify allegiance to a particular country or other political or ideological body, feelings of inclusion and belonging or exclusion, pride or contempt. Flags may also bear particular symbols – the swastika, for instance, is strongly associated with the right-wing ideologies of Nazi Germany, the Holocaust, fascism, regimentation, oppression, pure evil and a host of similar negative associations – although the ancient symbol that the Nazis used as their emblem originally signified the sun, and symbolized good luck.

In an obvious way the crown is a symbol of royalty, but this in itself may mean many things,

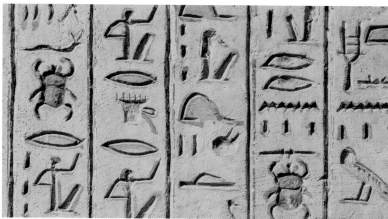

LEFT Some symbols, such as the Star of David, are imbued with an almost magical power due to their history.

LEFT Hieroglyphs are a good example of how subjective a language is. Although now an obsolete sign system, they still conjure up certain symbolic significance for us today.

such as authority, inherited power, immense wealth, status and responsibility. A monarch, like a parent, may be either a protective, benevolent authority figure, or a threatening and despotic character who reduces our own freedom. The second kind of monarch embodies an excess of power, wealth and so on, and highlights one's own relative poverty. The scales of justice suggest balance and impartiality, as well as the authority of judges and the legal system in general.

ALPHABETS AND HIEROGLYPHS

We use symbolic systems to communicate – whether they consist of the letters of an alphabet, which represent sounds of speech, the hieroglyphs of ancient Egypt, musical notation or a code such as semaphore.

If we dream of such symbols, whether we understand them or not is crucial. The symbols may be associated with a particular nationality or culture, and understanding them may signify access to that culture, or a denial of that access. Equally, the symbols may indicate that information is being obscured or withheld, or that the dreamer has a lack of clarity, an inability to "read" or "decipher" a situation.

ABOVE In older cultures, everything in nature held a particular meaning and was given symbolic value.

ABOVE Heavenly symbols, such as the sun, the stars and the moon, are a part of the richly symbolic language of religious imagery.
RIGHT Crowns, sceptres and thrones suggest the pomp and majesty of kingship and rule.
BELOW Even something simple and iconic can be given a lofty and weighty symbolism, such as the scales of justice.

STRENGTH AND WEAKNESS

IN OUR COMPETITIVE WORLD, IT IS NOT SURPRISING THAT DREAMS OF STRENGTH AND WEAKNESS TROUBLE OUR SLEEP AT TIMES. SUCH DREAMS MAY TAKE THE FORM OF CONVENTIONAL SYMBOLISM — THE STRENGTH OF A LION, A WRESTLER, IRON CHAINS OR AN ELECTRIC STORM, OR THE WEAKNESS AND FRAILTY OF A TINY CREATURE, AN OLD OR DISABLED PERSON, A DELICATE SPIDER'S WEB. OR THEY MAY HIGHLIGHT YOUR OWN PERSONAL STRENGTHS AND WEAKNESSES, EITHER LITERAL OR METAPHORIC. WHAT WE THINK OF AS STRENGTH IN OUR WAKING LIFE MAY MANIFEST COMPLETELY DIFFERENTLY IN OUR DREAMS AND WE MAY BE SURPRISED BY OUR OWN SYMBOLISM.

BELOW LEFT Rather than the obvious images of power or strength, images of gentleness, such as a tiny baby, may be used as a symbol for true strength.
BELOW RIGHT In our dreams, conventional metaphors for strength may appear as clear or distorted images.

COSMIC STRENGTH

The universe is immense, powerful and strong, and by comparison, we humans are almost absurdly tiny, vulnerable and weak. Cosmic dreams about strength underline the fact of this terrible fragility, as our unconscious tries to come to terms with the size, power, age and complexity of the universe.

We know where we begin and end as individuals, but any similar quantification of the universe is impossible. We know that we will die at some point in time, and that when we do so this immeasurable and intricate universe will continue in all its glory without a second thought.

Our passing and fleeting presence will leave not a trace in any way.

SECURITY

Dreams about strength may be our way of investigating how safe we feel in our waking life. They may be our unconscious mind's way of getting us to do something about feeling insecure. If we live in a dangerous neighbourhood we are likely to have a constant background preoccupation with safety issues and a fear of being threatened unexpectedly; to address this our best course of action could be to learn assertiveness or how to be physically stronger, to build safe zones where we can let down our

guard, or to be more cautious about entering dangerous circumstances or places.

The insecurity that troubles us may be of a more personal nature – in our relationships rather than in the sense of our physical wellbeing – so we should look at why these relationships make us feel that way. Our dream might also be the start of a search for a guardian angel of some kind who will protect us from being overwhelmed by the strength and size of the universe.

WEAKNESS

A dream of strength could be nature's way of drawing our attention to some aspect of our

defencelessness and vulnerability. If we feel threatened by stronger forces then it makes sense to seek ways of becoming stronger so we are better able to fight off the threat, or of compensating in some other way if this is not possible. The dream is flagging up the fact that we feel weak or frail or naked and we are being urged to do something about that. Where the threat comes from in our waking life is up to us to determine. It might be that we need to find a way of coming to terms with the imponderables of an immense and powerful universe, or it might be more mundane issues, such as our work or our relationships, that are threatening to overwhelm us. Either way, if we feel threatened by strength in a dream then it is likely that there is something that is making us feel threatened or vulnerable in our waking life.

PERSONAL STRENGTHS AND WEAKNESSES

It is probably physical prowess that first springs to mind when you think of strength, but just as important is the personal strength that we draw from being centred and knowing who we are. It may be that we express that centredness symbolically in an image of physical strength. We also describe as strengths and weaknesses the things that we do well or the things that we are not good at. And having a weakness for something means that we like it or are drawn to it so much that we cannot refuse it; although, say, having a weakness for chocolate may seem trivial, it could be a

RIGHT Powerful architectural forms may be used as symbols for strength in our dreams.
MIDDLE RIGHT An awareness of our mental strengths or fragilities may become apparent in our dreams and can cause worry.
BOTTOM RIGHT We may use immense symbols such as the power and strength of the entire universe to bring home a simple truth such as an acknowledgement that we are being used or abused in some way.

signpost to some other area of your life where you lack control. It is worth bearing all possibilities in mind when you are trying to understand your dream, as your mind may be using apparently frivolous concepts as a springboard for exploring more serious issues. How power manifests in our dreams can be a reflection on how secure we feel.

A COSMIC DREAM

"I was alone in the vastness of space but I could feel the sheer size and strength of the universe closing in on me. Everything was black and I couldn't see what forces were pressing against me – it seemed as though it was the very walls of the universe that were crushing me out of existence. I couldn't fight against this sort of strength.

The dream was really quite terrifying, and I woke up feeling small and helpless. It made me realize that I was letting a lot of people walk all over me and needed to be much more assertive, to learn to say 'no' more often, especially at work."

POWER DREAMS

POWER APPEARS IN MANY GUISES — FROM THE OBVIOUS FORMS AND TRAPPINGS OF POLITICAL OR MILITARY POWER AND WEALTH, TO PHYSICAL DOMINATION, OPPRESSION, VICTIMIZATION OR BULLYING, THE AUTHORITY OF AGE OR WISDOM, OR THE PERSONAL POWER OF A TRULY CENTRED INDIVIDUAL. POWER EXERTED OVER US CAN BE A SOURCE OF INSPIRATION, RESPECT, STIMULATION, ENCOURAGEMENT, DEFERENCE AND SAFETY. ON THE OTHER HAND IT CAN PROVOKE FEAR AND HOSTILITY. HOW WE FEEL ABOUT POWER AND INFLUENCE IN REAL LIFE WILL AFFECT HOW WE DREAM OF THEM. DOES POWER EXCITE OR DISMAY YOU? DO YOU FEEL INVIGORATED BY IT OR STIFLED?

BELOW A dream that involves a king figure, or even a godly one may well be a reflection of a feeling you have in your waking life that you are being dominated or controlled in some way.

Power can manifest itself on a cosmic level – divine, celestial, universal, collective – and also as an attribute of an individual or organization. Dreams in which power is a dominant theme tend to be unambiguous. We are likely to respond strongly to them and to remember them because of this. In them we may be enslaved or motivated; we may even be the source of the power itself.

Our society is highly stratified, and power in a social and political sense is an inevitable part of our lives. Monarchs and presidents wield it over their citizens, bosses over employees, parents over their children. Many people are preoccupied with power, seeking it, being dissatisfied with a lack of it, feeling the effects of the power that others wield. So it is not surprising that images of power crop up in dreams quite often. We may have power thrust upon us, such as when we are promoted to a position of responsibility, and be unsure of how to handle it or of how others will react. We may have bullied

someone and now be feeling guilty. If we pay attention to how power manifests in our dreams and how we respond to it, we may learn about how to deal with the real-life situation that is preoccupying us.

NUCLEAR POWER
We have all grown up in the nuclear age, in which the possibility of being wiped out by nuclear weapons or by an accident at a nuclear power plant has seemed very real. Such power is immense, and used properly, it can enhance the quality of our lives, but if anything goes wrong, and the containment of this power fails or is breached,

---

A DREAM OF GOD

"In my dream, God was sitting on a vast, unearthly throne. But rather than paying attention to being face to face with God, I was fascinated by the throne. Its construction was really important – it was made of some kind of metal, never seen on earth, which was grey flecked with red, and had a luminous transparency like crystal.

I realised that this throne was where the real power lay: whoever sat on it would become a god, and God Himself had only got his power from having been on it for so long. If anyone else sat there, they too would acquire that sort of power. There was no power in the person, only in the throne – the material trappings of power.

I'm not religious at all so I was quite surprised to have had what seemed at first like a religious dream, but I think it was more about knowing where power lies and how to access it than about the spiritual aspect of God. I'm very concerned with power and authority in my life as I am in the police force. My uniform represents these things, but it doesn't make me feel powerful from within; it also creates a negative reaction in some people, which I don't like."

disaster is virtually inevitable. The dreams of many people are affected by such fears, and they need to come to terms with the feeling of helplessness that this kind of threat generates. Because of the "all-or-nothing" feeling that nuclear war has, we may use it to represent in a more general or metaphoric sense the end of the world as we know it, or some personal calamity.

THE POWER OF NATURE

Sometimes nature unleashes its power on a spectacular scale: lightening storms, floods, forest fires, hurricanes and avalanches all put us in our place in the universe. We try to minimize the damage done by these phenomena, but ultimately we are powerless. An impending natural disaster in a dream – the moment before a dam bursts or a storm breaks – may show us the potential power that we have in ourselves; how we express it may make the difference between greatness and destruction.

COMING TO TERMS WITH POWER

In waking life or in our dreams, we might feel drawn irresistibly to some situation or event or person but cannot understand why. The power that draws us may be invisible and subtle but by careful analysis and observation we might begin to understand what is controlling us, and can assess what we are being manipulated or influenced by in our waking life.

By paying attention to power dreams we can literally empower ourselves in real life. Once we have pinpointed and understood the powers that we fear, find attractive or wish to develop in ourselves, then they can be tamed and put to use.

ABOVE FAR LEFT When you dream of power is it manifested on an individual basis, with a symbol of social control such as a monarch?
ABOVE LEFT Or does your dream of power involve forces such as those in large-scale industry?
ABOVE Or is it the power that might be unleashed by politicians and rulers that you fear you are unable to control?

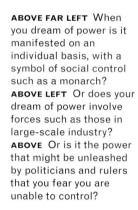

LEFT Nature has such awesome power, such highly destructive force, that it may appear in our dreams as a frightening power indeed.

COLOUR

THE MORE AWARE WE ARE OF COLOURS IN OUR LIVES, THE MORE WE ARE LIKELY TO DREAM IN COLOUR. BUT SOMETIMES IN A DREAM, COLOUR DEMANDS OUR ATTENTION, EITHER BECAUSE IT IS VERY STRONG OR BECAUSE IT IS UNNATURAL IN ITS CONTEXT. IN THIS WAY IT ACQUIRES SYMBOLIC VALUE, AND YOU SHOULD CONSIDER WHAT MEANING IT HAS FOR YOU. DO WE ALL DREAM IN COLOUR ALL OF THE TIME? THIS MAY SEEM IRRELEVANT IF YOU ALWAYS DO BUT WHAT IF YOU DREAM IN BLACK AND WHITE? HAVE YOU EVER HAD A DREAM THAT IS IN JUST ONE COLOUR? WHAT DO THE COLOURS WE SEE IN OUR DREAMS MEAN? ARE THEY REFLECTIONS OF OUR EMOTIONS OR OUR SPIRITUALITY?

Some colours we respond to in a very personal way, but many of the associations we have with particular colours are culturally informed – for example, white is worn by the bride on her wedding day in Western culture, but in the Far East it is the colour traditionally worn at funerals.

CREATIVE POWER OF COLOUR

We may be surprised by the intensity of colours in our dream, by the inventiveness of our imagination. But everything in our dream expresses ourselves – what we see is what we are capable of creating. These dreams can awaken in us a sense of our real power, can make us realize how impressive we really are, however much we get bogged down in our day-to-day lives.

EXPRESSING OUR INNER BEING

A dream that focuses on fantastic colour and form – whirling patterns and shifting shapes – may resemble an "acid trip", or it could be that you are making spiritual contact with your inner self. In a rainbow, all the colours are present, and are perfectly, naturally in balance. Strongly contrasting colours may signify either clear choices or a dilemma in some area of your life, while colours that merge and blend could signify an inner harmony, or, conversely, a lack of clarity.

Pay special attention if several dreams feature a particular colour, as this could be your unconscious trying to work with a particular issue that you are not addressing effectively in your waking life. Equally, if you stop focusing on this colour in your dreams then it could be that you have worked through something that was on your mind.

COLOURS BY ASSOCIATION

It is said that the colours we see in our dreams reflect the state of our unconscious mind. So if blue predominates, we may be feeling emotional, while green could suggest an interest in nature or environmental issues. These are only two possible meanings though, and it may be that your mind has randomly drawn on a catchphrase such as "feeling blue" or the Green Party of environmental politics. In the same way, blue has even been suggested as an indicator of futuristic travel because of the phrase "taking off into the blue".

COLOUR KEY

These are some associations people commonly have with particular colours. Remember though that your own personal experiences, as well as cultural differences, may mean that they do not always ring true to you – use them as a starting point to prompt your own feelings, rather than as fact.

Red: energy, fire, passion, love, sex, anger, danger

Orange/yellow: vibrancy, joy, life, sunshine, warmth, spirituality, jealousy

Green: calm, nature, illness, envy

Blue: peace, emotions, depression, space

Violet/purple: grandeur, royalty, rage

White: innocence, energy, emptiness, possibility, cleanliness, holiness

Black: death, mourning, depression, conformity, secrecy, obscurity

ABOVE Nature has her own colour symbolism which may not be for our benefit at all – flowers are coloured for the bees rather than for us.

ABOVE AND ABOVE RIGHT Natural colours, such as shades of green, have instant association with growth and renewal. If you dream of green your subconscious could be sending you a message about decisions that need to be made.
RIGHT Brightly coloured sweets attract children – do the colours have the same impact on you if you dream about them, or do they seem unpleasantly synthetic and confusing?

ABOVE The colour white in Western cultures is synonymous with purity and innocence. Dreaming of white weddings might therefore symbolize this.
LEFT Multicoloured objects in dreams may be a way for your mind to link with your emotions.
BELOW Perhaps there are no symbolic associations with colours in a dream. Vibrant shades might just be a way of your creative mind expressing itself.

The expression "seeing red", meaning to be angry, may well have come from the red mist you see before your eyes if in a severe rage, but it would be simplistic to say that this necessarily means that a dream involving the colour red always points to anger. Our conscious mind might make these easy associations of anger, violence, passion, fire and energy, but the red in your dream could also be the red of romantic love and passion, or a warning of danger. It could even be a "red herring" – perhaps before bed you saw the word "red", or a film in which colour was used for artistic emphasis. Perhaps you told your child the story of Little Red Riding Hood at bedtime. These triggers may lead your mind to cultural meanings that are commonly ascribed to the colour – the dangerous wolf is attracted by the girl's coat; her red coat may have pointed to the danger she was in.

DREAM COLOURS

"I was standing on a hilltop, and could see myself from above, turning round and round in slow motion. I was so aware of the vividness of the grass, the sky, my clothes, everything, and the colours were so bright, that I felt I was being told something. I woke up wanting to paint those colours, although I hadn't picked up a brush for years. I took up painting again because of this dream, and I'm so happy just doing it."

Shape, Form, Texture

Like colour, the shape and texture of objects and spaces can hold the key to the meaning of our dreams. Regular geometric forms carry associations similar to those of the number of sides they have, while proportions, such as how long, tall or short, and how fat or thin something or someone is, may also be significant. You may focus your attention on the texture of a surface in your dream, focusing on whether it is sharp or blunt, soft or smooth, and also whether it is whole or broken. How much do we draw on the sense of touch? Does each surface have texture?

Many of the above properties may be insignificant in the context of your dream, but if they particularly catch your attention or they are unusual in some way, you can be fairly certain that they are presented like this for a reason. You should ask yourself why it is that a particular shape is appearing in your dream, and if it is markedly different from what you would expect, then look at what the difference is and why your mind has formed the object in this way.

SYMMETRY

Regular shapes have a strong connection with numbers, and because they are so basic and are found in so many aspects of our waking lives – the sides of a geometric form, the number of petals on a flower, how many points a star has – physical shapes may often be used in dreams metaphorically, to stand in for more abstract or complex concepts.

For example, a circle – whether it is a golden ring or a round room – may suggest harmony, inclusion and femininity, while a square may bring feelings of order and symmetry, masculinity, conventionality or even military precision. A triangular shape to some people may allude to a representation of the perfect balance of the Holy Trinity, the mother-father-child relationship, or the tension of a love triangle. The pyramid, often thought to have a mystical significance, has a solid base, but in its pinnacle reaches for the sky. Dreaming of this form may show that you are aspiring to greater things.

CURVES AND SPIRALS

Wavy lines are more fluid and often more random than straight lines, and in this may suggest a freedom and unpredictability not found in a more regular form. While straight lines could suggest clarity of vision or thought, twists, loops and curves may indicate obscurity or confusion. Spirals have a strong sense of movement, notice whether they are spiralling inward or outward, and feel whether they are suggestive of something in your life "spiralling out of control" or whether they give you an exhilarating sense of moving outward and upward, away from confinement. By contrast, points and angles may indicate dead ends, especially if viewed from the inside, or show a concentration of energy.

BELOW RIGHT Dreaming of pyramid shapes might have a particular mystical significance for you, or it might be a more prosaic link with your aspirations. **BELOW** Dreaming of straight lines, such as a road with no turns or bends, might mean strength of purpose and clarity of vision. It might also mean predictability and lack of self-expression however.

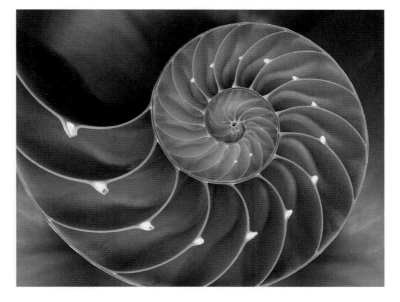

OPEN AND CLOSED FORMS

Whether the form is open or fully enclosed could also be highly significant. A box with its lid off, or an enclosed garden whose gate is open, has nothing to hide, and allows the possibility of moving out of a state of enclosure or confinement whether physical, intellectual or emotional, and of moving on to new experiences.

FAT OR THIN?

Our response to fatness and thinness in people is usually heavily influenced by widely accepted ideals and stereotypes. Your dream may use these stereotypes in a literal way, but you can also look at whether a person's size is associated metaphorically with some attitude to resources. In this way, a fat person – or object or animal – may symbolize plenty and a thin person a lack of resources; alternatively, size may point to a relationship to resources, such as whether you are hoarding or rejecting them, or using them up

faster than you can get hold of them. Fat may also have associations of cuddliness and therefore comfort, or alternatively may indicate lethargy or inaction.

PROPORTIONS

Tall people, buildings and other objects have a physical advantage in their height and can also be seen from a distance. Tall people have stature and can see farther, while from the commanding height of a tall building or hill, one has a greater perspective. Short people, on the other hand, can be looked down on both literally and figuratively, and may have difficulty in having their authority accepted. But smaller

can also mean more nimble or manoeuvrable or can offer the advantage of having an ear close to the ground.

TEXTURE

You may well have an emotional response to the texture of objects in your dream. Sharp edges and rough surfaces may be uncomfortable to the touch, or even threatening. Fuzzy surfaces may be comforting, a reminder of the cuddly toys of childhood, while smooth or reflective surfaces may be attractive but distracting or deceptive. Whether something is broken or intact is also likely to be significant, especially if it is treasured.

LEFT Dreaming of spiral shapes or movement can be an indication of how you feel about your life – is it spiralling out of control, are you on your way up and out, or are you trapped in ever-decreasing circles?

BELOW FAR LEFT Texture can feature in a dream. A feeling of roughness might be threatening but could also be attractive.
BELOW LEFT Curves can suggest freedom and self-expression. If you dream of them perhaps you feel you need less restriction in your life.
BELOW Formal patterns and straight lines might suggest constriction and a lack of imagination, but can bring a feeling of security and comfort if you feel life is too random and out of control.

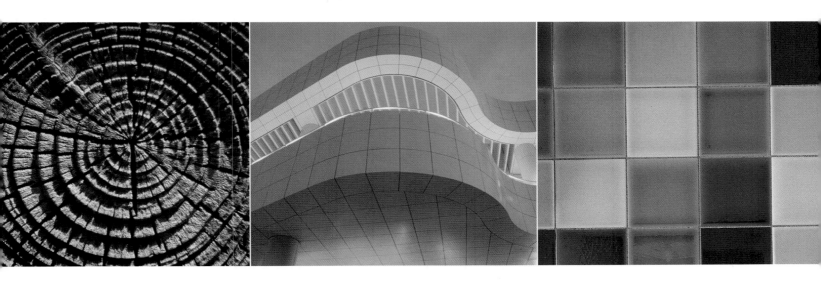

NATURE DREAMS

How we relate to the world around us and how secure we feel about being alive and part of our environment are revealed in dreams of nature. In nature we find the unspoilt, original state of our essential inner being, the truth of who we are as individuals. Landscapes, whether natural or urban, are highly evocative, and set the mood or tone of the dream. Together with the weather, they suggest the atmosphere and underlying impression of your dream, and give clues to your frame of mind, your disposition, your emotional states. The four elements, fire, earth, air and water, work as basic symbols for some key abstract concepts – principally passion, practicality, communication and ideas, and emotions. Animals and plants reveal some of our most primitive, instinctive feelings and fears, which arise from the deepest levels of our unconscious, and from the thoughts and understandings of the world that we formed during the years of our childhood.

DREAM LANDSCAPES

THE LANDSCAPE IS THE BACKDROP FOR THE ACTION OF THE DREAM. IT ANCHORS A DREAM IN TIME AND PLACE AND SETS THE GENERAL THEME AND MOOD, JUST AS SET DESIGN CAN ESTABLISH THE TONE OF A PLAY. CHANGING THE SET OR THE DREAMSCAPE CAN BRING ABOUT A COMPLETELY DIFFERENT EXPERIENCE FOR THE AUDIENCE OR THE DREAMER, EVEN IF THE STORY AND THE CHARACTERS REMAIN THE SAME. AS WELL AS THE PHYSICAL SCENERY ITSELF, THE QUALITY OF THE LANDSCAPE — FAMILIAR OR ALIEN, COMFORTABLE OR DISORIENTATING, OPEN OR RESTRICTED AND CLAUSTROPHOBIC — WILL HAVE EMOTIONAL SIGNIFICANCE AND AFFECT THE GENERAL FEELING OF THE DREAM.

NATURAL LANDSCAPES

Any given landscape can mean different things to different people, and you need to look at both yourself and the context of the dream to understand what it is trying to tell you. Many landscape elements, such as mountains and rivers, have very basic symbolic meanings. For instance, mountains commonly represent obstacles and rivers strong emotional currents. But even if this seems true for you, how you respond to mountains and rivers as well as how you cope with obstacles and emotions will put a personal spin on the dream images. Someone with a fear of heights will see a mountainous landscape quite differently from a mountaineer,

and their unconscious will use this image to express quite different things. Even two people who attach the same meaning to mountains may interpret the same dream quite differently if one views obstacles as frightening and daunting and the other as exciting and challenging.

Your position in relation to the landscape is also important – being on top of a mountain and gazing out over a glorious landscape of snow-covered peaks will probably give you an exhilarating sense of achievement, whereas standing at the base and needing to get to the other side may rather bring up feelings associated with challenges as yet unmet. A stream may symbolize something

relatively minor that needs to be overcome, and a bridge crossing it could give you a means of getting over that obstacle. Jungles can give rise to a feeling of being lost, alienated, emotional or fearful, but they could create a sense of being at one with the lushness and aliveness of nature in all its abundance. Being in a desert could symbolize barrenness, isolation or disorientation in some aspect of your life, or you may feel relaxed in such a vast open space if you easily feel hemmed in.

Chasms, ravines and abysses in their physical form can be frightening, as one stands on the brink, facing the possibility of falling in or losing things irretrievably over the edge. These

ABOVE What are you doing in your dream? If you are climbing a mountain you might be doing likewise symbolically in your waking life.
RIGHT If you dream of open plains and vast wildernesses then maybe you are feeling lost in your real world.
FAR RIGHT Wide open spaces in your dream could be intimidating, but perhaps mean that you feel hemmed in and wish to break free from constriction and restraint.

edges of nature may represent major difficulties you are facing in your everyday waking life, issues that you are afraid to look into a sense of no return.

Beaches provide a transition point between the solidity of terra firma and the vast sea of emotions. They are the threshold of opportunity to enter into deep emotional states, places where you have the freedom to revel in being yourself and recapture the simple joys of childhood.

THE MANUFACTURED LANDSCAPE

Not all landscapes are natural, though. Cities and big towns may symbolize complex problems that have to be negotiated, with straight streets and avenues helping to give you a clear sense of direction. Indeed how roads help or hinder your journey is very telling – if in your dream you find yourself lost in a maze of back streets and alleyways, then perhaps this dream is trying to bring to your attention a sense

of being lost and fearful, while forked paths represent decisions or choices, and twists and turns imply confusion and setbacks. Open roads could leave you feeling exposed and vulnerable on one hand or clear-sighted on the other. Or a road could be hemmed in by walls, fences, high banks or vegetation, giving a feeling of security or claustrophobia. Notice whether you stroll or feel the need to run, and how comfortable you are with the path you are on – it could be symbolizing your path through life.

Walls and fences are also ambiguous symbols. As they can close you in, they may serve as barriers, cutting you off from the rest of the world, or give a sense of security and ownership. Gates also provide openings in otherwise restricted areas, and opportunities to look outward into the unknown from a safe space. Noticing whether you look for a gate or avoid one can give you clues to your emotional state.

LONELINESS DREAM
"In my dream I was walking along a beach. This was no ordinary beach, though – it was located outside of space, a planet floating on its own. I felt unutterably sad there, like I was the last woman left in the universe and there was no one else. It made me realize how lonely I'd been and I resolved to do something about it."

ABOVE Where do you fit into the landscape? Are you part of it or an observer? This is important if you want to know what your dream means. Dreaming of cities and towns may represent complex problems in our life.

FAR LEFT If you dream of a stream try to remember its characteristics, is it bubbling and friendly, does it present an obstacle, is it flowing where you would like to go?
LEFT Are you comfortable in your dream landscape or do you feel alien and out of place; too large or too small?

THE WEATHER

LIKE LANDSCAPES, THE WEATHER COLOURS OUR DREAMS EMOTIONALLY, GIVING BROAD CLUES TO HOW WE FEEL ABOUT OUR
LIVES, AND WHAT SORT OF GENERAL MOOD WE ARE EXPERIENCING IN OUR EVERYDAY WAKING LIVES. WE GENERATE THE
WEATHER IN OUR DREAMS AS A WAY OF EXPRESSING OUR FEELINGS. BECAUSE WHEN WE ARE AWAKE OUR MOODS CAN BE
STRONGLY AFFECTED BY THE WEATHER AND THE SEASON, AND AS THERE ARE MANY WORDS THAT WE USE INTERCHANGEABLY
TO DESCRIBE BOTH THE WEATHER AND OUR MOODS AND FEELINGS (STORMY, GLOOMY, SUNNY, HAZY, TO NAME JUST A FEW),
THESE ARE RELATIVELY EASY SYMBOLS TO START WITH WHEN TRYING TO MAKE SENSE OF OUR DREAMS.

ABOVE Rain may
symbolize our problems
and worries raining down
on us – or it might just be
raining in our dream.
ABOVE RIGHT In your
dream you may be relax-
ing, taking time out to
enjoy the sunshine. Enjoy
this dream holiday.

FAIR OR FOUL?

Moods fluctuate, sometimes
unpredictably, in much the same
way as the weather. Usually the
weather in a dream is congruent
with how you are feeling, so
calm, sunny weather could
indicate a peaceful or happy
disposition, while a storm could
be expressing anger.

But it is worth taking a closer
look at weather that seems to be
at odds with your mood. You
might be raging in your dream
but if the background weather is
calm and pleasant you can be
fairly certain that your rage will
soon pass. On the other hand, if
you are being serene and
reasonable in your dream but
storm clouds are gathering and
the temperature dropping, this
could be a sign that you need to
focus your attention on feelings
that are being repressed.

RAIN AND SNOW

As water is widely considered to
be a symbol for emotions, rain
and tears alike are richly
evocative of your emotional state.
Grey skies and rain clouds cast a
gloomy shadow over your spirit,
and could indicate that your
unconscious is trying to work
with feelings of depression or
despondency. You may express
your tears as rain – the gentle
summer rain that clears the air
and feels good, the light drizzle
of a spring day, or the deluge of
the storm. The rain can be cold
and invigorating, or warm and
welcoming, and an unexpected
shower of rain could mean that
you feel your enthusiasm or
interest have suddenly been
dampened. Any kind of rain can
also have a cleansing and
rejuvenating effect. Snow can be
seen as rain in crystalline form. It

ABOVE Water represents emotions
and rain is often linked to tears – if
you dream of rain, is there
someone you are crying for? If it is
a natural expression of grief or
tension then you might find a
dream of rain is as beneficial as
a good cry.

provides another way of
expressing emotions, colder and
clearer, but also often softer and
gentler, and it dramatically
changes the appearance of the
landscape. It can mean the fun of
playtime, but it can also be
threatening – blizzards and
avalanches show the emotions
becoming overwhelming and
out of control.

STORMS

In the build-up to a storm, a
hush descends on nature along
with a feeling of anticipation of
the power to be unleashed when
the storm breaks. Dark, heavy

clouds can be oppressive and threatening, and people who bottle up their emotions will recognize in the calm before the storm the moments before an emotional outburst.

Torrents of rain, dark, heavy clouds, and rumbles or claps of deep thunder all express the charged emotional content of the dream, whether anger or passion or outrage. Because storms can be dramatic, attention-grabbing events, they are likely to be central to the plot of the dream. Having a stormy dream gives you a safe opportunity to play out powerful emotions that may be too difficult or too dangerous to express in real life. Lightning gives dramatic moments of clarity as it illuminates the landscape. The passing of a storm parallels the end of an emotional outburst – you may feel relieved and invigorated by having put out your feelings, or you may be surveying the damage caused.

MIST AND FOG

By contrast, dreaming of mist and fog, drizzle and gloom, all of which obscure the landscape, may suggest that you are unsure of how you feel about something. Pay particular attention to what you do in your dream to clear the air, to see the way forward, as this may give you clues to what you can do in your waking life to resolve a confusing issue. Weather that obscures things can also be hinting that you are in a state of denial about something, and you may need to ask yourself what it is you are not acknowledging.

RIGHT The seasons have their own rhythms which figure largely in our life. Do dark clouds in your dreams presage the coming of winter, or a storm? Does this resonate in your waking life?

MIDDLE RIGHT Nature is a powerful symbol, and a dream of sunshine is likely to hold pleasant connotations. It could also be a nostalgia for a lost golden age.

BOTTOM RIGHT Dreaming of a blanket of snow may symbolize a deadening effect in our waking life – all is cold and forgotten.

THE SEASONS AND THEIR RHYTHMS

The rhythms of nature can be seen in the cycle of the seasons. As the year progresses and the seasons change, the days lengthen and shorten, the weather and the landscape changes, and plants grow, wither and die. These patterns can also have a profound effect on our outlook, behaviour, and lifestyles. The sequence of the seasons can also symbolize the progression from birth to death and the experiences that we have at different times of our lives.

SEASONAL SYMBOLISM

Spring – birth and childhood, a time of innocence, growth, bursting forth, warming and reviving, love and romance
Summer – youth, vigour, warmth or heat (either giving or sapping energy), abundance, lushness, growth, happiness
Autumn – maturity, ageing, rich colours and experience, closing in, settling down, preparing for death, reflection
Winter – old age and death, barrenness, lack of colour, darkness, stillness, isolation, dryness and brittleness, loss.

THE ELEMENTS — EARTH

THE ANCIENT GREEK PHILOSOPHERS REGARDED FIRE, EARTH, AIR AND WATER AS PHYSICAL MANIFESTATIONS OF SPIRITUAL ESSENCES. THE PROPERTIES OF THESE FOUR ELEMENTS, AS THEY ARE COLLECTIVELY KNOWN, COULD BE USED TO REPRESENT ABSTRACT CONCEPTS — THE PASSION OF FIRE, THE PRACTICAL AND STABLE NATURE OF EARTH, AIR AS THE MEDIUM FOR THE COMMUNICATION OF IDEAS, AND THE DEEP EMOTIONS OF WATER — AND WERE USED TO UNDERSTAND OUR PHYSICAL AND EMOTIONAL WORLD. THROUGH THE CENTURIES AND IN DIFFERENT CULTURES AROUND THE GLOBE, THESE IDEAS HAVE A MORE OR LESS UNIVERSAL SIGNIFICANCE, AND AS SUCH ARE EXTREMELY IMPORTANT ELEMENTS IN OUR DREAMS.

Earth is where we make our impression: our boot leaves its imprint, and our hands mould and shape it. Earth symbolizes the reality of a situation; it is practical, sensible and stable, and represents conventional, traditional values, long-term goals and ambitions. It is also a powerful symbol for those aspects of our world that are timeless and unchanging. What we make from clay will become mud or dust once again when we have finished with it or discarded it and moved on in our lives. The earth provides the food that sustains us and nurtures us, but is also where we go when we have died, a dark and mysterious place where our physical being gradually disappears.

STABILITY

In our dreams, Earth usually plays a supporting rather than a starring role, and as the only one of the four elements that is solid, it represents stability and passivity. In the form of mud or dry dust, compost, clay or sand, gravel or rocks it can have different qualities; at the grand end of the scale it can even be the whole planet. How it appears as an element in our dream may say a lot about how stable we feel ourselves to be. Fields or meadows, for instance, show that we feel grounded and at peace with ourselves. Conversely, Earth may come to our attention dramatically as an earthquake, a mudslide or quicksand where we can be buried alive. Dreams of eruptions usually mean that our unconscious is troubled – we feel insecure, or fear that we are on the verge of turmoil and upheaval in otherwise stable areas of our lives. Be aware though, that stability taken to an extreme could manifest as rigidity and inflexibility, or as passivity.

MATERIALISM AND THE SENSES

The Earth element is a physical one: it is about holding energy in a material form, about creating, building and augmenting solid things or structures. Because of this, it is also about how we experience those things with our physical bodies – in Jungian terms, it is about sensation. It is likely to feature more in the dreams of people who focus on their body and their physical

LEFT Earth is a very powerful symbol – dust to dust, earth to earth, it's where we feel we come from and where our bodies are returned after our death. How does the earth figure in your own dreams?

ABOVE Flowers and meadows indicate a settled, rooted approach to life.

ABOVE Dreams of fields and farms may also indicate that we feel settled and happy and relaxed enough to enjoy such a dream.

surroundings, or in people who are realistic and pragmatic. We may well ask ourselves if the earth we dream of is being useful; gardening, for instance, shows that we are engaging with it in a practical and creative way, and providing the security of a food supply and a pleasant, nourishing environment.

EARTH AND THE OTHER THREE ELEMENTS

It can be revealing to see how Earth interacts with the other elements in our dreams. The heavy power of physicality found in Earth is the foil to Air's flight of the intellect. Being brought back down to earth means we must engage with reality and practical issues. Air dries out earth, turning wet mud into dust. While passionate fire burns the earth, melting the metals in it, water will turn dust back into mud, enabling seeds to germinate and grow.

By working in harmony with other elements the Earth element is creative in character – it allows the forces of the other elements to work upon it, to alter its dynamics in various ways.

ABOVE Earth is a very creative force, but in our dream it may appear as barren or destroyed. We need to look closely at exactly how the Earth element appears.
BELOW Sometimes we need to be earthed, to be grounded, and our dream may be directing us to do this in our waking world.

ABOVE Working the earth in any way may indicate a need to control, to have power over our destiny and fate.
BELOW Do you feel that our planet nurtures us or that you are in control of it? Do you feel it is our mother or our servant?

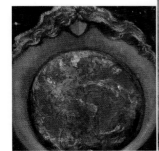

THE ELEMENTS – FIRE

THE CLASSIC SYMBOL OF PASSION AND VITALITY. FIRE IN A DREAM CAN TAKE MANY FORMS. IT CAN BE THE RAGING BLAZE OF A FOREST FIRE, THE TINY FLAME OF A CANDLE, THE HEAT OF THE MIDDAY SUN IN AFRICA, A ROARING FURNACE OR BONFIRE, AN OPEN LOG FIRE – EVEN A MATCH OR THE GLOWING END OF A LIT CIGARETTE. FIRE IS THE ELEMENT ASSOCIATED WITH OUR NERVOUS SYSTEM AND WITH MOVEMENT. IT IS OUR ENERGY, WHETHER PHYSICAL, EMOTIONAL, CREATIVE OR INTELLECTUAL. WHAT IS BEING BURNT, HOW IT IS BURNING, AND WHETHER IT IS A PRINCIPAL ASPECT OF THE DREAM OR MERELY BACKGROUND ILLUMINATION ALL AFFECT THE MEANING OF THIS SYMBOL.

SHAPES AND FORMS

Many things can produce a flame in our dream. An open log fire may represent romance and intimacy, or it could invoke feelings of comfort, of the warmth and cosiness of long, leisurely winter evenings, a warm haven protected from the cold outdoors. As a symbol of relationships, it can imply the security of a steady, warm love rather than an exciting and unpredictable new passion.

A bonfire, on the other hand, is usually livelier, more convivial and demonstrative. Bonfires are often celebratory events, and mark the purging of dead matter, of the accumulation of clutter in our lives. The ashy remains of an extinguished fire mark the end of a period of energetic activity, or of a passionate relationship.

CONTROL

Fire is a difficult element, dangerous and unpredictable. How much control you have over the fire may suggest the amount of control you have over a volatile situation or relationship in your waking life. A fire that is out of control may be pointing to a lack of constraint, or to fears about a fraught situation in your life becoming overwhelming or having devastating consequences. Tending a fire may show how we keep control over things, but it could also suggest an urge to interfere with a natural process.

Various agents may have an influence on the meaning of fire. Water quenching the flames or air being blown in to cause an inferno can change how the fire burns and the effects that it has, and so alter its symbolic value.

DESTRUCTION

Fire can often be seen as a destructive and irredeemable force; burning away or acting as a ritualized ending of some aspect or phase of your life. In its positive aspect, it purges, cleanses and purifies.

Whether what is being burned is valued or something you would like to get rid of is central to whether this is a traumatic destruction or one that gives a sense of relief and release. Your response to seeing someone burning books on an open bonfire, for instance, would say a lot about the nature of how you view learning, literature, culture, freedom of speech and so on. Many people prize books, holding them as a valuable source of information, inspiration and entertainment, and would be horrified by such destruction, but a person who cannot read may see this as a liberating dream. The destruction need not be dramatic, though – even blowing out a candle can symbolize the extinguishing of something.

ILLUMINATION

Fire also brings light and hope, dispelling darkness and revealing aspects of your life that need uncovering, bringing them to light. The steady flame of the candle gives constant

BELOW Fire is a difficult element – dangerous and unpredictable. How much control we have over it in our dream may indicate how much control we feel we have in life.
BELOW RIGHT Looking at what is burning in our fire dreams may indicate what our fears are in waking life.

illumination but little warmth, while a bonfire flares up and burns fiercely, casting great dancing shadows, then dies down again when its flames are spent. How it burns and how much attention you give it can tell you about areas of your relationships that you may need to work on.

CREATIVITY

The fire in a kiln or furnace or forge is immensely hot, and yet it is contained and controlled, and we put it to use to create things, both functional and aesthetic, that enhance our lives. We also use fire to prepare food. In these senses we can understand it as an expression of our creativity and productivity. By adding fuel to a fire we are giving our creativity greater expression.

SMOKE

A by-product of fire, smoke can be toxic or suffocating, making you ill or unable to breathe, and polluting the environment. As such it could be trying to bring to your attention the need to escape from a suffocating or unhealthy relationship before it destroys you. If there is a lot of smoke you may have difficulty seeing your way forward.

In a positive sense though, smoke signals could be giving you a message, showing you where the fire can be found or warning you away from it, and the smell of a fire or incense can bring good associations or be used deliberately to enhance your mood and bring about a feeling of stillness.

LEFT Fire can be warm and comforting as well as dangerous and unpredictable, a cosy fireside scene in your dream can be a totally unthreatening image. **MIDDLE LEFT** Fire can be controlled and is also vital as a tool for our wellbeing and comfort. Dreaming of fire that is under your power and is being used in some way can indicate a level of empowerment in life. **BOTTOM LEFT** Fire in the form of the small quiet fire of the candle can symbolize the tiny flame of spiritual progress.

THE ELEMENTS — AIR

Air is the very breath of life: without it we suffocate and die. It has no form, substance, shape or texture and yet it surrounds us, representing freedom and space and openness, both in a literal way and in the sense of free and open communication. It fills our lungs, giving us the capacity to breathe, speak, sing and shout — to express our emotions. As one of the four elements, it relates to the mind and the intellect, the generation and communication of ideas. We can't see air or wind, but we can feel and see its effects — drifts of smoke, leaves stirring, trees bent in a gale, clouds scudding by overhead, bubbles in water.

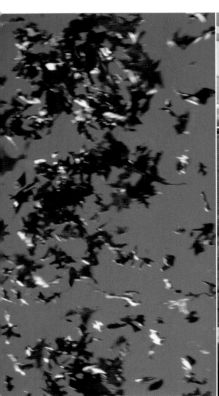

ABOVE We might not be able to see the air but we can see the creatures that use it and fly in it. If we dream of them, perhaps we are envying their soaring energy and freedom.

The current of air, whether it is a breeze or hurricane, is a vehicle for self-expression – like the air, our thoughts and emotions too are invisible but their effect is all too apparent at times. Smells are carried on the air, providing information about our environment and often generating an instant emotional response in us.

We should also look at how Air works in conjunction with the other three elements. Without air the fire cannot burn. Earth, water and air, together with the sun's

warmth and light, bring forth plants that sustain all living creatures on our planet.

THE INTELLECT

Traditionally, the element of Air symbolizes the intellect and our powers of communication. How clear the air is in our dream may show how clearly we are giving and receiving visual information and sounds. "Hot air" is a term meaning excessive verbiage, and we could see this as intellectual clutter. The mind does pick up puns, so dreams of hot air

ABOVE We can now use the air for recreational sports and doing so in our dreams could make us feel liberated and free. A dream of flying might mean we yearn for space and freedom.

ballooning, for instance, or jets of hot air, could well suggest communication overload to you – not surprising in this information age.

WIND

Air is often manifest as wind, and in our dream we should look at what effect it is having, what role it is playing. Is it sustaining and helping us, like a cool breeze on a hot day? Do we work with it – flying, soaring or being borne aloft by it – or is it a powerful and harmful force, like the strong winds of a storm that blow us flat and bring destruction in their wake? As a symbol of intellectual and emotional direction and force, the wind in your dream is an outward manifestation of your internal life.

SUFFOCATION

The lack of air is usually more noticeable than its presence, and suffocation is an important dream theme. Suffocating, feeling short of breath, or even being in a stuffy room may show that our emotional and spiritual expression is being stifled, or that our intellect is not being

exercised sufficiently. Likewise, if we are ourselves choking someone or something, this may be pointing to unconscious guilt at choking the life out of a relationship, not allowing another person enough space and freedom, not saying what we want to say or not giving the other an opportunity to speak and be heard.

OBSCURITY

Smoke, haze or mist all obscure the view, suggesting a lack of clarity in your thinking, or being unable to see your way forward. Equally, debris flying through the air could indicate distractions, a whirl of ideas, or being caught up with other people's ideas.

HOLY BREATH

As we breathe we feel the air entering and leaving our body. The Hindus talk of *prana* – holy breath, cosmic spirit. The same is true of the Taoists of China who speak of *ch'i* – again a cosmic spirit or energy that flows like air

– and feng shui – literally "wind and water", the two cosmic forces that shape the landscape in which we live and bring us health and life. In the Bible, the Holy Spirit is said to manifest in several forms, including as a wind and a flame.

> ### AN AIR DREAM
>
> "I was standing on a high hill with the wind blowing all around me. Then suddenly I was being shot upwards at tremendous speed through a plastic tube on a column of air. In a flash the hill was far below me, getting smaller and smaller, more and more distant. I was aware of how important the air was. It was holding me, shooting me upwards. Without it I would fall back to the earth again and be killed.
>
> As I realized I was reaching the top of the column I woke up and remember feeling incredibly grateful for the dream, and that I had to learn to breathe more deeply, to feel more alive."

BELOW LEFT The wind blowing through grasses is an evocative image. Are you dreaming of bending to forces that you find irresistible?
BELOW Smoke rising in misty swirls can be linked with holy breath, our spirit selves.

BELOW Wind can be frightening and destructive as well as dangerous, and our dreams can reflect our fears of the untameable, wild and erratic manifestation of air.

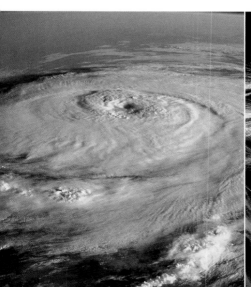

THE ELEMENTS — WATER

WATER HAS LONG BEEN THOUGHT OF AS THE SYMBOLIC VEHICLE OF EXPRESSION FOR OUR EMOTIONS, FEELINGS AND SENSITIVITY. IT IS, IN FACT, A PERFECT SYMBOL FOR THESE AS THE FORMS IT TAKES ARE SO VARIED. WATER IS THE SAME SUBSTANCE WHETHER IT IS A STILL POOL, A RAGING TORRENT, TOWERING WAVES ON THE BEACH, OR A DRIPPING TAP AT HOME. WITH THE SAME WIDE SPECTRUM, EMOTIONS CAN RANGE FROM SORROW, ANGER, JEALOUSY AND BEREAVEMENT, TO JOY, EXCITEMENT AND LOVE. ANY KIND OF WATER IMAGE IN A DREAM HOLDS THE POTENTIAL TO SYMBOLIZE OUR EMOTIONS AND OUR EMOTIONAL NEEDS, DESIRES AND CAPABILITIES.

BELOW Water is very evocative. It has a great power to move us, causes us to dream, and makes us reflective and contemplative. Eddying brooks and small streams are soothing, and to dream of any of these is a sign that we are relaxed and comfortable.
BELOW RIGHT The more we try to hold on to water – to our emotions and tears – the more it escapes from us; it is elusive and fluid.

Water represents the full range of different emotions, and it is immensely difficult to generalize when analysing the symbolism of water images. A scene that for some may be scary – say, a raging sea on a stormy night – might for someone else be exciting and exhilarating. Similarly, while for some people it is enough to feel emotionally comfortable and stable, others seek passion and new challenges.

BODIES OF WATER

Vast and deep, the sea is a particularly useful symbol for the enormity of our unplumbed, unconscious emotional depths. In some respects it is always changing, with the weather and with the ebb and flow of the tides and the constant movement of the great ocean currents – and yet it has its own rhythm and predictable aspects.

Rivers represent our emotional journey and can show us whether we let our emotions flow easily. Whether the river in your dream is strong and fast-flowing, a babbling brook or a brackish backwater could well be saying something about the strength of your emotions, and whether you are allowing them to be expressed fully and in a healthy way. Do you go with the flow, or swim against the current? Crossing a river may indicate that your emotions present some kind of obstacle, so having a means of doing so – a bridge, a raft, a ford – could be showing that there is a way forward. The stillness of a pool or pond can show the peace and tranquillity of a steady, reflective nature. A lagoon may provide a haven of stillness from the open sea without breaking contact with your emotional nature, and the protective, enclosing nature of the lagoon suggests a feminine aspect.

QUALITY AND QUANTITY

Our lives depend on water, but it must be pure to sustain and clean us. Dreaming of muddied, stagnant or polluted water may indicate that our emotions are confused or unhealthy, even harmful, and we may need to pay special attention to looking after ourselves, giving ourselves enough space to know what we are really feeling, and not engage in self-negativity.

A deluge may be completely overwhelming, and can wipe out everything in its path, but water

also evaporates, and the lack of it can equally be traumatic. Being profoundly thirsty or in a dry, barren place can indicate that our emotional side is neglected and is in need of reviving.

RELATIONSHIP TO WATER

Where are you in relation to the water in your dream, and how do you respond to it? You may be beside a body of water trying to skirt it, crossing it in a boat, or dithering about whether to get in, or perhaps you can't wait to take a running dive and feel the rush of bubbles past your skin. If you find yourself already in the water, are you floating, sinking or swimming? You may see water as a place to have fun, a place where you can be mesmerised by the easy, rhythmical movement of your body, or a terrifying place where you feel out of your depth or fear you will drown or be eaten alive.

BELOW Water can be exhilarating; if you dream of pounding waves, perhaps you are wishing for more excitement in your life?

We use water in a very practical way. Drinking it and cooking with it are positive, embracing tasks that nourish us, while washing ourselves and our possessions in it may indicate a need to rid ourselves of negativity and emotional debris. Dissolving things in water brings about complete transformation.

BIRTH, SEX AND LOVE

We are essentially made of water, and for the first nine months of our existence, the most sheltered, protected time of our lives, we live in fluid. We may be remembering or making sense of this experience when we dream of enclosed water or of being submerged. We talk of the waters breaking just before birth, when we are ready to make our traumatic journey into the world.

Fountains, hosepipes, geysers and so on can act as symbols of sexuality – in an obvious way they represent ejaculation, but in a more general sense they can be seen as metaphors for sexual energy and release. A dream of swimming with a lover, for example, may be sensuous in a more tranquil way, and speak of

the harmony of love as you move together in a slow, easy rhythm, at one in a buoyant medium.

TEARS

Dissolving in tears as salty as the sea, we express our sadness, grief, anger, tiredness, fear and insecurity, and in so doing, find emotional release. Many people have taught themselves not to cry, so dreaming of doing so may be particularly powerful if it breaks a personal taboo. If someone else is crying in your dreams consider whether this is an aspect of yourself that is trying to be expressed.

ABOVE Water dreams might contain water that has been harnessed as a resource, in the form of running taps or over-flowing bathtubs – or perhaps a lack of water, as in dry wells. All could have links with your waking life.

CREATURES OF THE LAND

ANIMALS SHOW US OUR MORE INNOCENT, INSTINCTIVE AND INTUITIVE SELVES. THEY SHOW US HOW WE MIGHT BE IF THE RESTRAINTS AND TABOOS WE LEARN THROUGHOUT OUR LIVES WERE REMOVED, AND THE VENEER OF CIVILIZATION, MATURITY AND SOPHISTICATION STRIPPED AWAY. OUR PLAYFULNESS AND CURIOSITY, AGGRESSION AND SEXUALITY MAY ALL BE EXPRESSED IN OUR DREAMS THROUGH IMAGES OF ANIMALS. OF COURSE WHAT EACH ANIMAL SYMBOLIZES WILL VARY FROM CULTURE TO CULTURE. IT IS EASY FOR URBAN WESTERNERS TO SAY A LION REPRESENTS STRENGTH, WHEN TO AN AFRICAN LIVING IN THE BUSH IT MIGHT JUST SYMBOLIZE DANGER AND FEAR.

CHARACTERISTICS

If there are strong cultural associations or stereotypes around an animal's character, such as the stealth of a tiger or the cunning of the fox, you may bring the animal into your dream to stand in for such meanings, but if it is a less distinguished creature or one you don't recognize, it could be its wildness, or some characteristic or behaviour it is exhibiting in your dream, that is important. Such characteristics show you something about yourself, characteristics that you should aspire to, or avoid, or eliminate. Whether the animal is behaving normally or doing something odd

BELOW What are the animals in your dream doing? Their behaviour is as important as what kind of beast they are.

or bizarre, may say how comfortable you are with what the animal represents, or that its natural qualities are present but are being subverted.

ASSOCIATIONS

When you dream of an animal, see what associations it has for you, as well as if there are any stereotypes around that animal. Baby animals often have different associations from those of the adult, but also bear the characteristics of the adult. Use the list provided to spark off your own ideas.

WILD ANIMALS

Freud held that dreams of wild animals represent our unbridled passions – lust, greed, jealousy and the like. It is possible that the animal in your dream represents your sexual fears (a bull or a stallion the loss of prowess, a crow unfaithfulness) but such a prescriptive interpretation fails to take into account either the characteristics of the animal or the personal response you have to it. It may make more sense to extend Freud's interpretation of wild animals to mean our unbridled nature – wild animals in their natural habitat are unconstrained, so like other elements of nature, they show us some aspect of our

true selves. In a zoo or cage, farm or game reserve, the animal is to a greater or lesser extent enclosed – for display, consumption or its own protection – and its natural impulses may be curbed. If the animal in your dream has been contained like this, see whether it is content or fretting, aggressive or apathetic, to understand your own relationship with being constrained. A wild animal being hunted may suggest a threat to your natural self, while an animal stalking or hunting may have connotations of strategy, self-sufficiency or single-mindedness.

PETS

The animals in our dreams are often domestic rather than wild animals, and our familiarity with our pets is likely to give us a greater feel for their range of characteristics. If the animal is our own pet, we may relate to it more like a family member than an animal, as we know its behaviours and moods intimately and have a strong emotional bond. Your pet's playful, devoted, aloof or mysterious nature may be what you are trying to work with in your dream.

FARMING

Farm animals have qualities of both wildness and domesticity, but the relevant characteristics of

these creatures may be that they are bred and reared for slaughter; they live in vast herds or flocks or stacked up in sheds, and they are contained in a limited and sometimes very unnatural environment. This processing of animals may seem acceptable to you, or you may regard it with ambivalence or abhorrence; your attitude will influence the meaning of the dream.

SPIDERS AND INSECTS

Tiny and alien in appearance, spiders and insects have quite a different set of meanings which often have little to do with their ability to harm us by stinging or biting us or spreading disease. Many people fear or dislike them at the best of times, often apparently irrationally, and in our dreams they can be monstrous and terrifying.

Spiders weave invisible webs to entrap their unsuspecting prey, so we may use both the spider or the web in our dreams to symbolize being trapped or betrayed in some way. Insects such as bees and ants live in colonies, and so teamwork is vital to their very survival. On its own a tiny insect may seem like nothing much, but collectively they can move large objects, build complex structures and strip a forest bare, providing powerful images for the value of co-operation and the lack of individuation. Insects also seem constantly active, so your dream may suggest a need to slow down, or to be more efficient.

ANIMALS AS FAMILIARS OR MESSENGERS

In some cultures animals are believed to come to people in their dreams as spirit messengers, and the shaman will identify a person's "familiar" – the animal most likely to communicate with them. It could be interesting to see if there is one particular animal that keeps cropping up in your dreams, and whether it communicates any message.

ANIMAL MEANINGS

Lion Raw strength, power, danger, pride, kingship

Dog Devotion, faithfulness

Cat Independence, mystery, love of comfort, hunting

Horse Intelligence, athleticism, strength, nobility

Butterfly Beauty, capriciousness, transformation

Cow Calm, slowness, maternity

Monkey Playfulness, mischief

Mule Stubbornness, bearing of loads

Rabbit Prolific breeding

Snake Deceitfulness, venomousness

Pig Greed, dirtiness

THE CYCLE
OF LIFE

No matter who or what we are, we all go
through the same cycle of life, from birth
through childhood, youth, maturity and old age
to death. And no matter how we approach these
different stages – whether we enjoy and
welcome them or resent and try to avoid them –
they are all inevitable, unless we die
prematurely. How they appear in our dreams
will reflect how enjoyable or difficult we find
the whole experience, and dreams about the
rites of passage associated with the different
stages in the life cycle – about puberty, leaving
home, getting married, having children, or
retirement, for instance – affect all of us and
show how we are in ourselves, whether we feel
secure and at ease with where we are in life, or
resentful and in denial. Indeed, these dreams
are often the way we prepare mentally and
emotionally for approaching rites of passage.
They may prompt us to ask some of the serious
questions about our existence that we may
otherwise avoid –about those stages we have yet
to go through, and especially about what
happens to us when we die.

BIRTH DREAMS

BIRTH IS A HIGHLY SYMBOLIC THEME WHEN IT OCCURS IN OUR DREAMS, AND IT IS ONE WHOSE MEANING IS USUALLY QUITE EASILY INTERPRETED — IT IS ABOUT ORIGINS, NEW BEGINNINGS, LABOURING, THE STRUGGLE FOR INDIVIDUATION AND DEVELOPMENT. OUR OWN BIRTH IS PROBABLY THE MOST MOMENTOUS EVENT OF OUR LIVES, YET VIRTUALLY NO-ONE IS ABLE TO REMEMBER ANYTHING OF IT. IT IS POSSIBLE THOUGH, THAT WE DO RETAIN SOME OF THE SENSE OF IT, THAT THE EXPERIENCE OF IT STAYS WITH US SUBCONSCIOUSLY OUR WHOLE LIFE. WHAT WE ARE TOLD ABOUT IT BY OUR PARENTS OR BY OTHERS WHO WERE PRESENT MAY ALSO AFFECT US DEEPLY.

BEING BORN

In dreams of your own birth it may be that your unconscious is trying to draw your attention to some momentous event that it feels is in some way as traumatic as your birth. Often the dream will give you the clues you need to decipher what this event is – if it is not already immediately obvious. The context of the birth in your dream, together with the feelings you experience around it, will probably reflect how your unconscious feels about the event in your life – apprehensive, excited, hesitant, or reluctant, perhaps – and your unconscious is trying to encourage you to look at why these feelings are coming up. Birth involves a momentous transition, and we may use it in our dreams to represent the shock of the new, the move into an uncertain and unsafe new world, but one that is full of potential.

As well as giving us the wherewithal to look at important events in the present, dreams about our own birth may also point to feelings or problems buried deep in our psyche. If we were abandoned at birth, or if for some reason we believe that our birth was a disappointment to our parents, we may carry this sense of being abandoned or of not being good enough with us all our lives.

OUR CHILDREN'S BIRTH

Men and women alike may feel apprehensive about their own child being born; this is a major event that brings immense change and responsibility to a person's life, and to dream of it is natural. But women in particular are visited by dreams of birth when they are expecting a child. Such dreams are a way of coming to terms with the new being that is developing inside a woman's own body, and preparing for the birth, as well as for the huge lifestyle changes that happen after the baby arrives. Fears that the unborn child will be somehow less than perfect are quite common, and this fear

BIRTH DREAM

"When I was about six months pregnant I dreamed of a space ship, all silver and spinning, with lots of portholes. It didn't land, but a ladder was lowered and a creature appeared, with spindly arms and legs and big eyes, a bit like the alien at the end of the film 'Close Encounters of the Third Kind'. The alien spoke to me and then somehow entered my belly. I think this dream was my way of accepting that something unknown was growing inside of me, and that I was approaching a new situation I had never been faced with before."

often manifests in dreams about giving birth to a monster or a changeling. Dreams of giving birth may also simply be a wish fulfilment if you want a child.

To dream of our child's birth long after the event may show we are worrying about them for some reason – perhaps they are going through transition, or we are worried about their progress.

BIRTH SYMBOLISM

Dreaming of birth or babies may have nothing to do with real life pregnancy or having babies, but can symbolize a variety of things, such as ideas, projects and plans for the future. A normal birth in a dream may symbolize new beginnings. But if the birth is premature or unnatural we should look at why events are not unfolding in the natural way. Perhaps there is some obstruction and we are too impatient for nature to take its course, forcing it to make its journey into the world prematurely. If this is the case, perhaps you are making something happen without adequate preparation, or putting pressure on someone to start something they are not ready for.

If the creature that is born is unnatural or deformed, this may well be related to stumbling blocks or problems in plans you have made; the nature of its deformity or the qualities that make it unusual are probably significant, so remember as much detail as you can. If you dream of a stillbirth you might be thinking about a project that won't come to fruition, while an abortion may be the plan's termination.

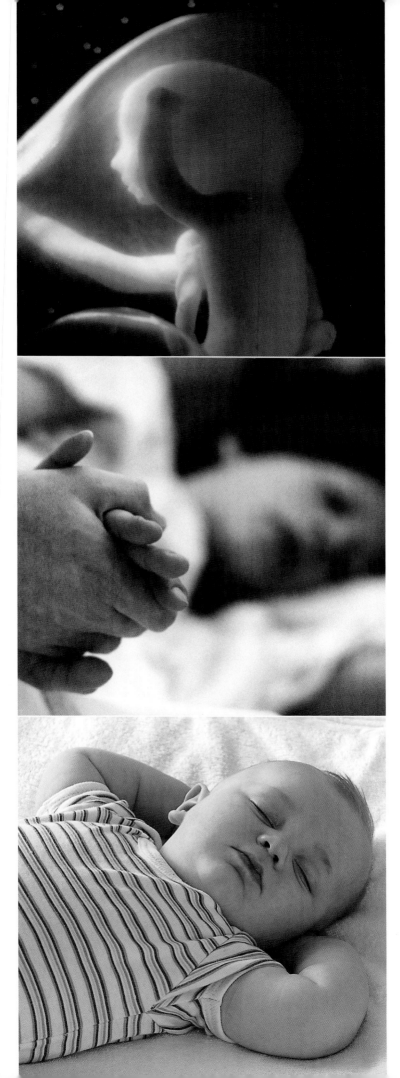

LEFT Dreaming of a baby in the womb could be reflecting your present circumstances, but might have nothing to do with babies at all. Perhaps it reflects ambitious plans and projects in your waking life that you feel need nurturing and bringing to life.

MIDDLE LEFT It is only natural to have lots of birthing dreams while pregnant – we all worry about a successful and happy delivery.

BOTTOM LEFT Dreaming of babies can mean that you are dreaming of the growth and maturing of something that is dear to your heart.

CHILDHOOD DREAMS

As we grow up we are influenced by many things. The people in our lives — especially our parents and siblings — as well as the environment we grow up in and the countless experiences we have during our childhood years, are all formative influences, giving shape to our personality and the way we approach the world. How we remember our childhood will influence how we see this stage of life in our dreams. When we dream of children we might be dreaming of our own childhood, but we might also be dreaming of the child we still are. Dreams of children might also symbolize ideas and plans we have that have yet to mature.

BELOW Dreaming that we are a child again may tell us a lot about how we feel about being grown ups,. Even if the dream is playful it may suggest feelings of unease or feeling ill equipped.

The terrifying moments of our childhood, the pain and trauma that we experience as we grow up get imprinted on our psyche and can scar us for the rest of our lives, surfacing in our dreams even when we are adults, and have "forgotten" the events. Alternatively it could be the freedom of childhood that we are yearning for in our dreams, a time when we could play to our heart's content, a time without the responsibilities and problems we face as adults. Childishness — silly, petty behaviour — may also be expressed in our dreams.

TOYS AND GAMES

Voices from our early years, familiar old toys and memories of games we used to play may all figure in our dreams as symbols of our childhood. This is a time to discover, and much of our learning is done through play, not only with toys and games but also by entering the world of make-believe through dressing-up and role play. These objects and activities are powerfully symbolic and thus easy for your unconscious to choose as representations of childhood – of fun and naivety, of curiosity, growth and development.

Particular toys or scenes may have a special meaning for you, for instance if you dream that

your favourite toy, from which you were inseparable as a child, is lost or taken away from you, it could be that your unconscious is using this as an analogy for possession or attachment, separation or grieving, or for a loss of security.

Games involving fantasy and role play could be a hint that we need to be more creative, see life from a different perspective, or try to change how we handle problems. Many children's games rely heavily on rules, and how the game is played can be as important as what is being played – making or breaking the rules, changing them as you go along, cheating or following them rigidly may say something about your relationship to laws and social expectations.

DREAMING OF CHILDREN

When we dream of a child or childishness we might be dreaming of the emotions we link to childhood. Young children are often more expressive than

adults, and feel less constrained by what others think when they want to cry or laugh or scream. They have the time and the freedom to play actively and to explore the things they enjoy or find interesting, and may also become completely immersed in the worlds they read about. On the other hand, children may be ignored when they speak, or punished for being noisy or angry, for making a mess or not sitting still.

When we dream of children we might be recalling something in our waking life that makes us feel in a way that we associate with the state of childhood, or we may be echoing something in our everyday life that has given us the status of a child in some way.

ADULTS AS CHILDREN

If we dream about someone else as a child we might be trying to find out what makes them tick, or perhaps to get to the root of why they are the way they are. Suppose you dream of your boss as a child. You may be trying to

understand what motivates them, or be attempting to reduce them to someone smaller and less powerful in order to make them less intimidating. You may equally turn an adult into a child in your dream because you want to attempt to exert some kind of control over them, or perhaps because you want to relate to them in a more direct and childlike way.

ABOVE If you dream of a teddy bear does it make you feel nostalgic for your lost childhood?

ABOVE LEFT Children are precious and usually very endearing and it is only natural to dream of such a wonderful gift.

ABOVE FAR LEFT To dream of toys can mean many things and you need to think carefully about the details of your dream, did the toy belong to you? was it broken, desirable, boring, symbolic?

A CHILDHOOD DREAM

"I was upstairs in a small room filled with sunlight, which streamed in through an open window. It was late afternoon towards the end of summer, and I was sitting on the floor, very still, very quiet. I'd been told that I had to stay here, and I had the feeling that something terrible would happen if I didn't.

I didn't understand the dream until I mentioned it to my sister. She told me that our mother would send me to my room when her parents came to visit, as they didn't know she had an illegitimate child and she was afraid they would disinherit her if they found out. She would tell me to go upstairs and stay there, and pretend that I didn't exist. When I heard this I cried and cried. Even though I hadn't remembered my mother doing this it must have made a huge impression on me, as all my life I've felt like I had to be bigger and better than anyone else – and make sure everyone knows I'm there! I like to think that the sunshine and the open window show my unstoppable outgoing nature, which existed even when I had to pretend I did not."

DREAMS OF YOUTH

ABOVE Dreaming of puberty might mean that we are working through crucial life changes in our dreams.

ABOVE RIGHT Adolescent and teenage years can represent rebellion and flux, and if we dream of this stage it may be that in our waking lives we are trying to find the right course of action to take.

YOUTH IS A TIME WHEN WE THROW OFF BOTH THE CONSTRAINTS AND THE INNOCENCE OF CHILDHOOD, TESTING AUTHORITY FIGURES AND TRYING TO FIND OUR OWN WAY IN LIFE. IN OUR TEENAGE YEARS WE EXPERIENCE THE PHYSICAL CHANGES OF PUBERTY, DISCOVER OUR SEXUALITY, HANG OUT IN GANGS, SUFFER FROM INTENSE PEER PRESSURE, AND DISCOVER OUR POWER AS YOUNG ADULTS. BUT OUR OWN EXPERIENCE AS TEENAGERS — GOOD AND BAD — WILL BE REFLECTED IN OUR DREAMS AS MUCH AS THE STEREOTYPES OF THIS LIFE STAGE, SO DREAMS OF YOUTH WILL MEAN VERY DIFFERENT THINGS TO DIFFERENT PEOPLE.

GROWING PAINS

Many people find adolescence to be a tumultuous and painful period, and some of us carry the scars for the rest of our lives. It is a time of transition from childhood to adulthood, and indeed the key take-home message of dreams about adolescence may well be metamorphosis. At this age we are not yet used to the changes in our bodies, and also often feel awkward and embarrassed at the errors we make in our quest to seem grown-up. To make things worse, we may be teased for the very mistakes we make and the changes we are going through, and withdraw as a result. Dreaming of youth later in life may mean that we are going through changes about which we feel uncertain or unconfident. We may be anticipating criticism or ridicule, or even fear that we will not be taken seriously by society. Even if your dream doesn't actually give you answers or guidance, it should be a useful way of making you aware of how you feel about the changes and what your fears are.

RIGHT The desire to be part of the "in-crowd" is probably at its most intense during youth, so if you dream about this it might reflect a feeling you have of being on the edge of things, of being not quite accepted.

PEER GROUP

At the same time as we begin to rebel against the adult world and leave our childhood ways behind, we turn instead to our peers, with whom we can identify more strongly, for ideas, support and encouragement as much as

friendship. Because the peer group becomes so important, many teenagers feel the need to conform – to adopt current fashions, have the latest gear, and even to use the right words, in order to be acceptable. In our youth we are testing out new roles, so there may be a lot of faking involved in our behaviour before we become settled in who we are. For this reason, dreams of adolescence may also be about inauthenticity, about following trends or trying to find a niche within an accepted set.

EXTREMES AND IDEALS

Because we have so many new experiences as teenagers and young adults, this period of our lives may seem to be one of extremes, especially in our feelings and behaviours. We may be more passionately in love at this time than at any other later time in our lives, or be filled with despair when things don't go our way. It is a time when we are most likely to feel prepared to step into the unknown, travel the world on a shoestring or take up

dangerous sports. This is when we are at our physical peak, and feel able to do all these things because we have a sense of being invincible, immortal. It is also a time of pushing the boundaries – partying all night long, getting very drunk or experimenting with drugs – and exploring social or political ideals. We may still do all these things or have the same feelings later in life, but as a stereotype, we are more likely to associate them with being young, and youth may be the theme of our dream to represent our desire to try new things, to step back from the mundane practicalities of life and remind ourselves of our own ideals.

LOOKING AHEAD

In our youthful explorations of the big wide world, we are in the process of finding where we belong in society and what we want to do with our lives. We leave school and have to make choices about work or further education, and begin to assert our own personal style and beliefs. While dreams about

youth may be about immaturity in yourself or others, they could also be about discovering and asserting yourself.

NOSTALGIA

Looking back at our youth, we may feel nostalgic, remembering the freedom, the fun, the passion and excitement, and forgetting the more painful moments. We may even be reconstructing a youth that we never really had, perhaps one that seems more fun and interesting than our own. If we are afraid of growing old, we may be rejecting the stereotypes of middle or old age and clinging to youthfulness, rather than embracing the positive aspects our current stage of life can offer.

ABOVE If you dream of a lack of financial freedom in youth perhaps you are admitting to a feeling that this has never really gone away, and that this is materially a real problem for you.

ABOVE LEFT The excitement and intensity of your first romance can never be matched. If you dream of young love perhaps it reflects a dissatisfaction with your love life.

ABOVE FAR LEFT Dreaming of the wilder side of youth culture might mean that you are yearning for a more exciting element in your life, whatever your age.

DREAM OF YOUTH

"In my dream I had dyed my hair red and wore a biker's jacket, and I was behaving like a teenager again. Not that I dyed my hair when I was a teenager, but in my dream it made me feel young again. Since I passed forty I've got it into my head that I must be wild, rebellious and wacky to recapture my youth and ward off middle age and all the implications of sedateness that that time of life has. I think I'm also a little jealous of my own teenage children and the fun they seem to have."

AGEING

WE ARE GETTING OLDER ALL THE TIME, AND GRADUALLY THE FEAR OF WHAT THIS MEANS FOR US AND OF WHAT COMES NEXT BEGINS TO PERMEATE OUR UNCONSCIOUS AND WORK ON OUR IMAGINATION. WE KNOW OR FEAR THE HORRORS OF THE FIRST GREY HAIRS, OF WRINKLES AND AN EXPANDING WAISTLINE. WE ARE AWARE THAT WE MIGHT BECOME INFIRM OR ILL, OR LOSE OUR MENTAL FACULTIES WHEN WE GROW OLD. BUT THESE FEARS CAN ALSO BE BALANCED BY THE WISDOM THAT A LIFETIME'S EXPERIENCE MAY HAVE BROUGHT US, AND OLD AGE CAN BE A TIME WHEN WE ALLOW OURSELVES TO ATTAIN A LEVEL OF PEACE AND CONTEMPLATION.

We dream of ageing for several reasons. It may be that we are worried about it, about losing our youthful looks and our physical strength and ability. It could also be that we are coming to terms with ageing, content with what we have seen and done so far in our lives and looking forward to the prospect of a comfortable and interesting retirement. A dream of old age may also be a metaphor for times past, and serve as a kind of nostalgia trip.

FEARS OF AGEING

We all react to the fear of growing old in different ways. We may face up to it, but often this is too painful and we choose instead to deny the unpleasant realities of old age, or to suppress them by ignoring them or

laughing them off. We try to reverse the ageing process by going for cosmetic surgery, dyeing our hair, applying anti-ageing creams, and wearing youthful clothes.

Our unconscious is not easily deceived though, and will deal with our fears in our dreams if we don't do so in our waking lives. It knows that we are terrified at the prospect of our lives ending and our bodies decaying, that we are afraid to confront the possibility that when we reach old age and drop the frantic activity of our younger years, we will discover that it has all been meaningless.

Dreams in which we see ourselves getting older, or already old, can be quite shocking, and act as a wake-up call for us to pay more attention to what we

are doing with our lives, to make us realise that time is passing. Sometimes these dreams mask a concern about our health, and may be taken as a cautionary note to make sure we remain as fit and active as we ought to. Recurring dreams about ageing may indicate an ongoing concern, and if you have them it is important to get to the bottom of what is bothering you.

RETIRING

Even if you are still fit and active, retiring from the working world can be the first step in starting to acknowledge that old age is not far off. You may dream about retirement in a literal way if you are approaching it in your own life, or if your partner or parents are soon to retire. This will provide you with a way to

BELOW RIGHT As time passes we can start to feel edgy, as if there are things to do that we need to concentrate on.
BELOW How we feel about our health will be shadowed in our dreams – if we are healthy while asleep it is pretty much how we will feel when we are awake.

A DREAM OF AGEING

"I was looking in a mirror and while I watched I saw my own teeth fall out and my hair turn white. The whole ageing process was immensely speeded up. I know I am getting older, but this dream really shocked me and made me feel that I wanted to hang on to my youth at all costs. But it also made me realize that I really have to enjoy what I've got because time goes so fast and I won't have it for long. And as it all slips away I have to keep reminding myself to enjoy each and every moment."

LEFT As we get older we do get more experienced, better equipped to be successful. If our dreams reflect this we can be reassured about how we fit in to the world around us.

explore possible anxieties you have around this transition.

How you see retirement will depend to a considerable extent on how well you are prepared for it, both financially and emotionally. It can be difficult to adjust to the lack of structure and activity, the loss of status, the lack of contact with your colleagues, and the sheer weight of idle time that you now have. But you may equally see it as a time to reap the benefits of your hard work, to enjoy a leisurely life or turn your hand to hobbies or other interests you have not had time for before.

WITHDRAWAL

Whatever your age, your dreams may also use retirement or old age as a metaphor for withdrawing – especially from society or from an overly active lifestyle. Indeed old age is for many a time when our contact with the outside world lessens as our ability or desire to get out decreases and our friends and siblings die. It can be a lonely time, and it may be this that your dream is trying to draw to your attention – either your own fear of becoming isolated, or guilt at not paying enough attention to an elderly relative.

WISDOM

Our stereotypes of old age are not all negative though, and while the elderly are often marginalized in Western society, we may find the archetypal figure of the wise old man or woman appearing in our dreams as a source of advice or understanding; we may even be that figure ourselves.

Grandparents or other familiar old faces may also crop up in our dreams as symbols of stability and continuity, allowing us to feel grounded and supported in our family, and giving us perspective on our lives.

BELOW FAR LEFT To dream of old or worn-out objects might point to something in our life that we feel needs to be rejuvenated.
BELOW LEFT Dreaming of possible loneliness in old age might reflect the way you feel about your life currently rather than a fear of the future.
BELOW But even when there is no hope of living forever we can rest assured that there is new life even in our dreams.

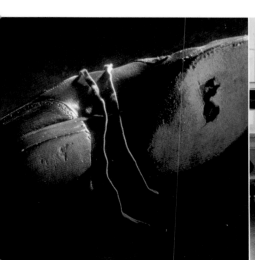

DEATH

WE ALL KNOW THAT SOONER OR LATER, DEATH WILL COME TO US, HOPEFULLY NOT PREMATURELY, BUT AS THE INEVITABLE AND INESCAPABLE LAST STAGE IN THE CYCLE OF LIFE. HOWEVER MUCH WE TRY TO AVOID THINKING ABOUT OUR OWN DEATH, OR THAT OF OUR LOVED ONES, OUR UNCONSCIOUS WILL AT SOME STAGE START TO ADDRESS THE ISSUE AND TRY TO PREPARE US FOR IT. THERE ARE MANY ISSUES ASSOCIATED WITH DEATH THAT MIGHT FEATURE IN OUR DREAMS: LOSS, LONELINESS OR RELEASE FOR EXAMPLE, AND WHETHER OR NOT THERE IS LIFE AFTER DEATH MIGHT BE ANOTHER THEME THAT WE MAY TRY TO SPECULATE ON AND EXPLORE IN OUR DREAMS.

COMING TO TERMS WITH MORTALITY

Dreams of funerals or graveyards, grief and mourning, dead bodies or skeletons may be quite literally about death and dying, and often show that we view this process in a negative light. If we are worried about death and dying then dreams of death probably happen to make us do something to try to come to terms with our own mortality. But if we dream of people celebrating, being happy,

BELOW Even if we never consciously think about our mortality it will be a source of worry to us on a deep level. We might also dream of death as a way of focusing on worries that we have of being separated from others.

remembering the dead person with pride and love, then perhaps we have made some progress in coming to terms with it. This doesn't necessarily mean we have to look forward to it, but merely that it holds no power over us to frighten us, and that we are as prepared as we can be for this event.

A LOVED ONE'S DEATH

Dreams about others dying may indicate a worry that they will die or leave us. Who we dream about may be telling us who we most fear will leave us, but it could also be that rather than a literal death, the dream represents some figurative termination of a quality that you particularly value (or dislike) in that person.

IMAGES OF DEATH

History has given us many morbid death images which our society seems to have taken eagerly on board – vaults and misty graveyards, mourners dressed in black, skeletons and gravediggers, crows, the Grim Reaper, and countless images of hell. People down the ages seem to have enjoyed frightening and torturing themselves with such images, and in your dreams they could point to disturbance and fear around death. Dreaming of being buried – especially being

buried alive – may have nothing to do with death but rather a feeling of having the life squeezed out of you, of being stifled in some way.

But death is not always disturbing – it can be very undramatic, even mundane, or very peaceful and part of the natural order. A graveyard in your dream may be a beautiful, calm place where you spend time remembering people you loved.

LIFE AFTER DEATH

Death is our biggest rite of passage, the one that takes us out of this existence and on into the next – whatever that might be. If we do believe that death is merely a transition into the next life, our unconscious may choose to show us images of change, of journeys and rebirth – which may indicate that it knows that death is not final but is indeed merely a symptom of great transformation. These dreams may be suggesting radical change or the need for such change, and not actual physical death.

How we dream about death reflects not only our views of the process but also our views of what we think happens to us afterwards. We may dream of heaven or hell as if we know what they are like, though such imagery is generally based on

LEFT Images of death don't have to be negative. They can also generate a feeling of ultimate peace and tranquillity that we may feel we need.

BELOW The religious trappings of death might suggest an awful state of nothingness, or inspire awe and acceptance. It depends on how we view death.

countless images that have been handed down to us by others. Such dreams may indicate some kind of self-judgement, seeking reward for good behaviour or fearing punishment for bad.

Whatever else it may involve, death means separation from the body, so may reveal a wish for release from ill health. It could also mean that we are coming to terms with our preoccupations with the body, or, less literally, the material world.

ABOVE Standard images of death in our dreams might actually be about some other kind of rite of passage, and perhaps something quite mundane in comparison.

LEFT Whatever religion we follow will give us plenty of imagery to fuel our dreams and visions of death and the afterworld.
RIGHT Dreaming of someone's death might mean you are reflecting on the passing of a relationship, or a phase of your friendship together.

DREAM OF DEATH

"I was in a foreign country like Egypt, being buried alive. I could feel the sand filling my mouth and my body sinking deeper and deeper into the ground. I felt I was suffocating. Just then someone uncovered my face with a spade and I could breathe. They said, 'look – some bones!' and I realized I had been dead for a long time.

I think the whole dream was about an inability to change. I felt it meant that I had to look at what was important to me, and get rid of a lot of things in my life so that I was not so stuck and held back by my possessions and rigid attitudes. I think there was also a fear that it might actually be too late to change."

MIND, BODY AND SPIRIT

Our emotional and physical experiences, together with the things we are told or learn throughout our lives, give us a framework for our beliefs, which we try, often unsuccessfully, to use to keep us safe in times of trouble and crisis. With experience we have the opportunity to develop an understanding of our limitations, to grow and change, learn and expand. Some say that through such experiences our "soul" also learns and grows; when we have learnt all we need to, we move on. At times these lessons are enjoyable, but often we learn best through adversity. We incorporate our experiences, our hopes and our fears into our dreams. It is here that our unconscious tries to come to terms with guilt or with the heartache of grief; explores our sexuality and faces our mortality; and endeavours to answer some of the great questions of our existence.

EMOTIONS

ABOVE Sometimes we are not aware that we feel angry or frustrated, but such feelings can surface in our dreams.
ABOVE RIGHT Our dream symbolism may indicate painful emotions. This image could suggest isolation and loneliness.
ABOVE FAR RIGHT Holding a baby's hand is a symbol of love and tenderness. It may also mean a need to protect or be protected.

OUR EMOTIONS COVER A VAST RANGE OF EXPERIENCES, FROM ANGER AND JEALOUSY THROUGH BOREDOM AND SADNESS TO LOVE AND HAPPINESS. WHILE WE ARE ONLY TOO GLAD TO HAVE THE POSITIVE EMOTIONS, OTHERS ARE UNCOMFORTABLE AND WE MAY TRY TO PUSH THEM AWAY. BUT WE CAN'T ALWAYS CONTROL THEM, AND THEY CAN WELL UP AND OVERWHELM US, TAKING US BY SURPRISE. IN OUR DREAMS WE EXPERIENCE THE FULL RANGE OF OUR EMOTIONS, OFTEN MORE INTENSELY THAN IN OUR WAKING LIVES, AND THEY MAY HELP US COME TO GRIPS WITH THE REALLY DIFFICULT ONES.

BURIED EMOTIONS

We often hide or lose track of our emotions because we want to appear mature or civilized or in control. At times strong emotions threaten to take us over and then we may be afraid of seeming weak or vulnerable, or of doing something that we will later regret, or simply of wasting time that we think we should be spending on something else. We develop coping mechanisms to make sure that our feelings don't show, and some people are so successful at this that they lose touch with their feelings. They may also divert attention from one emotion and express it as another that may seem more

socially acceptable – for instance, men who have been brought up to believe that "boys don't cry" may express sadness as anger, and conversely many women who have had their anger curbed by social or parental disapproval may cry when angry.

When we control or divert our emotions we may delude ourselves into feeling stronger, braver, wiser, or in some other way more acceptable, but there is often a price to pay for being cut off in this way. We need to feel and express our true our emotions if we are to be well-rounded and complete human beings, to find a balance between heart and mind. Our dreams can

help us to do this by unlocking unacknowledged feelings.

FEELINGS IN DREAMS

It is always worth looking at the feelings that come up in a dream. Usually they are consistent with what you would imagine you should be feeling in the context of the dream, but sometimes the feelings and the plot may be puzzlingly at odds. Events may occur in your dream precisely to provoke a response that you will take note of, to make you think about what is really going on inside you. Sometimes this can be hard – if you always play the role of the kind and loving mother, for instance, a dream in

Dreaming permits each and every one of us to be quietly and safely insane every night of our lives.

WILLIAM DEMENT

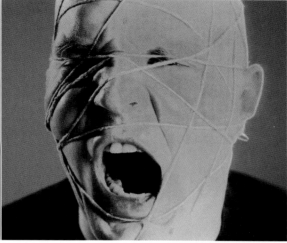

which you sit reading a book impassively while your children are tormented will be really shocking and hard to come to terms with, but it could be a reality check on your ability to be the saint all the time, and may bring to your attention your frustrations or the fact that your own needs are not being met.

EMOTIONAL POINTERS

In some dreams the emotional content will be the take-home message rather than any events or images, and it may even be that the only thing you

remember about the dream is that it was terrifying, or that in it you were extremely anxious about running out of time.

If you are not ready to deal with emotions square on, though, your mind may produce symbols to stand in for these feelings. Virtually all of your dream images can be read symbolically, or are present in your dream because they provoke some strong emotion or train of thought. Some are fairly obvious – for example a heart may stand for romantic love – while others are less clear but nevertheless

widely accepted – such as the notion that water in all its many forms represents our emotions. Many of the symbols we use to represent emotions are discussed more fully elsewhere.

The main thing is to look at the context of the symbol and your response to it in order to be able to access the emotional content. Once you understand what emotions are being brought to the surface and how they come across in your dream, you will probably have a clearer idea of how to deal with them in a useful and positive way.

ABOVE Expressing strong emotions can have a knock-on effect in our dealings with others.
ABOVE LEFT Dream imagery is often bizarre. Feeling tied-up in knots is frustrating and can make you feel like screaming.
ABOVE FAR LEFT Emotions that are held back or suppressed in your waking life may surface later in your dreams.

LEFT To dream of a macho man may suggest that it is hard for you to own your feelings as you like to appear "cool".
FAR LEFT The context of our dreams is important. A mother with her baby will mean different things for each of us, depending on our circumstances.

LOSS AND GRIEF

When death enters our lives it often comes as a complete shock, and we are left bewildered, lost, angry and confused. Added to the pain are feelings of regret and guilt, the sense of "If only I'd known", "If only I'd been able to say all the things I wanted to", or "I didn't get a chance to say goodbye". But it isn't just death that generates feelings of loss. Divorce, redundancy and even the loss of prized possessions can bring their own sudden shocks to our life. How we cope can affect how much finds its way into our dreams, and it is here that we will try to come to terms with this loss if we are not facing up to it in our waking life.

GRIEVING

The word "bereaved" is from an Old English word *bereafian*, which means "to plunder". And that is the feeling we have when we have lost someone or something close to us. We feel plundered, we feel that someone or something precious has been carried off without our permission or knowledge.

The experience of bereavement is not only triggered by a person's death, but other significant life events, such as divorce, separation and redundancy. The loss of such things as our health or our youth – or even our personal possessions – also have associations with grief and loss, and may affect us quite deeply.

Whatever the reason for our grief, we may try to work it out in our dreams. A lot of people are shocked and surprised if grieving continues in their dreams when they think they have "got over it", but the stronger the emotional tie, the longer the process is likely to go on. After someone you were close to has died, they may return to your dreams from time to time for the rest of your life.

BELOW It is very common when someone close to us dies that they continue to appear in our dreams – for months, or even years afterwards. This may be to help us work out aspects of our relationship with that person.

ABOVE Although we may chide ourselves for being silly, the loss of a precious possession is likely to stir up our emotions. If you dream of your lost treasure, consider what it symbolizes for you.

FUNERALS

A funeral is an official ending. It gives us a chance to say "goodbye" and to mourn our loss. In some cultures, open displays of crying and even wailing are perfectly natural at funerals, and grieving can be expected to last, and be marked with ceremonies, for months. In western society we are expected to "pull ourselves together" or "put on a brave face" and get on with our lives as quickly as possible, and far too little time or emotional energy is given to grieving. Yet if we have not fully come to terms with someone's death, they will in a sense, haunt us. Once there has been a proper grieving process, our dreams will by and large return to normal.

WORKING IT OUT

In our dreams the person or object we have lost may appear in glorious technicolour. They may seem perfectly normal and present, just as they were in life, and on waking we may feel the shock and sadness all over again when we realize it was "just a dream". This process is essential to our unconscious even if it is difficult and confusing for us. To our unconscious it is a way of working out what has happened and laying the ghost to rest. It also gives us the opportunity to say things that we feel were left unsaid, or to replay events in our unconscious mind so that we can be with our loved one once more. It is a hard and sometimes wrenching process but essential if we are to be able to get on with our lives and become as whole and as healed as possible.

DREAMS OF LOSS

Losing things in a dream may indicate that you need to mourn a loss or achieve closure on some aspect of your life. It may be something physical, such as a valuable object, or it could be more abstract, such as the loss of freedom, or of a particular phase in your life that has ended – for instance the transition from being single to being married. Even something frivolous, like having your hair cut, can be traumatic if it represents a loss of identity,

In all these cases there is a period of adjustment as you come to terms with losing something that is integral to your self-expression, or that reminds you of someone you love.

LEFT There is no easy way to mourn, but spending quiet time alone each day in reflection can help you come to terms with your loss.
MIDDLE LEFT A graveyard appearing in your dreams could be a reminder to lay the past to rest and move on with your life.
BOTTOM LEFT Piles of money in a dream may represent concerns with material security. What do you fear to lose?

GRIEF DREAM

"The year that my grandmother died I saw her in my dreams every night for months. Every morning when I woke up, I was convinced she was still alive and would run into my parents' room to tell them the good news; every morning they had to tell me she was dead. I felt the shock anew each time. It was terrible and sad, and for a good while I was frightened to go to sleep at night because I didn't want to face the shock in the morning. I even left notes to myself by my bed saying 'Granny is dead'. Each morning I woke grieving the loss. I think it helped. I feel that I can talk about her now and remember her with warmth and love."

GUILT AND BLAME

MANY PEOPLE ARE SURPRISED TO ENCOUNTER GUILT AND BLAME IN THEIR DREAMS, BUT THEY ARE AMONG THE COMMONEST OF DREAM THEMES AND PERMEATE BOTH OUR LIVES AND OUR DREAMS ON MANY LEVELS. WE MAY THINK THAT A DREAM IN WHICH WE ARE A CONVICT OR AN ADULTERER IS JUST OUR UNCONSCIOUS EXPLORING FACETS OF OUR CHARACTER THAT WE MIGHT NOT LIKE TO OWN UP TO IN OUR WAKING LIFE, BUT IT IS OFTEN GUILT THAT OUR UNCONSCIOUS IS EXPLORING. EVEN IF WE SEEM TO BE DREAMING SOMEONE ELSE'S GUILT OR BLAMING SOMEONE FOR SOMETHING, IT MAY WELL BE A DISPLACED REPRESENTATION OF OUR OWN GUILT AND SELF-BLAME.

MIND, BODY AND SPIRIT

FEELING GUILTY

Our conscious minds are very experienced at justifying our actions or blaming others so that we avoid uncomfortable feelings of guilt and self-blame. If we know we have been cruel or difficult to someone, or mishandled another person in some way, the unconscious may try to make us more aware of our behaviour so that we can see what we have done. For deep down we know what is right and wrong, and we know that we need to understand the implications of our actions and make amends for them. Part of

the role of the unconscious in our dreams is to drive us towards a greater self-awareness and understanding.

Even people who are by and large decent and honest will have the occasional lapse, and may feel disproportionately guilty and remorseful as a result. Our guilt may be misplaced too; children are often punished for being angry, and as they grow up, and even into adulthood they may continue to feel guilty when they feel anger. Adults who have this kind of problem with anger may also carry a subconscious fear of retribution as a result of anger.

CRIME AND PUNISHMENT

The greater the offence, the more intense the dream is likely to be, and we may wake feeling we have actually committed a crime, even if whatever is making us feel guilty is not the same as the dream scenario. The nature of the offence in our dream will usually give us enough clues to identify what it is we are feeling guilty about. It may be that you are being caught – or simply blamed – for a wrongdoing and you feel guilty until proven innocent. Take note of whether the punishment fits the crime – if you are given a hefty penalty for a mere peccadillo, it may be that you are feeling victimized by injustice rather than actually feeling guilty.

CONFESSION

Confessing in a dream, whether to a priest, a confidante or to the person you have wronged, also indicates that you feel guilty for something. It may also show that you are trying to purge yourself of your guilty feelings and regrets, or offload the burden of guilt on to someone else.

We treat ourselves badly at times and we may feel compelled to double the damage by "beating ourselves up" about it. Such guilt and self-blame may manifest as

BELOW Sometimes our inner voice must shout to be heard and can be symbolized in our dreams as threatening, or aggressive figures. Ask yourself what it is that you don't want to hear. Maybe you have a fear of being punished?

LEFT Fragments of our dreams are often all that we recall, but only you can decide if they make you feel guilty.

LEFT To be standing accused in your dream may tie-in with harbouring a guilty secret. Who is it that you are wronging and what is it that you fear from them?

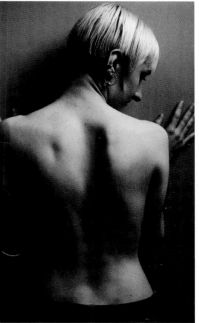

dreams about being punished. It doesn't have to be crimes that we feel guilty for. Sometimes we feel bad about withholding love, or for not responding to someone's distress, or for failing to rise to a challenge. We may even feel guilty whenever we please ourselves rather than pleasing someone else and judge ourselves "selfish".

Guilt is one of those insidious feelings that seem to spill into every area of our lives. It has the power to go on eating away at us forever and it is often extremely hard to get rid of. But our dreams may give us a clue as to what we can do to work through such feelings, and learn from them. Ask questions of your dream and the answers will emerge.

ABOVE Feeling guilty and being a victim often go hand-in-hand. Who or what would you like to turn your back on?

DREAM OF BLAME

"I was riding a motorbike and saw my son riding towards me. We both pulled back on our handlebars and did 'wheelies'. The strange thing is my son is only five but in my dream he was a young man. I feel really guilty towards him because his mother and I separated. Even though it was his mother that left, I still feel so much of his pain at not having her there, at having to grow up ahead of his time. I feel responsible for this because I must have played a part in her decision to leave."

ABOVE To dream of a prison cell may symbolize being punished for some misdemeanour. Could it be your guilt that has imprisoned you?

RIGHT Our guilt can make us feel small and trapped. It can remind us of how it felt as children to be accused of a crime we didn't commit.

FALLING IN LOVE

MORE SONGS, POEMS AND LETTERS HAVE BEEN WRITTEN ABOUT LOVE THAN ANY OTHER SUBJECT, AND IT IS ONLY NATURAL THAT SUCH AN IMPORTANT EMOTION SHOULD FIGURE SO LARGELY IN OUR DREAMS. WE ALL NEED TO LOVE AND BE LOVED, AND WHEN WE FALL IN LOVE WE LITERALLY CAN'T STOP DAYDREAMING ABOUT OUR CHOSEN ONE, SO IT IS COMPLETELY UNDERSTANDABLE THAT THIS CARRIES ON INTO OUR SLEEPING WORLDS TOO. FALLING IN LOVE AND HOLDING THE STEADY LOVE OF A REAL PERSON ARE TWO DIFFERENT THINGS, BUT BOTH REPRESENT OR CONTAIN POWERFUL EMOTIONS, AND MAY DOMINATE OUR DREAMS FROM TIME TO TIME.

160

MIND, BODY AND SPIRIT

In our dreams our partner may take on a new dimension – not who they really are but who we think they are, or who we would like them to be. They may be wilder, fiercer, bossier, kinder, more or less loving, but their essence remains the same. Our unconscious may amplify an aspect of their character to draw our attention to some particular point of view so we can adjust our relationship accordingly, or in order to flag up characteristics that we don't want to see.

FIRST LOVE
For teenagers, falling in love is often a painful experience. Our first love affair can be very formative, as all our future relationships may be built on the lessons we learn in those first few soulful gazes or fumbling

embraces. Likewise, that first ever love affair will probably feature prominently in our teen dreams.

It is also quite natural, especially at this young age, to fall in love with someone who is unattainable – someone we adore from afar, or who is forbidden – perhaps because they are too old for us, or are already in a partnership. This person is likely to appear in our dreams, which may have a sexual or erotic bias. Such dreams can be very realistic and make us feel confused and embarrassed, particularly when we meet the person in daily life.

ROMANCE
A kind of scene-setting for love, romance usually features more prominently at the beginning of a relationship when our feelings

are based more in fantasy than in the reality of the person on whom we have focused our attentions. At this stage it functions as wish fulfilment – we want everything to be wonderful and so we put all our effort into impressing the other person and making them feel special. We also want to be made to feel special ourselves. Romance provides a smoke screen, a context and loose set of rules and rituals in the framework of which we can get to know the other person, but it may also serve to distract us from who they really are.

The symbols and activities that we associate with romance – anything heart-shaped, candlelit dinners, sunsets on the beach, love poetry and so on – are many and wide-ranging, so dreaming of these things, whether they

BELOW RIGHT When we are in love, it can feel as if we are floating on air and our dreams may have a romantic feel to them. **BELOW** Falling in love is an exciting experience and it is most likely that our lover will keep on appearing in our dreams.

RIGHT Dreams of falling in love with someone in a very physical way might reflect something that you feel is lacking in your love life, or might recall the intense feelings that are associated with first love.

involve a particular person or not, may point to a wish for romance in our lives or the possibility that it is on the horizon. Men in particular may find themselves feeling particularly vulnerable if they show their softer side, so a romantic dream may have more to do with getting in touch with vulnerability and owning your feelings than with any kind of actual partnership.

Whether the romantic dream scenario will hold together coherently or is flawed in some way may also be taken as a hint as to how you should be approaching love and relationships. Ask yourself whether you are looking for a person to have a real relationship with or merely someone who will make you feel better by distracting you from areas of dissatisfaction in your life.

THE FOOD OF LOVE

Love and food go together in many ways, so you could consider whether food images in your dreams are linked to love. For many people food and drink are an intrinsic part of the rituals of romance and courtship, and

are also the subject of fetishes. Your unconscious may make reference to expressions such as "all-consuming passion" when it dreams of eating, to suggest the nature of how you relate to a lover, and perhaps to warn you not to become too obsessive.

DREAM OF LOVE

"I was madly in love with my girlfriend's mother and dreamed of her every night for months. Every morning I would walk my girlfriend to school. Her mother would see her off, and I would barely be able to talk to her. In fact I only really went out with the daughter so I could see the mother every morning. The dreams were all quite erotic, although we never made love either in my dream or in real life. There was no way I could ever have had a relationship with her in reality for lots of different reasons, so this was my substitute."

BELOW LEFT Red roses and champagne are popular symbols of romance.
BELOW FAR LEFT Our dreams may dwell on the physical intimacy we share with our lover. This may be the actual reality or else represent some kind of wish fulfilment.
BELOW Almost everyone can remember their first kiss and what it was like to fall in love for the first time. Teenage love is an emotional roller-coaster where feelings are experienced intensely.

SEX

THE MASTER OF THE EROTIC DREAM IS UNDOUBTEDLY FREUD, WHO HELD THAT MUCH OF WHAT WE DREAM, EVEN IF IT SEEMS TO HAVE ABSOLUTELY NOTHING TO DO WITH SEX, SYMBOLIZES SUPPRESSED SEXUAL DESIRES. IN THE FREUDIAN MODEL, A SNAKE, LADDER, KNIFE, STAIRCASE, CANDLE OR PEN REPRESENT THE PENIS, AND CAVES, BOXES, TUNNELS OR DARK ROOMS ARE THE VAGINA. BUT WHILE IT IS POSSIBLE THAT SUCH OBJECTS MAY ACT AS SYMBOLS IN THIS WAY, THEY ARE NOT NECESSARILY DOING SO IN EVERY CASE, AND AS PREVIOUSLY DISCUSSED, SYMBOLS WILL HAVE DIFFERENT MEANINGS FOR DIFFERENT PEOPLE. WE MAY ALSO WORK WITH OUR SEXUALITY DIRECTLY THROUGH OVERTLY EROTIC DREAMS.

ABOVE Erotic and stylized images may appear in our dreams, but only you will understand how they relate to you.
ABOVE RIGHT The kinds of things you dream about might be symbolically, or overtly sexual.
ABOVE FAR RIGHT For both men and women, snakes are a traditional symbol of sexual power and energy. Are you comfortable with your sexuality?

Many dreams contain symbolism that only you will understand. Certain things may have become associated with sex for you by dint of your experiences – for example, if there was music playing the first time you made love, the same tune may always trigger the memory of your first sexual experience.

SEXUAL FANTASIES
Two common sexual fantasies are of having sex in a public place and having sex with a stranger. Such dreams will tend to have different meanings for men and women because their basic sexual needs and responses differ.

Dreaming of making love in a crowded stadium, for instance, may reflect the tendency of men to boast about sex, or a woman's desire to be less inhibited. In this kind of dream a woman may be showing a need to be cheered on or encouraged by others to express her sexuality in a full and satisfying way, or she may enjoy the fact that she is capable of doing so and wants to let the world know about it.

If the dream is of having sex in a lift or on public transport, it may highlight the fun and thrilling aspect to sex, and remind us how it feels to do something "naughty". Such a dream may bring into question your attitude to rules and social behaviour and may show a desire to break a taboo.

For men, the biological imperative to spread their seed widely is met with confusingly divergent attitudes in society – on the one hand it is frowned on as infidelity and on the other it is prized as prowess. So dreams of sex with a stranger may reveal a yearning for just this model of

People don't fall in love with what's right in front of them. People want the dream – what they can't have. The more unattainable, the more attractive.
XANDER

behaviour, either to escape social restrictions and enjoy the taste of forbidden fruit, or to reassure the man of his virility.

WISH FULFILMENT

Your sexual desires and urges do not simply go away if you are on your own, and you will probably find other ways to express them. The more cut off you are from a healthy sex life, the more likely it is that sex will appear in your dreams as a substitute for the real thing. If there is no-one special in your life you may dream of sex with a stranger, or perhaps you have met someone you desire and can't wait to be intimate with in real life. Even if you have a relationship, you may be expressing your desire for something better if your present situation is unsatisfactory. Whatever the case, these dreams are usually healthy explorations of possibilities or expressions of our needs, and we can use them as a guide to how we are feeling.

SEXUAL PROBLEMS

We may have erotic dreams that help us deal with our sexual difficulties. Our problems could be quite obvious – for example frustration at not having a sexual partner – or your unconscious might be drawing to your attention something you haven't even admitted to yourself yet. Even if you feel unable to talk about a problem, you will still need to process it and try to overcome it or come to terms with it, and your dreams can provide a useful framework for doing just this.

DISCOVERING OUR SEXUALITY

Adolescence is a time of sexual discovery and exploration, but our need to understand ourselves as sexual beings doesn't end here. Throughout our lives we may use our dreams to help work out particular aspects of sexuality of which we are unsure, or to release sexual urges that may be

buried under taboo, or that we have not had the opportunity to express. We may dream of fetishes, or have homosexual fantasies, and in so doing uncover sexual impulses that are real for us, or play with ideas that we are curious about but don't want to act out in real life. Acting out the role of the opposite sex may give us an understanding of how our own sexuality may be experienced by our partner. Many people are self-conscious about their bodies, and it can be liberating to have dreams in which they can enjoy sex. Our erotic dreams can enable us to discover and fulfil our sexuality in a positive way.

ABOVE Our sexual fantasies will often be played out in our dreams. Having sex on a train is a fairly common fantasy.
ABOVE LEFT Talking about sexual problems is a sensitive area, so we may dream about them to help us work them out.
ABOVE FAR LEFT Our dreams can provide a "safe space" where we can allow and explore sexual feelings.

BELOW It may be easier to enjoy "perfect" sex in our dreams than in our actual relationships. This could be because our inhibitions don't get in the way and our partner seems to know exactly how to give us pleasure. Sharing intimate dreams with your partner can help build trust.

IMPOTENCE DREAM

"I was in a fencing tournament, and my opponent was my boss. I had already donned my mask and jacket, but while my boss was ready and waiting with his sabre raised, I couldn't find mine anywhere.

I had been unable to have an erection for some time, but this dream made me realize that it was the stress of work that was making me impotent."

HEALTHY BODY

Our relationship with our body is often fraught, as our society seems to become more and more obsessed with the way we look rather than how healthy we are. We have manic sessions at the gym, or go on faddy diets and worry about being overweight or dislike parts of our body. These anxieties may come through into our dreams. On the other hand, a general sense of health and vitality in a dream may indicate emotional wellbeing, or at least the desire for it. In dreams where our attention is drawn to a particular part of the body, it could be a reference to what it enables us to do rather than the organ or limb itself.

BELOW FAR RIGHT
Therapeutic dreams where you are pampered and cared for might point to an absence of this in your life.
BELOW RIGHT Dreaming of a fast-moving sport might indicate that you want more action and movement in your life.
BELOW A dream in which you are enjoying the invigorating effect of exercise might simply be a dream to enjoy and nothing more.

HEALTH AND WELLBEING

Occasionally we might get dreams in which we are healthy, vibrant, and full of life. Our unconscious does throw up unexpectedly good dreams from time to time to make us realize what we do in fact possess, and although they lack drama and are easily overlooked, these dreams are just as important as dreams of pain or illness.

If we suffer from ill health, such dreams can seem cruel, but they are our unconscious mind's way of instilling hope in us, of showing us that we can overcome anything, even if only in spirit. Dreams such as this can be seen as a call to get better, to find out what is behind our condition and do something about it if possible. If, in our waking life, we are in good health then these dreams may unfold to give us clues to what our unconscious believes is our true potential.

DIET AND EXERCISE

Achieving and maintaining a beautiful, healthy body is a major preoccupation in Western society, and as such it may figure strongly in our nightly dreams if we are dissatisfied with ourselves in some way. The dissatisfaction could be an expression of low self-esteem or of control issues, as both diet and exercise involve discipline and perseverance.

While obesity may signal hanging on to comforts, dieting could suggest that you are depriving yourself in some way, and breaking a diet may be either a loss of control or a defiance of restrictions in your life. If you are exercising in your dream, this could be an indication that you are taking your own needs seriously and feeling the power of your physical being.

THE BODY

Focusing on a particular aspect of your body generally shows a preoccupation with the functionality of that body part or associations commonly made with it. So the head may symbolize your ability to think and rationalize, while the face can be seen as the front you display to the world, as well as being the most intricately expressive part of your body. The heart was long thought to be the seat of our emotions and still holds that association; it can also be thought of as our essential self, associated as it is with the

bloodstream, the life force of the body. Hands and feet, arms and legs may be equated with action, movement and dexterity, with being able to go places and do things. Focusing your attention on the eyes, ears, nose or tongue is probably to do with the senses of sight, hearing, smell and taste, and the process of taking in information. Dreaming of the mouth or tongue might also suggest the power of speech.

We may pick up on common metaphors to do with the body when dreaming – "swallowing" information indicates gullibility, while being able to "stomach" something shows a level of tolerance for something we may not like – that we find "distasteful" or "unsavoury".

In our dreams our organs or limbs may not be in their normal state – perhaps they are injured, enlarged or shrunken, or unable to do their job properly. We may dream of having something stuck in our throat, of losing blood or seeing a pool of it. Perhaps images such as these are trying to draw our attention to some level of dysfunctionality, obstacle or imbalance in our lives.

PARALYSIS

Much like a woman who came to Freud's practice complaining of inexplicable paralysis, we are expressing our feelings of powerlessness and vulnerability in our dreams when we lose our ability to move. It may be that we are stuck in some undesirable situation and need some kind of impetus to get ourselves out of it, or that despite all the efforts we have made, we feel frustrated at getting nowhere. Dreams like this may not offer up a complete solution but might help you focus on the problem.

ABOVE Dreaming of being at one with your body and mind is a good wake-up call. Perhaps our dreams can disengage us from our obsession with weight, youth and beauty and help us value what we have.

BELOW FAR LEFT Dreams of ill health often flag an underlying worry we have in our waking lives.
BELOW LEFT Dreaming of the pleasant glow after exercise may start you on the road to a fitter life.
BELOW If you dream of healthy food perhaps you need nourishment. You might also dream of food if you are obsessed with diet and weight control.

Madness and Irrationality

DREAMS ARE SOMETIMES THOUGHT TO BE THE WORKINGS OF A MIND GONE TEMPORARILY INSANE, BUT ACTUALLY BEING IN THE GRIP OF INSANITY RARELY SHOWS ANY SIMILARITY TO OUR DREAMS. THE DREAMING MIND USES METAPHORS AND ALLEGORIES, IMAGES THAT MAY BE QUITE FANTASTICAL AND DISTORTED, AND OPERATES FROM A DIFFERENT LOGICAL BASIS, WHILE IN MADNESS IT IS RATHER A PERSON'S PERCEPTIONS OF WHAT THEY SEE OR HEAR OR FEEL THAT MAY BE DISTORTED. MADNESS IS NOT ONLY USED AS A MEDICAL TERM. WE MAY ALSO BE REFERRING TO OBSESSION OR PARANOIA IN OUR DREAMS; EVEN EXTREMES OF ANGER AND EMOTIONAL INSTABILITY MAY IN SOME CASES BE TERMED INSANITY.

LOGIC AND RATIONALITY

Some of our dreams may seem just like scenes from our waking lives, but at times a different logic from that of our daily lives operates, and rationality and reason seem to be suspended. But if we look more closely, within what seems to be random and meaningless nonsense there may exist a less obvious form of rationality, and within apparently demented or uncontrolled behaviour there is a degree of meaning and purpose.

Our dreams talk to us using symbols and metaphors, and we must try to understand them with our heart, not our head, to feel intuitively what these dreams might mean rather than trying to reason them out. However odd they may be, they are seldom a sign of actual madness. Rather they show the unconscious mind hard at work, producing attention-grabbing images and situations that give us a new way of looking at ourselves, however strange they may seem to our rational mind.

MADNESS

It is hard for sane people to comprehend what it is to be mad, and so in their dreams they may resort to stereotypical imagery to convey the impression of it. Even still, the terms "mad" and "sane" are difficult to define absolutely, as what is right and normal for one individual may be completely wrong or highly bizarre for another.

Madness can take many forms, and in our dreams, being insane may be showing us in an extreme way the levels of distress or confusion we are enduring in our lives and warning us to take action. If you are rather confused, dazed and incoherent in your dreams, you may need to look at how confusion may be distressing you in your waking life, or why you are unable to express yourself clearly.

ASYLUM

Finding ourselves in some kind of mental institution, or asylum, in our dreams may mean that we have acknowledged that we need help, and that we have given ourselves permission to devote our full attention to working through why we feel mad or unstable. Here we will also find ourselves thrown together with others who are insane, and this becomes the normality within the context of the asylum, and gives us a chance to benchmark our feelings and behaviours against others. By dreaming of being institutionalized, we may be showing a need to be helped or looked after, or we could be fighting against the label of madness or the norms of society.

BELOW It is hard for some people to understand the fears that other people have about mental illness, fears that may surface in their dreams in the most negative ways. Try to examine these fears if you suffer from such dreams.

ECCENTRICITY

Odd behaviour in a dream may be disturbing, especially if it is manifesting in someone you know well. Examine how the behaviour is different from that person's normal way of being, as it could be showing you some aspect of your own character that is asking for greater expression. For instance, dreaming of aggression in a person who is normally calm and controlled, or childish behaviour in someone you regard as mature and responsible, may be a way of letting yourself "try out" these behaviours, to see how they feel and how you respond, before you deal with them in reality.

OBSESSION AND PARANOIA

Being fixated on something or someone in our dreams is relatively common, and may reflect a naturally obsessional personal style, or it could be a signal to your conscious mind that there is something you either need to focus your attention on or have been paying too much attention to – only the contexts of your dream and your life will tell you which. The irrational fears that all too often visit our dreams may seem like paranoia, but are likely to be an accentuated form of some real fears, or an indication that we are overly concerned with other people's views of ourselves.

BEING POSSESSED

Madness can take more frightening forms though. Being possessed by devils, or wreaking havoc in a frenzy of unbridled anger, may well affect people who have difficulty coming to terms with their own anger, or who have not found appropriate and satisfying ways of expressing their anger.

SPLIT PERSONALITY AND THE PSYCHOPATH

Sometimes a person's negative feelings can be so strong that they can only cope by cutting off from them. In a way this is what we often do in our dreams by using another character to represent an aspect of ourselves, but if we actually dream of having a split personality then it could be that reconciling two aspects of ourselves that are at odds with each other is our prime task, and it is important to find out what these are. In extreme instances, being cut off from our humanity can manifest as psychopathic behaviour: unstable and violent, the psychopath is unable to form normal personal relationships and may act in anti-social ways, indifferent to his effects on people or his obligations to society as a whole.

RIGHT Extreme flights of fancy and levels of absurdity can seem quite unremarkable in our dreams but totally ridiculous when we wake up and remember the details.
MIDDLE RIGHT However strange a dream may be it is rarely a sign of actual insanity. Instead they present an alternative way of looking at reality.
BOTTOM RIGHT A dream that focuses on some kind of distortion of reality that you find disturbing might be pinpointing your fear of being out of control or letting yourself go.

ENGAGING WITH PEOPLE

Of all the elements we are likely to encounter in our dreams it is people that will feature most often. At times in our waking life we respond to people strongly, falling passionately in love or running into conflict, and without them we can become lonely. Usually when a person appears in a dream their significance is unique and relevant in the context of that dream alone, although if you have a series of dreams on the same theme they might become representative of something particular – some aspect of ourselves, or an archetypal figure. Besides the characters that we meet in our dreams there is always you, the observer or participant.

Many of the activities that fill our lives revolve around people. We keep busy for many reasons – sociability, fun or fitness, out of curiosity or necessity – and in our dreams we can continue to explore, to do things we can't do in real life, or to work through issues that are troubling us in our day-to-day lives.

FRIENDS

THE FRIENDSHIPS WE HAVE OCCUR AT MANY LEVELS, FROM SUPERFICIAL ACQUAINTANCES TO LIFELONG COMPANIONS.
CIRCUMSTANTIAL FRIENDSHIPS – SUCH AS THE COLLEAGUES WE LIKE AND WITH WHOM WE MAY OCCASIONALLY HAVE A
CHAT, OR THE PEOPLE WE MEET AT NIGHT SCHOOL – MAY DEVELOP, BUT BASICALLY THEY ARE ON THE OUTSIDE OF OUR
NETWORK. AT THE OTHER END OF THE SPECTRUM ARE THE PEOPLE WHO ARE OUR CLOSEST COMPANIONS, PEOPLE WE REALLY
CONNECT WITH ON A DEEP LEVEL, OR WITH WHOM WE HAVE SO MUCH SHARED HISTORY THAT OUR DIFFERENCES BECOME
IRRELEVANT. DREAMS OF FRIENDS MAY BE OF EITHER SORT, AND WILL HAVE SIMILARLY DIFFERENT LEVELS.

We relate to our friends on different levels, sharing deeply personal things with them and relying on them in difficult times or simply having a good time and a laugh with each other. We may have a lot in common with them, or be completely at odds with them in many ways but still value their companionship. Because our relationships with our friends are so diverse, they can mean many things to us when they appear in our dreams.

FRIENDS IN OUR DREAMS

We choose our friends, responding to aspects of their personality or shared experiences that we can relate to, and because of this they may sometimes be closer to us than our relatives. Friends become all the more

important if your family is not loving and supportive, and can in some cases provide a kind of substitute family. But we also befriend people with whom we share common activities or interests, and this may be the focus of the relationship rather than any deeply shared personal connection with them.

We may dream of friends for many reasons – out of love or guilt, or in order to resolve

conflict issues. If the friend you dream of is associated with an activity such as a sport or hobby, then it could be some aspect of the activity rather than the qualities of that person that you are investigating. With closer friends though, we often dream of them because they have a particular quality on which we need to focus our attention, perhaps to understand it, adopt it ourselves, or reject it.

> **DREAM OF A FRIEND**
>
> "I hadn't seen my friend Paul for a long time. He'd been abroad teaching and I guess I missed him. I dreamt that he was back and we were on his motorbike together. He turned to me to say something and didn't see there was a lorry coming towards us. We crashed and I woke up. I was concerned at the time because I hadn't heard from him in such a long time and I think I was worrying that something might have happened to him. I didn't know if anyone would think to let me know. On another level it could have been that I was worrying about our friendship having 'died'."

BELOW RIGHT We all need friends and companions to be a healthy part of society. We might take it for granted in our waking lives, but celebrate it in our dreams, however bizarrely.
BELOW A friendship dream doesn't have to be particularly profound, but might simply highlight the importance of a friend's presence in your life.

FRIENDS OR STRANGERS?

Sometimes in our dreams our friends will be transformed into unfamiliar people – so much so that we are not sure whether or not they are still the same person that we know and love. Such transformations draw our attention to the differences – so for example, if a friend who is always bouncy and jovial appears in your dream in tears, this may be a sign that you have lost touch with the positive things in life, that you need to reconnect with what makes you happy and perhaps with the people that you really enjoy being with.

LOSING A FRIEND

Such transformations may also be our unconscious mind's way of working out how we feel about relationships. Friendships are often fragile and changeable, and can easily evaporate if we don't take care of them or if our circumstances change or we develop in different ways.

Having friends can make us feel valued, and the loss of a friendship can be a heavy blow. If we do lose contact it might be no more than an accident but it still hurts, and we still feel the loss. Dreams may be a way of coming to terms with such losses, or of bringing determination to putting a friendship back on track.

LEFT A good social life is an essential part of a happy and wholesome life; it emphasizes the positive. Just as close one-to-one friendships are vital, so are groups of friends where a different dynamic exists.

BELOW LEFT We may feel the loss of friends long after they have grown away, and remember them in our dreams.
BELOW In childhood we begin to establish friendships that may last us a lifetime.

Let us learn to dream, gentlemen, and then we may perhaps find the truth.

F. A. KEKULÉ

LOVERS

FINDING AND RELATING TO A LOVER IS ONE OF THE BIG PREOCCUPATIONS OF ADULTHOOD. IF WE DON'T HAVE A LOVER WE PROBABLY WANT ONE, AND IF WE DO, WE MAY DREAM OF THEM TO REINFORCE HOW WONDERFUL IT IS TO BE IN LOVE, OR TO WORK THROUGH THE CONFLICT ISSUES THAT INEVITABLY CROP UP FROM TIME TO TIME. WE MAY DREAM NOT ONLY OF OUR CURRENT PARTNER, BUT ALSO OF PAST LOVES, OR OF PEOPLE WE ARE ATTRACTED TO BUT WHO ARE UNAVAILABLE; WE MAY EVEN HAVE FANTASIES ABOUT COMPLETELY UNATTAINABLE LOVE OBJECTS. IF WE STIFLE OUR LOVE FANTASIES OR AVOID LOOKING AT DIFFICULT RELATIONSHIP ISSUES CONSCIOUSLY, THIS MAY WELL SURFACE IN OUR DREAMS.

PAST LOVERS

It is quite common to dream of past lovers. It may mean that you are hankering after being with them again, but often it is simply your unconscious mind's way of cataloguing and storing away experiences and memories. Often it is important that you process why a relationship ended so that you don't make the same mistakes again with the next person. You may need to regain a level of self-esteem after a damaging or abusive relationship, and realize that it is alright to be just who you are.

Whatever it is you need to work through, dreams give you the opportunity to do so.

BELOW Our notions of what makes a romantic situation are often conditioned by our culture, and the standard ideals may surface in our dreams as our mind replays the images we have absorbed.

PRESENT LOVERS

Just as we dream about our friends and family on a fairly regular basis, so too do we dream of our present partner. There are many reasons for this. It can be our unconscious mind's way of reassuring ourselves that we are still loved. Even playing with notions of being unfaithful or out of love, or being cruel, hurtful, or distant may be our unconscious mind's way of checking that things are in reality alright, or of experimenting with ideas or situations without us having to try anything out for real.

Unpleasant dreams about a lover may also hint at a certain dissatisfaction in a relationship, and give you an opportunity to see how it might be to behave differently from the way you do in real life.

POTENTIAL LOVERS

Our unconscious likes to keep an open mind on what is around us. This may be unsettling if you are in a good relationship, but it is also normal and natural. Just because we dream about people we fancy doesn't mean we would do anything about it in our waking life or even that we want to. It may be just a way of experimenting with the idea without having to go there. It may also mean that unhappiness in your relationship is prompting you to see a way to finding a more satisfactory partner.

FANTASY LOVERS

The most common fantasy lovers in our dreams are real people whom we might, in an ideal world, make a play for, but with whom a relationship is at best extremely unlikely. These might be people in the public eye, like pop stars or actors, or people with whom it would be too risky to have an actual relationship, such as a boss or married person.

When we are asleep there is no limit to our imagination, and occasionally the lovers of our dreams may be really bizarre and

RIGHT Dreaming of having an affair might reflect a desire you have for the unknown.
MIDDLE RIGHT Dreaming of your love life could be a way of working through the everyday concerns of any relationship.
BOTTOM RIGHT Dreams of a romantic new affair can simply be highly enjoyable escapism.

completely unobtainable. We may also dream of breaking taboos, and have sexual dreams involving incest, or animals, for instance. Many people might be shocked by having such fantasies, and for some they may be an indication of disturbed psychological states, in which case professional help may be needed. For the most part though, our unconscious likes to slip the leash occasionally and dream of things we would simply never do – it does not mean that we would want to act these out in reality. Our dreams are a way of approaching taboos in safety, experimenting or letting off sexual steam. The meaning will depend on who we are – it could be that we are reacting to social restrictions and trying to find greater freedom of expression; in fact breaking taboos in dreams may be a liberating experience.

If you are the kind of person who worries what others think of you this may be disturbing. In our dream we may need to deal with others being judgemental, or even with our own self-condemnation, if we take unusual or inappropriate lovers. But a taboo lover may also be a companion on your journey to self-fulfilment and have qualities that you don't find elsewhere.

DREAM OF LOVERS

"I had about half a dozen dreams about my boss, who I rather fancied. They were never exactly the same, but they always involved being physically intimate, and always one or other of us was a reluctant partner in this intimacy, usually because we were afraid of discovery.

I think that this dream was my way of attaining something that in reality would never be possible. I think that the reluctance was to do with my fear that my own partner would find out that I was attracted to someone else, as well as with the fact that my boss was in reality very happily married. "

PEOPLE IN OUR LIVES

IN GOING ABOUT THE DAY-TO-DAY BUSINESS OF OUR LIVES, WE ENGAGE WITH COUNTLESS PEOPLE. OUR ENCOUNTERS WITH THEM MAY BE INSIGNIFICANT OR TRIVIAL — THE FELLOW PASSENGERS YOU SIT BESIDE IN SILENCE DURING A TRAIN JOURNEY AND NEVER SEE AGAIN, THE CHECKOUT OPERATOR IN AN UNEVENTFUL VISIT TO THE SUPERMARKET — OR THEY COULD BE MORE INVOLVED, SUCH AS THE RELATIONSHIPS THAT DEVELOP WITH COLLEAGUES OR NEIGHBOURS. WE EVEN HAVE A RELATIONSHIP OF SORTS WITH FAMOUS PEOPLE WHOSE FACES ARE FAMILIAR AND WHOSE LIVES WE MIGHT READ ABOUT, BUT WHO WE MAY NEVER MEET.

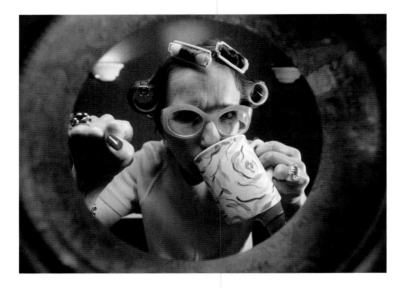

RIGHT Whoever we are intimidated by in our everyday waking life is likely to "visit" us in our dreams in a similar way. If this happens repeatedly you might want to work with why this person affects you so deeply.

Any of these people could appear as characters in our dreams, whether they are playing supporting roles or taking the lead, and although at times they may simply be a necessary part of the scenery, like extras in a film, they will often appear in our dreams for a reason. Notice what role they play, as well as how you behave towards each other in the dream and how you feel during and after the interaction.

FAMILIAR FACES

In going about the routine of our lives, we get to know many faces in the places we frequent – neighbours, the people who work in the local shops or bank, the people we work and socialise with and countless others. When such people appear in a dream,

try to establish whether it is their role that seems important or their personal qualities. For instance, a neighbour may have to do with having your privacy and personal space invaded, or it may be reminding you that there are friendly people about who are always willing to help you. Dreaming of your boss is quite likely to be about issues of power, authority, status and so on, but it may be that the formal relationship you have with each other is secondary to particular personality traits that you feel he or she exhibits.

IN THE PUBLIC GAZE

Royalty and politicians, media celebrities, and others who have made it into the public arena may all feature in our dream

world. As we only know them from a distance, it will be the qualities they present to the outside world – their public face – that we probably focus on. This may be simply the fact that they have achieved fame and fortune or infamy, that they have reached the pinnacle of success on their chosen path, or it may be more specifically about what it is that they have done, or how they have gone about getting what they want. We may want their success to rub off on us, to use them as a role model, or to engage with them and turn the one-way relationship into a more personal one.

STRANGERS

What does it mean, though, if the people we encounter in our dreams are not familiar faces, but apparently arbitrary individuals? Realistically, strangers are likely to appear in our dreams as often as they do in real life, but if we do engage with them or something about them grabs our attention particularly, it may be worth looking at whether they have a particular significance to us. It may indeed be the very fact that we don't know them that is salient – we may feel uncertain or wary of them, they may behave in unpredictable or mysterious or dangerous ways, or they may be

BELOW If you dream of people who are famous in real life you are probably dreaming of what they represent to you. Alternatively, maybe there is something about fame itself that intrigues and attracts you?

ABOVE We might all fear crowds, especially if they are made up of strangers, but being part of a mass gathering can also be quite exhilarating.

people we are attracted to and want to get to know. Look at the kind of interaction you have in the dream and how you feel about the contact you have with them. Obviously, a stranger chasing you with a loaded gun will bring up quite different feelings from one who shows you the way when you are lost.

In particular, see what qualities are dominant in your dream, as a stranger could present some aspect of yourself that you have yet to bring to awareness. Also look at whether the person seems to conform to any stereotypes – the tall, dark and handsome stranger who may be the lover of your dreams, or the wise old man or woman who can be your guide or angel.

Strangers who are obviously foreigners or people of different races may bring issues of difference or prejudice to the fore, and whether the person is a man, woman or child could be drawing your attention to your own personal masculine, feminine or childlike qualities that may be useful for you to focus on right now.

ABOVE You have to look at what qualities each person brings to your dream to understand them and their impact on your life.

RIGHT Fear of getting to know people may figure in our dreams and we may seek ways to get round this in our waking life.

BELOW Work colleagues might not be our best friends but we spend a disproportionate amount of time with them, and this dominance in our lives might be reflected in our dreams.

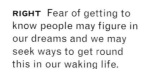

GATHERINGS

ABOVE If you dream about a party at which you feel out of place and lonely, then analyse why this might be so. What kind of party was it? Who was there? What made you feel peripheral?
ABOVE RIGHT A gathering of lots of people in a dream can act as an indicator of how we think we fit into society.

WE GATHER BECAUSE WE ARE SOCIAL BEINGS. WE ALL BELONG TO COMMUNITIES OF VARIOUS DESCRIPTIONS — FAMILY, NEIGHBOURHOOD, WORKPLACE, NATION — AND SHARE RESOURCES, INFORMATION AND COLLECTIVE EXPERIENCES WITH EACH OTHER. WE GET TOGETHER AS A FAMILY, WE MEET COLLEAGUES TO DISCUSS BUSINESS, AND WE JOIN THOUSANDS OF STRANGERS IN PUBLIC FOR A CONCERT OR TO CELEBRATE A NATIONAL EVENT. THE GATHERINGS OF OUR DREAMS REFLECT THIS DIVERSITY, AND THEY ALSO EXPRESS HOW WE FEEL IN THE CONTEXT OF SOCIAL GROUPINGS.

HARMONY

Gatherings where people understand and support each other, and want to be together, can give a tremendous sense of belonging, and help you to feel safe, supported and sustained. If you have been struggling with such issues, dreaming of such a gathering may show that some aspect of your personal sense of community is now being satisfied in some way.

Harmonious gatherings can also be an expression of general consensus on society's norms and values. Looking in on them from the outside, though, or being excluded from them, could indicate a rejection of these norms, or that you still have some kind of unresolved social issues – isolation, a lack of confidence about your role in your community or workplace, or uncertainty about how accepted you are by the people you value.

Unfortunately, gatherings can also be fraught with discord. Antagonism, dominance or bullying are all too present in our society and you may be using the gathering in your dream as a metaphor for these. If this is the case, look for any signs of resolution, and also see who is present and what their dominant characteristics are. If you are involved in the dream rather than an onlooker, see what role you are playing.

ROLES

The characters in your dream gathering are probably playing particular roles, perhaps in some kind of hierarchy, or at least contributing to the group identity. They may be people you know or complete strangers – leaders and followers, teachers, diplomats trying to keep the peace and finding solutions to problems, jokers defusing situations with their humour, and the black sheep, pulling in a different direction and at odds

---

A DREAM OF REJECTION

"I was looking through a window into an expensive restaurant. All my friends were gathered together, eating and drinking and having a good time. I became very distressed at not being amongst them. Were they talking about me? Had I not been invited? Had I lost the invitation or been turned away? I banged on the window but no one could hear me. In the dream I became anxious that this was all an elaborate joke; they were pretending to ignore me, and wanted to hurt me.

I had just split up with my partner, who had been quite hurtful. I was feeling insecure and shut out, and my self-esteem had taken a blow."

with everyone. Gatherings may also speak to us of individuality, whether suppressed or given freedom. See what your own role is within the group, how others perceive you, and how you respond to that role as well as to the goals or beliefs of the group.

FORMALITY
Some people like the informality of an unstructured gathering, with its sense of companionship, freedom and youthful energy, while others prefer the more formal circumstances of an organized event. Formality can give us the safety of structure if we understand and feel comfortable with it, but it can also be intimidating if we don't feel we belong.

CROWDS
Being in a large crowd, such as at a major sports match or a New Year celebration, can be an exhilarating experience as the happy, excited mood of the people rubs off on you. But it can also be immensely stressful – even downright scary if the

crowd becomes a mob. Your relationship with the crowd in your dream is important in understanding what it means – does it give you a sense of belonging or community, a unity of purpose, a celebration, or is it threatening, in which case you may panic at the thought of getting crushed, or feel that you need to escape and be alone?

Try to relate this to your everyday life – crowd dreams could be telling you something about the amount and type of contact you are having in relation to your needs as an individual, or

about your relationship with conventions and the mass of opinions. If you tend to need time alone to recharge your batteries and aren't getting this, you may be expressing a need to get away from people for a while. Conversely you may be feeling isolated, and need people around you to make you feel human again. A crowd dream where you can't escape or where the attention of the crowd is focused entirely on you may indicate that you feel pressure to conform rather than taking your own direction in life.

ABOVE Really big crowds can be scary – but that is true in waking life as much as dreams and we shouldn't read too much into such fears.
ABOVE LEFT In a social gathering we may feel "small", which might represent that this is how we feel about ourselves in real life.

BELOW Any crowd scene can represent how we feel about being part of a group. Do you blend in or are you singled out in some way as being other than the norm? Does this please or daunt you? Do you want to conform or rebel?

CELEBRATIONS AND CEREMONIES

CELEBRATIONS CAN TAKE MANY FORMS — FROM SPONTANEOUSLY OPENING A BOTTLE OF CHAMPAGNE WITH A FEW FRIENDS, TO THE FESTIVITIES AND RITUALS OF A RELIGIOUS HOLIDAY OR A FORMAL AND HIGHLY REHEARSED NATIONAL CEREMONY. WHEN WE DREAM OF SUCH CELEBRATIONS THEY ARE LIKELY TO BE EVENTS IN WHICH WE ARE PERSONALLY INVOLVED, ALTHOUGH THE GRAND CEREMONIES OF CELEBRITIES AND LEADERS — A ROYAL WEDDING, THE FUNERAL OF A STATESMAN, OR AN INAUGURATION — MAY FEATURE TOO. OUR DREAMS MIGHT ALSO FEATURE THE SYMBOLS OF THESE CEREMONIES RATHER THAN THE GATHERINGS: A WEDDING RING, AN ELABORATE CAKE, BALLOONS OR STREAMERS MIGHT MAKE AN APPEARANCE.

ABOVE We all like to celebrate and we enjoy having our friends around us to help us party. Our dreams are no different and are to be enjoyed.
ABOVE RIGHT There are a lot of cycles in our life that need to be marked as a rite of passage. You might dream of the symbols that are linked with an event rather than the event itself.

ANTICIPATING AN EVENT

In the build-up to a major life event such as a wedding or the birth of a child, the excitement and apprehension can spill over into our dreams. In dreaming of the event our unconscious attempts to work out the fears we have around it — saying the wrong thing, forgetting something crucial, or making a fool of ourselves in some way. With weddings in particular, we are publicly entering into a social contract and may be anxious about having made the right decision. Perhaps we are even responsible for the administration of such events, in which case it might be sheer nerves that makes us dream about them. On the positive side, such dreams give you a chance to rehearse and familiarize yourself with the event, and to anticipate things that could go wrong.

CEREMONY AS SYMBOL

Dreams of ceremonies are not necessarily about real events though. If the dream seems to spring out of nowhere we should view the ceremony as a symbol — probably for the achievement or event that it is designed to mark, or for the feelings that the prospect of such an event evokes. So a 21st birthday party may mean that we are maturing in some way, or feeling the increased freedoms or the responsibilities of adulthood, while a wedding could be prompting us to ask ourselves about our relationship — perhaps about how committed we feel — or if we are single, to explore what kind of person we would like to settle down with.

The exact purpose or structure of the celebration may be less important than the feelings that it brings up in you, and it is worth asking yourself if you fear such events or anticipate them happily. Maybe you want to be the centre of attention but have difficulty reconciling this with being shy or modest, or perhaps you find it stressful making speeches or playing the host or hostess — roles that also put you firmly in the spotlight.

If in your waking life you are being caught up in routine and yearn to be more spontaneous, your dream celebrations could give you the opportunity to let your hair down. If you think this is true then try and create a time where you can do it for real, and live the dream.

THE PARAPHERNALIA OF CELEBRATIONS

More subtle indications or symbols of ceremonies may be present in your dream – a wedding ring standing in for the unity and commitment of marriage, a coffin for the death of a loved one, a crown or sceptre for a coronation, balloons for a festive occasion.

Clothes are an important part of many traditional ceremonies, and if in your dream the clothes are wrong for the occasion, you should look at what makes them so – wearing casual clothes to a formal occasion, for instance, may indicate your resistance to the event, or a feeling that you are not ready for it.

Gift-giving can be fraught with difficulty and evoke a strong emotional response. Look at what the gift is and how appropriate it is, the spirit in which it is given and received, who the recipient and giver are, and, if many presents are changing hands, whether they are comparable or unfairly distributed. Gifts can represent our talents and opportunities, so receiving them or being disappointed by them may hint at how you feel about broader issues in your life.

RIGHT A dream that involves a dramatic or epic celebration on a large scale might indicate that you are fretting about a real-life one you are involved with, or might be highlighting a desire you feel to live a little wildly for a time, and forget about your usual routines.
MIDDLE RIGHT By letting off steam we can release a lot of the tension that such events may induce.
BOTTOM RIGHT A symbol of celebration, such as popping corks, might be a sign or expression of happiness.

RITUAL

Many ceremonies are highly ritualized. Their stylised and formulaic nature means that everyone has a role and knows how to behave. Some rituals are extremely taxing, such as some complex and physically exacting initiation rites, which are a test of stamina, physical prowess and ultimately, of whether the initiate is ready for his or her new role.

In dreams we may try to resolve issues around a role we need to play, and so our unconscious will replay this and try to analyse our response to it. Rituals are often able to give us the comfort of predictability, but they may also be markers of change. Look at whether you are a creature of habit or if you enjoy change, and consider why change features in your dream.

DREAM WEDDING

"I was getting married and all the invitations had been sent out, but in my dream I was trying to post them and they kept turning into scorpions in my hand. The harder I tried to post them the more they fought back and tried to sting me. It was quite terrifying. Although I really wanted to get married, I had had to invite a whole bunch of people that I didn't know – my fiancé's relatives and a lot of my mother's friends and distant relations – and this was where the problem lay. I didn't want them to be there on my big day, and the dream was my way of resisting having to invite them."

SEPARATION

WHETHER IN OUR DREAMS OR IN WAKING LIFE, SEPARATION ALWAYS IMPLIES CHANGES IN OUR LIVES, LETTING GO AND STARTING ANEW. WE MAY TYPICALLY THINK OF PARTING FROM LOVED ONES, BUT THE IDEA CAN EQUALLY BE APPLIED TO LEAVING HOME, ENDING A JOB, GOING ON A JOURNEY, OR A PHASE IN LIFE DRAWING TO A CLOSE. WE MAY HAVE SADNESS AROUND THE SEPARATION AND THE LOSS OF THE LOVED AND THE FAMILIAR, BUT MANY A SEPARATION WILL INSTEAD BRING HAPPINESS, RELIEF OR EXCITEMENT AS WE LOOK AHEAD. DREAMS OF SEPARATION WILL REFLECT ALL THESE ISSUES DIRECTLY, AND CAN ALSO PINPOINT ANXIETIES WE ARE FEELING THAT AREN'T NECESSARILY OBVIOUSLY LINKED TO SEPARATION ANXIETY.

PARTING FROM OUR LOVED ONES

It is inevitable that we will at some stage be separated from people we love. As well as coping with the loss, we are afraid of being lonely and having to become self-reliant when perhaps we lack the confidence to do so, and we may give vent to these fears in our dreams. The loss of a long-term relationship is likely to affect us particularly strongly as we grow increasingly dependent on the person whose life is intimately involved with our own, although for some it may come as a relief or a blessing, a way to flourish. Either way we may use dream time to come to terms with the changes and the feelings they bring up.

LEAVING HOME

When leaving our family and home, even temporarily, we have to discover our independence, perhaps for the very first time, we need to stand on our own two feet without the support we are used to. While being a valuable and important voyage of discovery, this may also be hard to deal with.

Students often report disturbed dreams during their first year away from home. These dreams are often about their childhood, as if by dreaming it they can recapture some of the security they felt then, and are possibly missing now. Leaving the past behind in this way provides an opportunity to discover yourself as an adult, without parental constraints, and you may well use your dreams to engage with new issues and lifestyles as much as to separate from and lay to rest your childhood.

DIVORCE

Going through divorce is almost always a traumatic experience, and if you are experiencing this process your dreams will probably reflect your distress. Conflict and haggling over possessions may be scary and worrying, especially if you stand to lose a lot in the divorce. You may feel guilty about having caused your marriage to fall apart, or about not having put in enough effort to make it work – or you may blame your partner for exactly the same things. You

BELOW LEFT Separation leads to an emotion that goes very deep indeed; we may carry over such deeply held scars all of our life.
BELOW RIGHT Our dreams may reflect such feelings of separation and loneliness, and may need addressing when we are awake in order to find the source, and hopefully alleviate the pain.

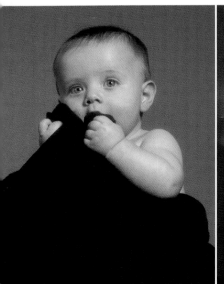

may even be angry with yourself for having wasted time in the relationship. Coming to terms with our own role in a divorce is part of the long painful process to a new normality, to achieving independence for ourselves.

For many people the worst part is having to be separated from children – both the loss of their presence and guilt at abandoning them. The partner with custody may feel anxiety around having to look after them unaided. How you feel about these issues will affect the quality and content of your dreams.

Divorce is also a traumatic time for children, as they get caught in the cross-fire between the adults involved, and have immensely strong feelings that they are often not able to express or deal with fully. They may feel responsible for the split, abandoned by the parent that leaves, and in some cases fearful and unsettled around the other changes that are happening at the same time, especially if these are not explained fully to them. Children are more prone to nightmares than adults, and may be particularly affected by them at these kinds of stressful times.

MOVING ON

Long-term separation requires a major adjustment, even if there are positive spin-offs. Moving on may mean coming to terms with past issues and letting go of them, and the new start in life could provide the chance to gain or regain our freedom and sense of self. Dreams that involve objects strongly associated with your past, such as favourite childhood toys or gifts given to you by your partner, may well be showing you what you need to let go of.

LEFT Dreaming of going away somewhere, perhaps alone, might point to feelings of separation anxiety that you are trying to subdue. It might also point to a desire to get away and move on.

SEPARATION ANXIETY

At the age of around seven or eight months, a baby starts to show signs of having a strong attachment to its primary carer, and distress when separated from that person, especially when upset or ill.

At first the infant may protest by crying, but can be comforted by another. If the separation is prolonged, the child may despair, seeming calmer but becoming apathetic, no longer looking for its carer and trying to comfort itself by thumb-sucking or rocking. In the most extreme cases of separation anxiety the infant becomes detached and unresponsive, and will even ignore the return of the caregiver.

These very human reactions we have to separation might be at their most acute when we are young, but they can carry on to adulthood, and can perhaps be as traumatic and damaging. Dreams may well bring up these issues, and if you dream of them often, perhaps you need to examine where your anxieties come from.

ABOVE When it is time to move on from an unhappy relationship, the grief of separation can be hard to bear, for all concerned, even if we know it's the best course of action. If a separation you were involved with happened long ago, but is still part of your emotional baggage, you may well deal with it in dreams.

PERFORMANCE

ABOVE In our dreams, the trappings of the ballet could symbolize a desire for fame and a glamorous and "artistic" life.

ABOVE RIGHT To dream that we are taking part in a theatrical performance can reveal how we feel about being on display in the many public roles we play in life.

WHEN WE THINK OF PERFORMANCE WE PROBABLY HAVE SOME KIND OF DRAMATIC PRODUCTION IN MIND. BUT THERE IS A SENSE IN WHICH WE ARE ALL ACTORS PLAYING MANY DIFFERENT ROLES, WITH LIFE ITSELF AS A STAGED PERFORMANCE. OUR DREAMS MAY SHOW US THE STYLIZED AND PUBLIC ASPECTS OF OUR LIVES AS MUCH AS OUR PRIVATE INNER WORLDS, AND DREAMS IN WHICH PERFORMANCE FEATURES COULD WELL BE GIVING US IMPORTANT INFORMATION ABOUT THE TYPES OF ROLES WE ARE ACCUSTOMED TO PLAYING IN DAILY LIFE.

THE WORLD OF STAGE AND SCREEN

Theatrical or film productions are artificial and stylized portrayals of reality. The breakdown of a play into acts and scenes gives it a structure and predictability lacking in normal life; scenery and props are usually pared down to the essentials and actors may speak in a noticeably dramatic way for emphasis, showing and saying only what is essential to get the story or the message across. Films contain a different type of artifice, tricking us into believing that what we see is real by virtue of their detail, or abandoning any pretence at reality altogether in special effects or animation.

When theatre and film appear in our dreams, there are several aspects we need to look at.

Having a dream that features a stage or screen performance can be something of a conundrum – the entertainment is often a fictional scenario played out within the fantasy of the dream, and it can be difficult to tell where one fantasy ends and the other begins. The performers are dream characters one step further removed from reality than usual – what is being highlighted is that they are in a sense not real people even in the dream reality; they are in role, they are not what they seem. Their exaggerated movements and speech may be stressing things that we particularly need to notice. Such exaggerations, together with the fact that the actors are presenting a persona or donning a mask, may also be trying to express how ill at ease

we feel in ourselves, in that we are choosing to project an image rather than being authentic. They may also allow us to take on roles that we ordinarily cannot or will not assume – being a king or tyrant, a jester or fool, a child or even a fantasy figure.

Mime figures may be there to underscore our inability to be heard, although their exaggerated body movements could be telling us that we are more in touch with expressing ourselves physically than verbally.

PERFORMING FOR AN AUDIENCE

Asking yourself how the audience responds could give you insight into why your unconscious is using the performing metaphor. Do they like the performance, or are they chatting among

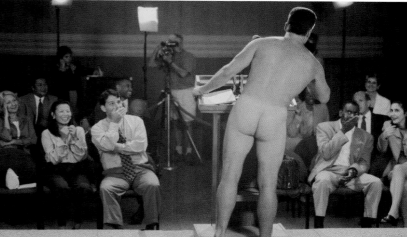

themselves, heckling or walking out? Is the performance an audition? We are constantly being assessed in our daily lives, measured against standards that may be beyond our control, and rewarded in our jobs for "performing" well. It is tempting to measure our self-worth in the light of such standards, and we will work hard towards getting a positive response. In our dreams we may be looking for this response, or may fear being challenged by others when we put ourselves forward. If the audience is ignoring you though, this could be saying something about you not getting a message across or not being noticed. If they are laughing or you are performing badly, it can reveal a fear of failure.

In a dream performance you may forget your lines – losing the thread of why you are performing, or perhaps feeling anxious or over-challenged. It may be that you are being required to say something that goes against the grain, and are having difficulty internalizing it.

CIRCUSES AND CARNIVALS

There is something intriguing about circuses and carnivals. We relish the glitz and glamour, and get an adrenalin rush from watching the daring feats of the high wire. Running away to join the circus is a classic example of escapism, and dreaming of such performances may point to a lack of adventure in our lives – we desire to be part of the show, to become a travelling player and see the world. If you do dream of a circus, look at which roles or acts dominate – the ringmaster, lion-tamer, trapeze artist tightrope-walker, or clown, may provide clues to the issues you are trying to address.

BEING FAMOUS

In our dreams we may dream that we are playing to a packed house, that we are feted as a superstar. This may be because we desire the fame and fortune that stardom brings, or it could represent a desire for attention or recognition of our talents, or a need to be praised just for being who we are. It could also indicate something we long to achieve.

ABOVE Appearing naked in front of a laughing audience is a classic nightmare scenario. Such a dream may be about performance anxiety.
ABOVE LEFT If you have a performance dream, notice if you are a solo player or part of the chorus. Which role suits you best and what does this mean for you?

Be not afeard; the isle is full of noises,
Sounds and sweet airs, that give delight
   and hurt not.
Sometimes a thousand twangling instruments
Will hum about mine ears, and sometime voices
That, if I then had waked after long sleep,
Will make me sleep again: and then, in dreaming,
The clouds me thought would open and
   show riches
Ready to drop upon me that, when I waked,
I cried to dream again.

WILLIAM SHAKESPEARE, THE TEMPEST

COMMUNICATION

HUMANS ARE SOPHISTICATED COMMUNICATORS. WE HAVE EVOLVED NUMEROUS COMPLEX LANGUAGES THAT WE CAN USE TO EXPRESS THE MOST DETAILED NUANCES OF OUR FEELINGS AND EXPERIENCES. WE HAVE DEVELOPED INGENIOUS SYSTEMS OF RECORDING INFORMATION AND TRANSMITTING IT ACROSS TIME AND DISTANCE. WE ALSO COMMUNICATE WITHOUT WORDS — BODY LANGUAGE AND TONE OF VOICE SOMETIMES GIVING MORE INFORMATION THAN WHAT WE UTTER. DESPITE THIS, OR PERHAPS BECAUSE OF THE COMPLEXITY OF OUR AVAILABLE COMMUNICATION CHANNELS, WE ARE OFTEN FRUSTRATED BY MISCOMMUNICATION, A LACK OF INFORMATION, OR BY CONFUSION OVER MIXED MESSAGES.

In trying to decipher our dreams of communication, we need to pay attention to what is being said, who is saying it and in what way, as well as to what is happening at the same time. Are people shouting or whispering? Are they looking at us? Do we understand them? Is what they say compatible with what they are doing? Also consider whether the communication is happening face to face or at a distance.

BELOW Shouting in a dream can indicate that you need to speak up for yourself. Does it feel as though no one is listening to you, or that in order to make yourself heard you have to raise your voice?

SPEAKING WITH A PURPOSE

To give information and express our feelings and opinions are probably the most important reasons we communicate. But we also speak and write to change or manipulate others – to persuade them round to our point of view, by preaching or dictating to them or by using our expressions to intimidate them. We may feel uncomfortable with silence, and feel we need to fill the void with chatter to hide or deny our insecurity. And of course we talk for the pleasure of it – to make or maintain contact, or to entertain.

Get a feel for the purpose of the communication in the dream and relate it to how others speak to you in real life, as well as how you use communication yourself.

If your communication is not straightforward in the dream, try to understand why this is – perhaps you don't trust that others will accept you or agree with you if you say what you mean. If this is the case, it could be worth looking at your beliefs and checking if they are still true for you so that you can feel more confident in them or dispense with them.

LANGUAGE

We often use our dreams to try to decipher situations we don't understand, and may use language as a metaphor for our confusion – indistinct speech, riddles or foreign tongues, for example. There may be clues in the dream to why we are not communicating effectively or

---

COMMUNICATION DREAM

"I was at a noisy party where everyone was talking at the same time. I couldn't understand what anyone was saying – but I realized I could understand what they were thinking. They were thinking really rude thoughts, criticising each other's clothes, making personal comments. But their words were all jumbled as they came out. I was too embarrassed to say anything and I wanted to run out. I was afraid that someone else could understand my own thoughts – namely, that they were all animals. I woke up feeling completely lost and disoriented.

I am quite perceptive about what is going on with others, but don't always trust my intuitions and get confused by lies and subterfuge. I have also always had a problem saying what I mean and this dream was showing me my fears and frustrations around this – often I just keep quiet when I am angry with someone and really feel like being very rude. "

BELOW What would a child shouting mean in your dreams? Could it be that you are afraid to say what you think for fear of being judged as childish or rude? Or perhaps you have a child who is struggling to be heard?

LEFT We adapt the way we communicate to fit with the situation. Talking to our work colleagues is different from talking to close friends or family. How you communicate tells you a lot about how you relate to other people.

RIGHT Pay attention to body language and subtle signals as well as what is being said. Looking away while someone is talking to you could mean many different things.

understanding others, and it could be useful to see if you are in contact with people in your daily life who are hard to fathom, or who are not what they seem.

RIGHT Children love to whisper and share their secrets. Is there something private that you would like to say to someone? What is holding you back?

SELF-EXPRESSION

In our dreams, we may be involved in the communication process or perhaps we are onlookers seeing others interact. Watching ourselves talking can be very revealing. Are we at ease talking? Or do we find it difficult in the dream? Are we happy with what we are saying or are the words stilted and awkward? If we can't see ourselves but we are still part of the dream how do we interpret what people are saying to us? The whole secret to good

or accurate dream interpretation is asking questions: why are we saying this? Who are we talking to? What is their response?

SHOUTING

We cry out to make others hear, or express intensity. It is not uncommon, especially among children, to dream of shouting at the top of your voice but barely a whisper comes out. This is almost certainly to do with feeling you are not heard, that your voice doesn't count.

The meaning of every dream is the fulfilment of a wish.

SIGMUND FREUD

ENERGY AND POWER

ENERGY TAKES A MULTITUDE OF FORMS, AND IN OUR DREAMS WE ENCOUNTER IT IN THE CATACLYSMIC ERUPTIONS OF
NATURE – VOLCANOES, LIGHTNING, EARTHQUAKES – AS MUCH AS IN OURSELVES. THOUGH WE CAN EXPRESS OUR ENERGY
POSITIVELY THROUGH DANCE, SPORT AND VERY MANY OTHER ACTIVITIES, IT IS OFTEN CHANNELLED INTO AGGRESSION AND
VIOLENCE. LEARNING HOW TO CHANNEL VIOLENT, AGGRESSIVE ENERGY CAN BE A LIFELONG STRUGGLE AND WE MAY NEVER
FEEL TOTALLY CONFIDENT THAT WE HAVE IT UNDER OUR CONTROL. THE TRICK IS TO ALLOW THE FEELINGS WITHOUT
ACTING THEM OUT. IF WE SUPPRESS THEM AND TURN THEM IN OURSELVES, WE WILL DO OURSELVES HARM.

ABOVE The universe is born out of energy and our powerful responses may be much more natural than we think. To dream of nature's forces may mean that you have personal power issues to work out. How do others see you?

VIOLENT ORIGINS

Stars are born out of cosmic explosions on an unimaginable scale. Fiery forces deep within our own planet erupt as volcanoes so destructive that they can engulf entire cities and set up far-reaching tidal waves. Our entire universe was created in violent energy reactions, and continues to evolve and be transformed in this way. Even our own birth is an energetic and sometimes violent moment, a dramatic experience for mother and child alike, and the baby's first gasp of breath is a struggle.

It is not surprising, then, that we may be troubled when such images occur in our dreams. It is as though we are struggling with the violence inherent in our existence, and trying to reconcile this with the passivity and control that are in many ways esteemed in our society.

VIOLENCE CURTAILED

The struggle with energy and violence is so instinctive that it permeates our unconscious, but there are precious few socially sanctioned outlets for this in our normal waking lives. Being civilized, controlled, elegant, and sophisticated are prized at the expense of emotional expression. We still have the same instinctive reactions and negative emotions as our primitive forebears, but the "fight or flight" response is often not appropriate in our modern world. We are not allowed to be violent, no matter how incensed we are, and if we do become violent or if we have temper tantrums, we are punished, and we may feel overwhelmed, frightened and guilty at the very thought of it.

We need these dreams as safety valves for our unexpressed violence, anger and frustration, and to give us an opportunity to find alternative ways of dealing with the world so that these feelings don't well up in the first place. Sometimes our unconscious presents us with dreams of energy or violence in its raw and awesome state in order to forge a safe link between our calm outer persona and our turbulent inner self, between our civilized, rational exterior and the anger and passions that many of us tend to bottle up. In this way, having violent dreams can be a healthy experience.

The more elaborate, complex and impenetrable the mask of sophistication a person wears, the bigger the gap between feeling and response. Conversely, the more instinctual and expressive the person, the less likely they are to be troubled by such dreams, as they have already found ways of venting their energy safely in waking life.

ATTACK AND DEFENCE

If violence is a real part of your life, you may be constantly in fear and on your guard against being attacked. The trauma of even a single attack may linger for years. It can prompt feelings of anger and violence, and you may want to act these out on particular individuals. However, the feelings may be unfocused and you are simply searching for a target for them. But if you are powerless to act on your feelings in real life, you may well have these encounters in your dreams instead. You can also actively use your dreams to deal with violence in a positive way – it can be beneficial to replay the scene of an attack in your dreams in such a way that you successfully defend yourself. This can give you the strength and feeling of self-worth you need to move on.

The physical attacks of your dreams can be metaphors for many other ways in which you might be attacked. Perhaps your ideas or actions have been harshly criticized and you take this personally, or you have to bear the brunt of someone else's anger, even when you haven't deserved it. In these cases it is useful to look at the role you play – are you aggressive, taunting, or an innocent bystander, a victim of circumstances? How you respond to an attack is also important, and your dream could give you clues as to how to deal with aggression in others.

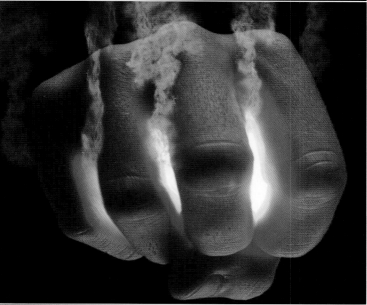

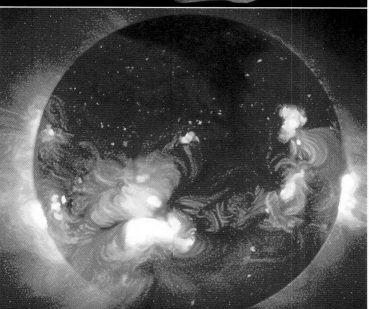

LEFT We may think ourselves cool and calm, yet our dreams may show what is bubbling beneath the surface, like a volcano waiting to erupt.
MIDDLE LEFT The tighter the grip on our natural responses, the more likely we are to "blow up".
BOTTOM LEFT Cosmic explosions are what sets the universe in motion. Powerful, violent energy is part of life – we can use this force to create or to destroy – it's up to us.

ENERGY DREAM

"I could see worlds in collision, entire galaxies erupting in fireballs and glorious colourful explosions. It was staggering, mind-blowing, and I could see how the world was made out of conflagration. It seems strange that such violent destruction can result in so much beauty.

I think that my dream was trying to tell me that I had to put more energy, more passion, into making things happen, that I had to get rid of the apathy that was holding me back."

Living in the World

From the moment of our birth until we die we build up a wealth of experiences through our interactions with the "world out there". These experiences shape who we are and guide our behaviour. How we feel, how we express ourselves, how we react with the world and the people in it, combine to produce a unique experience for each of us. Often we peg our self-worth on external factors, such as our level of wealth, or our achievements or social status, and we expend a great deal of time and energy trying to gain more of these things. Our aspirations become preoccupations and we try to work out aspects of these things in our dreams. In comparing ourselves with others, we may set ourselves up for competition and conflict. But sometimes the world delivers experiences over which we have little or no control – change is part of life and accidents can happen – and our dreams can help us adjust and warn us of potential trouble.

AMBITIONS AND GOALS

WE ALL HAVE OUR AMBITIONS AND GOALS, HOPES AND DESIRES, AND ENJOY THE SATISFACTION OF SUCCESS WHEN WE FULFIL THEM OR DISAPPOINTMENT WHEN WE CANNOT. BUT IF WE GET TO A POINT AT WHICH WE ARE CONSUMED BY UNFULFILLED AMBITIONS, OUR UNCONSCIOUS WILL TRY TO WORK WITH THEM IN OUR DREAMS, TO SEE A WAY FORWARD OR TO ACCEPT SOMETHING DIFFERENT FOR US. IF WE FAIL TO ACHIEVE SOMETHING THAT IS REALLY IMPORTANT FOR US OR TURN OUR BACK ON A BURNING AMBITION, OUR UNCONSCIOUS WILL PRODUCE DREAMS THAT MAKE US FOCUS ON THAT GOAL AND FIND A WAY TO MAKE US SUCCEED.

REACH FOR THE SKY

We don't have to put a limit on our hopes and aspirations. If we aim for something in our dreams that we have no hope of actually achieving, it may not matter that our ambitions are unrealistic. Such fantasies can be liberating – they give us scope to stretch our self-imposed limitations, and to make possible things that might otherwise seem far-fetched.

BELOW A lock and key is a powerful symbol. Do you have an unfulfilled ambition locked away inside of you, and if so, what is the key to realizing it? Perhaps the key is just out of reach, or maybe it doesn't quite fit the lock.

If an ambition remains out of reach because we have aimed too high, however, it can cause distress. It may leave us feeling that we will never achieve what we want and make us feel like giving up. In which case we may need to take a closer look at it, at the symbolic value of what we are failing to achieve. In asking questions about a dream symbol we may find out why we are being so unrealistic and aiming too high. We can gain more insight into what makes us set ourselves up for failure and find ways to set ourselves more realistic targets.

STUMBLING BLOCKS

There may well be valid reasons for not achieving an ambition – perhaps deep down inside you know that achieving it may not be as beneficial as you might like. For example, you may have been offered a fantastic job that will mean moving abroad, but because it offers you things you really want you may well be blinded to the attendant

BELOW To dream that you are doing a tedious, repetitive task may suggest that your goals are set too low. Perhaps it's time to get your ideas in order, rather like the bottles on the assembly line, and review your ambitions.

disadvantages or dangers – your family doesn't want to go, your parents would miss you, the company is not as stable as you want to believe, or your expertise isn't up to a high-powered job.

These unconscious realizations may manifest themselves as something stopping us in our dreams. This could be a locked door or a fence that stops us going along a certain path. A guard is another common symbol; this is usually someone impassive, anonymous and immovable who bars our way. If we don't find a way past the obstacles in our dream, then perhaps we ought to reconsider our ambition. But if we do manage to get through, this may give us a clue as to what our best course of action should be. We can relate it to our waking lives and find a way of achieving our goals and ambitions. On the other hand it may show us that although achieving our goal is possible, it is going to be very difficult, so perhaps it would be better to scale back or drop what it is that we are after.

SYMBOLIC IMAGERY

Literal images of goals and targets may appear in our dream to symbolize our personal ambitions. Games involving scoring goals, or aiming accurately for a small target, such as golf or darts, can show us how focused we are and whether or not our ambitions are fixed or keep changing. As well as looking at the nature of the

RIGHT Some ambitions are not easy to achieve but require great skill and tenacity if we are to make it to the top.
MIDDLE RIGHT A dream could suggest that achieving your goal will require total commitment, just like an athlete preparing to race.
BOTTOM RIGHT Our dreams may tell us to take control and put ourselves forward, rather than sitting in the background waiting to be asked.

goal, notice whether the game in your dream is a team effort, and if so who is helping or opposing you, or whether you are solely responsible in some way.

THE SCALE OF OUR AMBITIONS

Remember that our goals may be anything from major lifelong ambitions to relatively trivial targets, such as tidying up a messy cupboard, so if the dream does appear obviously to be about goals or ambitions but you are unable to see immediately what it could be referring to, think laterally about the nature of what you might be trying to process. Even small goals may take on greater significance than they deserve if they link into personal hang-ups – if your mother was always pestering you to tidy your room when you were a child, for instance, you may feel obsessed, angry or resistant about tidying up. Being goal oriented may also mean that you will tend to turn ordinary activities into goals, into something you can check off a list, rather than just being a regular part of daily life.

Dreams are a dress rehearsal for life. ALFRED ADLER

JOBS AND WORK

WE SPEND A LOT OF TIME AT WORK, AND EARNING A LIVING IN A SATISFYING WAY IS ONE OF LIFE'S GREATEST CHALLENGES. IT IS ONLY NATURAL FOR WORK TO OCCUPY AN IMPORTANT PART OF OUR DREAM LIFE. BUT WORK IN A DREAM IS NOT ALWAYS ABOUT AN ACTIVITY THAT WE DO – WE ENCOUNTER PEOPLE WHO ARE OPERATING IN THEIR WORK ROLES ALL THE TIME, AND OUR COLLEAGUES MAY ALSO FIGURE PROMINENTLY. ENJOYING OUR WORK MAY BE REFLECTED IN POSITIVE, HAPPY DREAMS ABOUT IT, OR DREAMS IN WHICH WE GRAPPLE WITH INTERESTING REAL-LIFE PROBLEMS THAT WE CAN'T BEAR TO LET GO OF EVEN IN OUR SLEEP. SOMETIMES STRESS AND ANXIETY RELATED TO WORK WILL ALSO SURFACE.

ABOVE When work seems like drudgery, it could be time to review your career options.
ABOVE RIGHT Your dreams may reflect what it is you really want to do with your life.
ABOVE FAR RIGHT You might dream about the work of others rather than yourself. Is this a reflection of someone in your life who has authority over you? Is the authority justified or does it worry and frustrate you?

WORK AND EMOTIONS

Unfortunately, for many people work means stress, boredom, frustration, unhappiness, and anger; we may feel unchallenged or abused or taken for granted, and our dreams may well reflect such feelings. We may say or do something extreme in the work environment of our dream, and wake worrying that we might act out such stuff in real life. But the point of these dreams may in fact be to address just that possibility – to let off steam in the safety of our dreams so that we don't cause a scene at work.

Work dreams may seem fairly realistic, but at other times our unconscious will create a memorable scenario to draw our attention to what is bothering us.

Dreaming of work might also be symbolic of more general issues, such as survival or money, how to rise to a challenge or deal with pressure, feelings of inadequacy, subservience or anger and a myriad other experiences.

PEOPLE AT WORK

We do not always dream about our own jobs, however. As in our daily lives, we are constantly in contact with or seeing images of others as they go about their work, from shopkeepers to bank managers, newsreaders to teachers, factory workers to artists and chefs. We probably hold countless attitudes about those roles – wishing we could be in the other person's shoes, or thanking our lucky stars that we

aren't. We may admire people for their work, thinking that they must be clever or talented or courageous to do what they do, and envy the satisfaction or prestige or fame that goes with their wonderful-looking jobs. Or perhaps we hate the idea of the tedium or lack of status of a particular job, the confinement of an office or the uncertainty of contract work.

Engaging with strangers in our dreams may often be in the context of their occupation, and our attitude to that occupation. Teachers, bosses and policemen, for instance, tend to be authority figures, and your experiences in real life will be crucial in forming your attitude to such figures. As a child, did you have teachers who picked on you, inflicted corporal punishment or made you feel stupid? Or did they inspire you, understand and encourage you, satisfy and nurture your curiosity or give you a love of reading?

People at work can symbolize many different things. To dream of a cleaner, for instance, may indicate you need to get your house in order and to "clean up", while an accountant might suggest that you take stock of your affairs and get organized. An artist on the other hand may suggest that you need to relax your attitudes and think laterally or engage more with your intuitive, creative side.

COLLEAGUES

We spend much of our waking lives with colleagues, so it is not surprising if we dream about them. Often their function in our dreams will be similar to that of friends, in that they will appear because they have particular characteristics that we need to address. But in many cases their role will be more important – bosses in particular may bring up important issues relating to authority, power and status.

RIGHT Some workplaces are big and imposing. Dreaming that you are in such a building can make you feel small and insignificant, especially if you are alone.
MIDDLE RIGHT Sometimes it feels as though you are just going round and round and not getting anywhere. Your dream may be showing you that progress does not always follow a straight line.
BOTTOM RIGHT Repetitive work is not necessarily boring. Your dream may be a reminder to take a pride in all your endeavours and know that every job has its part to play.

WORKPLACES AND RESOURCES

If you find in your dream that you are unable to do things because the equipment you have for doing your job is inadequate or the work environment is unpleasant, it could be saying something general about your material wellbeing or your ability to get things done.

Do you feel that you get what you want out of life, or that there are constantly obstacles to what you want to do? Our physical environment can have a major impact on our emotional state, so it is worth noting how you feel about the workplace of your dream as much as what you are doing or the people you are with.

WORK DREAM

"I was due to go on my first business trip, to the headquarters of a major bank. In my dream I arrived at their imposing building and went up in the lift. The doors opened directly into the boardroom, which contained a massive table surrounded by middle-aged men in suits. As they looked up I realized to my horror that, although I was wearing a smart black jacket and smart black shoes, I was also wearing a frilly, homemade nightdress.

This dream was clearly to do with not feeling confident in myself or comfortable in the imposing and masculine setting of the bank. I was afraid that I couldn't pull off the meeting successfully, that I would somehow make a serious gaffe, be intimidated or not be taken seriously."

SPORTS AND GAMES

FUN, PHYSICAL WELLBEING AND A SENSE OF ACHIEVEMENT ARE JUST SOME OF THE REASONS WE TAKE PART IN SPORTS AND GAMES. THEY ALSO PROVIDE A WAY OF ENGAGING WITH OTHER PEOPLE IN A VERY ACTIVE WAY, AS BOTH TEAM MEMBERS AND OPPONENTS, AS WELL AS HELPING US RELEASE STRESS AND CHANNEL OUR AGGRESSIVE IMPULSES. FOR ARMCHAIR SPORTSMEN OR TEAM SUPPORTERS AT SPORTS FIXTURES, THERE IS THE EXCITEMENT AND CAMARADERIE OF WATCHING A FAVOURITE TEAM OR FAVOURITE SPORT IN ACTION. WITH THESE DREAMS, WE NEED TO ASK OURSELVES ABOUT THE SPORT WE ARE ENGAGED IN, HOW WE PLAY, AND OUR MOTIVATIONS AND FEELINGS, AS WELL AS WHAT ACTUALLY HAPPENS.

GAMES PEOPLE PLAY

The various forms of sporting and leisure activities represent many qualities. For instance, a violent rugby match may have more to do with aggression and teamwork than the leisurely, non-contact style of a round of golf, while an intellectually absorbing chess game is mainly concerned with strategy and has almost nothing to do with physicality. There are also many games that we play simply for fun, such as beach volleyball or the role-playing games of a child's make-believe world where the rules are made up as they go along.

SUBLIMATION OF AGGRESSION

For many people, sports and games provide a much-needed way of working through aggression and frustration. The positive effects of strenuous physical activity on the emotions are well documented, and in some sports, hitting or kicking a ball can be a great substitute for doing the same to someone who has made you very angry! By analysing how we feel and how we are behaving and reacting to others in our dream, we can try to uncover the real cause of our aggressive feelings and work through them or lay them to rest.

OPPONENTS

Who are you playing with and against in your dream? Your opponents may be real people, they may represent abstract qualities – luck, fate, challenges, opposition – or they may be an aspect of yourself that you are at odds with.

Often opponents will be people with whom we are having some kind of power struggle or conflict. Who wins is often a vital question, as it could indicate what is actually happening in an important relationship, what you wish for or what you fear. Look at how seriously you take the game – you may want simply to put your opponent in their place, to hurt them badly, or even to eliminate them altogether.

TEAMS

Being part of a team gives a great sense of belonging, going beyond our individual needs to unite in a common goal. Teams give us a place, a role, a bond with others. They show us who our friends are and how much we rely on others to achieve our goals. Sports teams can also be a

BELOW What sport are you pursuing in your dream? Is it something that you normally do? **BELOW RIGHT** What are the items of equipment associated with a game or sport? Perhaps these have a significance in your dream. **BELOW FAR RIGHT** Dreams of running a race may raise issues of winning and losing in your life.

RIGHT Dreams of top sports people are fairly common. Such dreams may represent a wish-fulfilment, an ambition to be the "best" at something, or to be famous and admired. What could this mean for you?

metaphor for other social groups in our lives, such as the family or work team, and looking at how they pull together and the roles people play may be significant in relation to these units.

COMPETITION AND RESULTS

Competition is an all-pervasive feature of our society, and the games we play are often about proving who is best, who has the greatest talent, skill or intellectual ability. For many people, getting ahead gives a feeling of self-worth that they may otherwise be not capable of feeling. Winning or losing a dream game could be crucial to how you see yourself – your confidence or assertiveness, what your role is in relation to your opponent or your team, or how you view your skills and talents. If you have a relationship

where you are constantly racking up points against each other, this may show up in your dreams as a competition of some sort.

PLAYING THE GAME

Cheating or rule-breaking may hint at an unfair situation in your life, or one in which someone is being underhand with you. Rules may be about social restrictions, so check whether you know what the rules of the game are, and whether it is you or someone else who is breaking them.

COMPETITIVE DREAM

"I was playing chess against my father, using life-sized pieces. Although we laughed and joked as we played, I knew we were playing for big stakes and this created an underlying seriousness, a feeling of menace that affected my game. Behind the laughter I was in crisis: I wanted to win so badly it hurt, and I wanted to hurt him, even kill him, by winning. This was a very powerful dream and it made me realize that I had a lot to work out about my relationship with my father. We have always been competitive, and he is also very pushy, expecting me to do well, earn well, and drive myself as hard as he does. I've always felt I have a lot to live up to and although I don't like it, I've always done what he wants. In this dream I realized that I didn't have to be dominated by him forever, but that I would need to be more assertive for that to happen."

LEFT Every sport has its own set of rules and we need to understand them before we can enjoy the game. Are you a player or a spectator in your dream?
FAR LEFT Very physical team sports can be a good way of letting off steam. Being part of a team in your dream is a sign of belonging, or wanting to belong.

MONEY

WHAT DOES MONEY REPRESENT TO YOU? WHEN IT COMES TO WORKING WITH OUR DREAMS THE ANSWER TO THIS IS CRUCIAL. MOST PEOPLE WILL ACKNOWLEDGE THAT THEY WANT IT, AND ALMOST CERTAINLY THAT THEY NEED IT, BUT BEYOND THAT OUR RESPONSES CAN DIFFER MARKEDLY FROM PERSON TO PERSON. PERHAPS YOU SEE IT AS A MEANS TO AN END, OR AN END IN ITSELF; MAYBE YOU THINK THAT IT REPRESENTS FREEDOM AND CAN LIBERATE PEOPLE, OR YOU MIGHT SEE IT AS AN ENSLAVER. OUR OWN AND OTHERS' ATTITUDES TO MONEY IN REAL LIFE WILL INEVITABLY BE REFLECTED IN OUR DREAMS; HOW MUCH THERE IS, WHERE IT CAME FROM AND WHAT WE DO WITH IT WILL ALSO BE SIGNIFICANT.

ASSOCIATIONS

Money is generally said to point to opportunity and reward or power. Some associate it with relationships, so in this way receiving it is linked to the birth of a child, finding it could suggest benefiting from a prosperous marriage, and wasting or losing it may mean that you are wasting your love on someone unworthy.

Using a Freudian model, hoarding money implies anal fixation. Money can also be used to represent resources in general. Bear in mind that it could be denoting riches in terms of time, energy, knowledge, love and so on, rather than material or monetary wealth. Consider your relationship with these other resources too and think about how rich or poor you feel.

Some of these money associations may make sense to you and help you to understand what your dream is really about. If not, you will need to dig a bit deeper, and really try to understand what money means to you on a much more personal basis, and thus what it symbolizes in your dream.

BELOW Think about what money may symbolize to you. Love? Security? Status? Freedom? Success? It is important to understand your own reactions before you interpret your dreams on the subject.

WHAT MONEY CAN BUY

It is what we can have and do with money – as well as what is unavailable to us if we don't have it – that gives it much of its value. We may feel that it gives us the freedom to have the things we want, including leisure time and opportunities to see and do things that aren't free. But having acquired wealth, we may feel burdened by our possessions and afraid of losing them, and we may also feel trapped by the need to carry on generating it.

Dreams of money may be simple wish fulfilment, or we may find they show us how to get it, the frustrations of not having it, or the fear of being suddenly deprived of it. But we can also use money dreams as a more general symbol for greed and materialism, opportunity, the loss of something we value, or even of being trapped.

STATUS AND POWER

Money can convey power and status. We can add to this the idea that money is a reward, so having or not having it differentiates us further and makes us feel more or less worthwhile as people. These issues may well bother us, keying in to our inherent sense of self-worth, and dreams of money – especially in relation to a salary

or wage – can be about this idea of our value, of how much we are being appreciated.

GIVE AND TAKE

If you are hoarding or counting money in your dream, you may be afraid that it will run out or be feeling insecure; similarly putting it in the bank may be to do with security,. Holding on to money can also represent holding on to ideas, rather than putting them into action. If you are giving money away, do you do so with a spirit of generosity, or because you simply want to get rid of it? Spending or giving money freely can imply a certain faith or trust in things working out, that your own needs will always be met, and this can be tremendously reassuring if you normally worry about such matters.

Owing or being owed money in a dream could be a worry about literally being burdened by debt. Looked at in a broader sense though, ask yourself if you are concerned about being indebted to someone in a more general way – perhaps they have done you a favour or you feel guilty about asking for help. You may also feel taken advantage of.

TYPES OF MONEY

The form the money takes in your dreams may hold another layer of significance. Cash is readily available, and whether it comes in the shape of coins or notes may indicate how much you value whatever it represents to you. An IOU or cheque may signify indebtedness, delayed gratification or uncertainty around whether you will be repaid; gift vouchers may suggest generosity, but may also hint that whatever they represent has some specific value or limitation placed on it. If you dream of foreign money it could be that you are unsure of the value of something.

MONEY DREAM

"I was being asked to pay admission to the cinema. I had brought a single coin in my pocket, but couldn't find it anywhere – it had slipped through a hole. A terrible grief washed over me. I couldn't understand why it should pain me so much – it was only a trip to the cinema after all.

This dream was about having given up a successful career in film-making to devote myself to my family. My children were growing up and needed me less and less, and I was aware that in the meantime my precious career seemed lost. Although I didn't regret having had children, I was experiencing pain at having let my career slip through my fingers."

AUTHORITY AND DISCIPLINE

WHEN WE ARE CHILDREN OUR PARENTS AND TEACHERS TELL US WHAT WE CAN AND CAN'T DO. OFTEN THE AIM OF THIS IS TO TEACH US SOCIAL NORMS OR PREVENT US FROM HURTING OURSELVES. BUT MUCH OF THE AUTHORITY THAT ADULTS WIELD OVER CHILDREN IS TO DO WITH THEIR OWN INTERESTS – PROTECTING THEIR BELONGINGS, THEIR NEEDS, THEIR FEELINGS. AS ADULTS WE MIGHT ASSOCIATE PUNISHMENT WITH AN ELEMENT OF UNFAIRNESS AND IMPOSITION, OR WE MIGHT SEE IT AS SOMETHING WE DESERVE MORE OF. AUTHORITY FIGURES MIGHT BE SEEN AS UNJUST AND REPRESSIVE, BUT WE MAY ALSO PRODUCE THEM IN OUR DREAMS AS A SYMBOL OF SECURITY, OR OF WISDOM AND GUIDANCE.

In punishing a child the stated aim may be to teach the child what is safe or dangerous, right and wrong, and acceptable or unacceptable, but from time to time, punishment may be meted out that has nothing to do with a child having done something "bad", but rather with an adult venting frustration or simply being a bully, and this can be frightening and perplexing.

INNER DISCIPLINE

When we grow up our attitude to authority and punishment can be quite complex, so we may use dream time to unravel how we feel, especially if we come up against problematic authority figures, moral dilemmas or confusion in our daily lives. As adults, there usually isn't the same sort of immediate authority

figure standing over us like when we were children. Hopefully we will have developed an innate sense of what is right and wrong; we have a greater understanding of the consequences of our actions and are able to exercise our own judgement and discretion. Laws and the fear of punishment keep most of us in check where our self-discipline or morality may otherwise slip.

Over the course of our lives, our unconscious takes note of the countless rules and injunctions laid down in our early years by parents, teachers and prefects; as we grow older we become aware of other authority figures and bodies of law, and we notice how others respond to these as well. We also develop subtle ways of avoiding punishment and guilt. If we are acting in a way our

unconscious thinks doesn't suit our own interests, it will let us know through the symbolism of our dreams by creating a figure who can tell us how to behave.

PUNISHMENT

Our experience of punishment and how we respond to it is also a personal one. Being given detention at school may have been immensely shameful and humiliating for one person, but for another merely irritating or even a fairly normal occurrence. Indeed for some, being punished by "the establishment" establishes "street cred". In some societies beating a child for a wrongdoing may be considered a normal – even essential – part of their growing up, whereas in others it is anathema, and thought to be damaging. So to understand what

BELOW RIGHT As children we soon learn who is in charge and this may be reflected in our dreams. Who was the dominant authority figure when you were growing up?
BELOW How we respond to authority in any of its smallest forms is very revealing. Even a red traffic light can trigger issues around sticking to or breaking the rules.

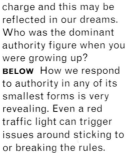

RIGHT Laws and the fear of being punished keep most of us in check. This can make us feel that we are under surveillance or living in a police state, and may show up in our dreams. Who is watching you?

punishment means in your dreams may mean coming to terms with how you view it in real life. Does it make you feel angry, guilty, submissive or humiliated, or does withstanding it give you strength? Did you feel you deserved it? If you are meting it out, look hard at what you were feeling and who you are punishing. Note what the punishment is, how severe it is, and if you feel it is deserved. Also try to discover why it is being meted out, and what it achieves.

REBELLING

What if you don't want to be told what to do, or you believe that an authority figure is wrong or evil, or you feel that someone is acting in an authoritarian way towards you but shouldn't? If your boss tells you to forge a signature or your partner dominates or controls your relationship, you may well feel resentful but unable to be assertive or to inject a reasonable balance. If you can't deal with the matter in an adult way, you may represent the dominant person in your dreams as a teacher or parent. Your powerlessness may reduce you to a small child or even animal, or your resentment may manifest in your dreams as a symbolic rebellion or mutiny.

AUTHORITY FIGURES

The area of our lives in which we are having difficulties, together with our upbringing, social standing, beliefs and cultural background, will determine who the authority figure in our dream will be. It may be a police officer if we are in danger of breaking the law, or a priest if religious or moral principles are at stake. For others it might be a judge, lawyer, traffic warden, headteacher, monarch, even a god. Each of these represents something different, and we need to look at what they mean to us to find out what their presence in our dream means.

> ### AUTHORITY DREAM
>
> "In my dream I couldn't find my car keys, and realized my wife had hidden them. I asked her for them back but she said no, it wasn't my turn to drive the car. She told me to go and stand in the corner for being naughty, that I'd asked for the keys before she had told me to. I stood in the corner and she was standing behind me flicking my ears and telling me I had been naughty and deserved to be punished. I felt like a small boy and was really seething inside but I couldn't do anything. In real life my wife is in control, and I guess I hate this."

BELOW LEFT Sometimes we may wonder who is pulling the strings. Our dreams can show us who is running the show and what we can do to take more charge of our lives.
BELOW It is easy for an adult to overpower a child when he wants to assert his authority. This can create a fear of authority, which we carry as adults.

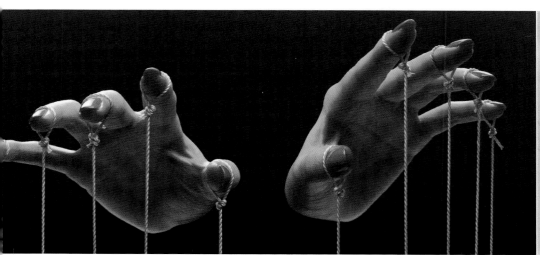

TROUBLE AHEAD

OUR DREAMS OFTEN DROP HINTS ABOUT HOW THE FUTURE MAY UNFOLD. ALTHOUGH THERE ARE OCCASIONS WHEN PEOPLE HAVE HAD DREAMS THAT SEEMED TO PREDICT SPECIFIC EVENTS, MORE USUALLY THE INFORMATION IN OUR DREAMS IS OUR UNCONSCIOUS MIND'S WAY OF TRYING TO ALERT OUR ATTENTION TO THINGS THAT MAY HAPPEN IF WE CARRY ON DOING WHAT WE'RE DOING, RATHER THAN PREDICTING THAT SOMETHING IS DEFINITELY GOING TO HAPPEN. SYMBOLS OF WARNINGS IN OUR DREAMS MAY BE AS SIMPLE AS THE WARNINGS WE RECEIVE IN DAILY LIFE. SUCH DREAMS CAN BE TRICKY TO INTERPRET AS IT MAY NOT BE CLEAR WHAT THE SYMBOLS RELATE TO.

WARNINGS

In general, the modern Western view is that our dreams exist primarily as a means of communication between our unconscious and conscious selves. Other cultures, however, have believed that our dreams can tell us of impending trouble and have used the information as a basis for their subsequent actions. There is plenty of anecdotal evidence to support this view. Famously, the American president Abraham Lincoln dreamed of his own death, which to the great interest of dream analysts ever since, he left an account of.

Unfortunately Lincoln did not heed the warning the dream contained, and met with an early demise. Still, we have no proof that it was not mere coincidence, or evidence of what must be a common fear among those with a high political profile. While dramatic dreams such as Lincoln's are the ones that seize our imagination, part of our fascination with predictive dreams lies in how we are able to foresee such an event, and what, if anything, we should do about it. If we were to alter our behaviour to protect ourselves from the possibility that every negative dreamt experience will come true, our lives would be blighted by paranoia and become an impossible nightmare.

READING THE CLUES

Our dream warnings may be less clear than a scenario of impending death, though. More typically, the warnings we receive in dreams will be of conditions or future events of which we are already aware but are trying to ignore, or that we could foresee if we took the trouble or the courage to notice the signs. Our lives are filled with stimuli, so it is not always possible to notice everything consciously, but these dreams allow us to become aware of the fact that we are not seeing or hearing something that we need to. In fact our unconscious may remind us of this by literally making us blind or deaf in our dreams, or by giving vivid or exaggerated pictures – either symbolic or literal – of our situation.

DANGER SIGNS

In real life, dangers are often helpfully signposted using fairly universal symbols. Traffic signs warn of hazards on the road, the

LINCOLN'S DREAM

It is easy with hindsight to interpret a dream as a precognition. These are the words of Abraham Lincoln as he recounted his dream in which he had foreseen his own death at the hand of an assassin.

"There seemed to be a death-like stillness about me. I heard subdued sobs, as if many people were weeping. I feel that I left my bed and walked downstairs. I went from room to room. No living person was in sight, but the same mournful sounds of distress met me as I passed along. I kept on until I arrived at the East Room, where I met with a sickening surprise. Before me was a catafalque, on which rested a corpse wrapped in funeral vestments. Around it were guards and a throng of mourners, many weeping pitifully. 'Who is dead in the White House?' I demanded of one of the soldiers. 'The President,' was his answer. 'He was killed by an assassin.'"

stylized image of the skull and crossbones is used to signify poison and other similar dangers, while "keep out" signs warn you that you are about to trespass on private property. If such symbols appear in your dreams, you can take them as an indication of some danger or difficulty you are headed for, given your present circumstances or actions.

An alarm fitted to your house or car may point to feelings of insecurity or vulnerability, either around your physical being or possessions, or around your sense of self. You may feel that you need to protect yourself from attack, or from losing things that are significant. If the alarm is ringing, there may be more of a sense of urgency in these feelings, as though you are already in danger, it is important to take such a clear warning seriously.

DECODING A SITUATION

Sometimes the benefit of heeding a warning lies in the process of working out what it is about. The next step is to actively take on board the significance and

implications of a situation, and in such cases our unconscious may present us with more obscure signs. If we can decode them, we will understand how to adjust our lives. For instance, you may dream of a realistic situation in your present life getting out of control. From this you may conclude that you need to make some adjustments about how you relate to the people in that situation; or that your life is going too fast and you must slow down; or that you need to take control of this aspect of your life.

RECURRING DREAMS

If you repeatedly dream of something that worries you, take whatever action you feel necessary to set your mind at rest. It doesn't mean that your dreams are foretelling things that will definitely go wrong, they are merely drawing your attention to a possible problem.

Recurring dreams can be an attempt by our unconscious to point out when we are ignoring danger; the dream may be repeated over and over again until we do something about it.

DANGERS

EVERY NOW AND AGAIN OUR DREAMS SEEM TO COME TO US SPECIFICALLY TO TELL US OF DANGER, USING METAPHORS FOR WHATEVER DIFFICULTIES OUR UNCONSCIOUS BELIEVES WE MIGHT BE IN. WHEN PLANE CRASHES, NATURAL DISASTERS, OR ACCIDENTS IN THE HOME FIGURE IN OUR DREAM NARRATIVE THEY MAY SIGNAL SPECIFIC PROBLEMS IN OUR LIVES THAT COULD LEAD US INTO TROUBLED TIMES. THEY MAY BE TELLING YOU ABOUT SPECIFIC FEARS THAT HAVE ARISEN BECAUSE OF THE SUPPOSED DANGERS THEY MAY PRESENT, OR TIE IN TO EVENTS THAT HAVE ALREADY OCCURRED IN YOUR LIFE AND WHICH YOU ARE AFRAID MIGHT HAPPEN AGAIN. THEY MAY EVEN BE COMPLETELY IRRATIONAL.

DANGEROUS PEOPLE

Threatening behaviour by other people is a common sign of social or emotional trouble. We might dream of being attacked – an intruder with a knife, a crazed lunatic rushing at us out of nowhere, someone grabbing us from behind. The attack may represent a personal threat rather than a physical one, for example if you have a bullying or critical boss or a domineering partner. Such scenarios may well be warnings, indications that our unconscious actively believes we are under attack or being overwhelmed by someone, and it is best to take notice of what such dreams are telling us.

NATURAL DISASTERS

In some dreams we might be threatened by dramatic events of nature – lightning, avalanche, storm, flood, earthquake, meteor strike – and again we should take note of these dreams. They have a symbolic intent, to warn us that we may feel insecure, out of control and at the mercy of fate, or overwhelmed. Different types of disaster are likely to place emphasis on different aspects of our being – for instance flooding can relate to the emotions, fire to passion or anger, an avalanche or earthquake to the stability of our lives – although the details will vary from person to person. All are disruptive, but in their upheaval they may also suggest a purging of some central aspect of our lives, sweeping away all that has gone before so that we can start afresh.

DANGER IN THE HOME

The dangers of our dreams can be minor domestic mishaps like getting an electric shock from a faulty plug, losing or breaking something we value, or the kitchen being flooded due to a blocked drain. Such dreams could be warnings of real dangers

---

DREAM OF DANGER

"I was walking along a dark, rural lane. It had been raining and the trees were dripping black water. Suddenly I felt myself grabbed from behind and thrown to the ground. I remember, in my dream, worrying more about my coat getting wet than about what was to happen to me. I felt I knew the person who had attacked me, even though I couldn't see his face. He stood over me in a very threatening attitude with his fists clenched. This dream seemed so real that I didn't feel I could ignore it, and I spent ages trying to work out who my attacker was. I came to the conclusion that he represented a colleague I worked very closely with but had never really trusted. I had a quick look at his work later that day and found he had been taking my ideas and passing them off as his, and I had been literally 'in the dark' about his behaviour for some time."

that could actually occur in our waking lives. We may have seen but ignored the signs of an "accident waiting to happen" – a frayed wire, a blocked drain – and this is our unconscious mind's way of bringing these defects to our notice and making sure that more serious mishaps don't happen. But they may also be symbolic rather than literal – pointing to discord in the home or fears around a multitude of issues to do with loss or damage or danger.

A more calamitous event, such as the house falling down, could indicate difficulties around your security, stability or domestic situation, while a dream of being trapped in a house on fire may be a powerful metaphor for how you feel about some central aspect of your life.

EMOTIONAL OUTCOMES

The accident or disaster in your dream may be intended as a catalyst for some behaviour or emotion rather than a sign of danger. For instance, you may have feelings of guilt or blame around some completely different scenario in your life where things are not working out – maybe you need to express these feelings and work with them. Or you may be contemplating failure, especially of something that you see as being very important – perhaps your plans or dreams for the future are going awry and the life journey you had envisaged for yourself is being abruptly curtailed. But in every disaster a hero emerges, and it could be that you are seeking to take on this role – to gain recognition for strength or bravery, or love.

ABOVE Our unconscious is infinitely creative in the way it produces its dream images. Being in a precarious situation is highlighted by this image. It may indicate things slipping out of control.

LEFT In dreams, as in waking life, danger can come at us from any direction and from where we least expect it.

CHANGE AND IMPERMANENCE

WHEN THINGS ARE GOING WELL IT IS FAIRLY NATURAL TO WANT THEM TO LAST THAT WAY FOREVER. BUT CHANGE IS ACTUALLY ONE OF THE FEW CERTAINTIES WE HAVE IN LIFE AND OUR DREAMS OFTEN DROP HINTS ABOUT HOW THE FUTURE MAY UNFOLD. WHATEVER OUR SITUATION IS NOW, IT IS SURE TO BE DIFFERENT SOON. WE MIGHT BE ENERGIZED BY THIS PROSPECT AND FIND IT EXCITING, OR WE MAY FIND IT THREATENING AND SCARY. WE MAY EVEN REFUSE TO BELIEVE IT COULD BE TRUE. BUT NO MATTER WHAT OUR ATTITUDE, THERE IS NO GETTING AWAY FROM THE FACT THAT CHANGE IS A NATURAL AND INEVITABLE PART OF LIFE AND OUR SUBCONSCIOUS MIND WILL BE DEALING WITH IT IN OUR DREAMS.

CONSTANT CHANGE

There is a story of a king who asked his advisers to come up with a saying that would be true for all time, no matter what situation we find ourselves in. The advisers thought long and hard but were defeated, so the king turned to a Buddhist monk who said, "This too shall pass." This was the phrase the king had been looking for.

This story illustrates the point that change is inevitable. The changes we experience may be more or less noticeable at different points in our lives.

Some, such as having a baby, getting married or divorced, or leaving school, will be major and will alter the course of our lives and the roles we play. Other changes will be more subtle and may have more to do with our inner world – our feelings and perceptions change over time and affect the way we relate to others.

RESPONDING TO CHANGE

Some changes are self-generated, and we have some control over them. We are able to decide what happens and when. But often change is out of our control and can take us on a journey that we didn't intend. These sorts of changes, such as losing a partner or a job redundancy, may be scary as we have to adjust to an unknown that is not of our choosing. Changes that are forced on us can be useful and welcome or they can provide setbacks – whether we resist or "go with the flow" will make a huge difference as to how well we cope.

How we respond to change is reflected in our dreams. If we cope well, then change may be symbolized by something that is fluid or flowing, such as a running brook or clouds moving across an open sky. If the change is dramatic or important, then an image of transformation, like that of a caterpillar turning into a butterfly, or a chicken hatching from an egg, may appear. If we are finding it difficult to cope with change, then the symbolism may be more intimidating, such as dreaming that our teeth are falling out. Our unconscious will always provide the clues about what is happening.

TRANSITION

As we move through life, we leave behind the behaviours and attitudes of one phase to move into something new: when one door closes another opens. Such

BELOW Our dreams will reflect how we view change and how we adjust to the unknown. Do we hanker for the past, or are we able to move with the times? Consider what an image like this steam train could mean in your dreams.

times of transition are not always easy. We may find it hard to adjust to losing our youth for instance, or when we discover that our thoughts and feelings are outdated. Like a bird learning to fly, we have to find new ways of coping with life as we settle into each different phase.

At such times, our dreams may be filled with images of running away, travelling or exploring; in such activities we may be searching for the energy of more youthful pursuits; trying to escape from the narrowing of focus that often goes with the ageing process; or, in a more positive light, we may be

discovering the value of our present lives and looking forward to some kind of transition.

TRANSFORMATION

Some dream images can be frustratingly fluid. In a second our surroundings may have transformed, through the shapes and colours of objects, the size or layout of a room, or a person's character. We are more flexible than we imagine, and often it is a

matter of courage or imagination to see how wonderful change can be. On the other hand, we may use our dreams to confront or justify our fears of change and difference, or of uncertainty about the stability of a situation. Transformation in our dreams can guide us in how to make positive changes in our lives and overcome our resistance to things being different.

ABOVE All change is a metamorphosis of one sort or another – things changing from what they were to what they will become. Some of these changes will feel weird or unsettling in our dreams. **ABOVE LEFT** Change lies hidden beneath the surface of what we can already see, and is something of a mystery.

RIGHT Whether we find change easy or difficult will depend to some extent on our attitude. Our dreams may show us scenes from nature to remind us that every ending also contains the seeds of a new beginning.

DREAM OF CHANGE

"I was chasing mice, trying to get them back into their cage, but each time I caught one it suddenly rotted in my hand. I was panicking and running everywhere trying to keep these mice in. I wanted to scream at them 'Stay in the cage or you'll go to pieces'.

My children were leaving home, and it was very unsettling; I didn't know what to do with myself and I felt left behind. Each mouse in the dream was a child. I wanted them to stay in the cage with me. If I have to stay why shouldn't they have to as well? I also worried about how they would cope in the big wide world and wanted to stop them from leaving, but I suppose in my heart I knew that this was a change they needed to make whatever I felt about it ."

MOVEMENT, MACHINES AND STRUCTURES

Our dreams are often signals of change and progress, and movement, machinery and structures can be connected with these things. We all use machinery of one kind or another. It enables us to effect changes, and mould our environment to our needs and taste. Technology means that both the machinery and the things we can do with it are constantly evolving. This evolution may be challenging and exciting, but for many it is stressful and bewildering. It is easy to feel lost as if in a maze of new ideas. Alternatively we seek security in the structures we create – the comfort and safety of our homes or other buildings. Sometimes we don't know whether we are coming or going and we may try to escape from it all by flying or running away, or going on a journey. Indeed movement, whether of ourselves or of things in our surroundings, can signify change and show us how at ease we are with ourselves and our environment.

FLYING AND FALLING

OUR DREAMS RELEASE US FROM THE CONSTRAINTS OF OUR EARTHBOUND LIVES, AND SO IT IS NOT UNCOMMON IN OUR UNCONSCIOUS FANTASIES TO FIND THAT WE CAN FLY. AS WELL AS A SENSE OF RELEASE AND FREEDOM, FLIGHT MAY GIVE US A DIFFERENT PERSPECTIVE ON OUR WORLD, THOUGH IN MANY DREAMS IT INVOLVES LITTLE MORE THAN SKIMMING OVER THE SURFACE OF THE GROUND. DREAMING OF FALLING IS LESS LIKELY TO BE A PLEASANT EXPERIENCE, BOTH IN THE PHYSICAL SENSATIONS IT MIGHT CAUSE, AND ALSO BECAUSE FALLING OFTEN POINTS TO THE PRESENCE OF TROUBLES AND A SENSE OF BEING OUT OF CONTROL THAT WE MIGHT BE CARRYING IN OUR WAKING LIVES.

BELOW RIGHT Flying in our dreams can be a positive experience and we can learn a lot from it. It can feel very liberating to find ourselves free from the constraints of the everyday world.
BELOW Dreams of flying or falling can be so scary and realistic that some people are too afraid to go to sleep in case they have such a dream.

CONFRONTING OUR INNER FEARS

For some people dreams of flying and falling may be an attempt to confront a fear of heights or to deal with vertigo – the dizziness we experience when our sense of balance has been disturbed. You can actually reprogramme your subconscious before you go to sleep with an instruction like "if I dream of flying or falling I will have wings and come to no harm". If you repeat this instruction to yourself often enough, then in your dreams you will indeed develop wings and cope better with the sensations in the dream.

There have been cases of people so terrified of having dreams of flying or falling that they resist the onset of sleep. For some, learning to sleep with a pillow or cushion pressed up against the soles of their feet helps, as this stimulates the sensors in the feet and the sense of balance is restored, so there is no unconscious worry about being in freefall.

THEORETICAL INTERPRETATIONS

Freud and his followers maintain that for men dreams of flying are often associated with sex, while for women falling dreams may indicate succumbing to sexual temptation. Another school of thought says that flying and falling dreams point to the existence of a soul which can leave the body while we are asleep, and that such dreams are merely echoes or memories of these out-of-body experiences. Others still have said that falling dreams indicate the presence of internalized fears around our ambitions – the fear of falling from power or position.

PERSONAL INTERPRETATIONS

Any of these interpretations may be true in some circumstances, but since our dreams are personal to us, we also need to take into account our situation, experience and feelings, together with the details of the dream itself, before we can try to understand what it means.

Flying in our dreams is often quite a positive and liberating experience, as it suggests that we have shed the physical limitations of being earthbound. Flying high can be aspirational – think of the concept of "soaring to new heights" – or it could suggest that

we are seeking a new perspective on some aspect of our lives. We may find ourselves "flying in the face of something", trying to escape from the narrowness of social conventions or the dull routine of daily life perhaps, or it could be something more urgent or threatening that we are trying to escape from. Our dream flight could just be the frustrating business of not being able to get airborne, despite a monumental effort to do so, in which case you should look closely at what is holding you back; similarly see if there are any obstructions or other difficulties in flying, as these could indicate things that are hindering you in your life.

Falling may be liberating, but it is more likely to be linked to a loss or reduction of some kind, such as falling from power or from grace. It may represent loss of control – hence the expression "falling in love" – or it may be about getting into trouble. We talk of "falling out of favour" or even just "falling out" with someone, and any of these could be suggested in your dreams. The

RIGHT Dreams of falling may jolt us awake with a start as we come to "land". Notice what it is in your dream that breaks your fall – is it something soft and safe or is it more precarious? What does this mean to you?

feeling of falling into an abyss may point to the actual process of falling asleep, losing consciousness, or losing awareness or sensation. In any case, note whether you catch on to something while you fall, which could indicate a reprieve or point to something that might help you. Also see whether the landing – if it happens – is hard or soft, and what you land on – you may land in a safety net or plunge into a pool of water.

FLIGHTS OF FANCY
If you lie down and close your eyes, the resulting loss of visual stimulation means that you concentrate much more on your other senses. Physical sensations are particularly intense. But within a few minutes your body will probably be so relaxed that you will feel little other than your breathing. Concentrating on the

rhythm of your breathing in this way gives a sensation of movement. Add to this the lack of visual stimulation, the relaxed bodily posture, plus sleepiness, darkness and quiet, and you have pretty well all you need to imagine you are flying. The same goes for falling. If you lie down, close your eyes and roll your eyes upwards, the sensors in your feet that tell your brain about your spatial orientation and position get turned off, and your brain assumes that you are in freefall. The feelings of flying and falling that the brain generates may get translated into dream material.

BELOW LEFT The desire for flight has always been a source of fascination for us. Until we invented machines to help us fly, we could only experience it in our dreams.
BELOW It is not by chance that we use the phrase "falling asleep". The physical sensations are similar to falling, which may explain where some of our falling dreams come from.

MAZES AND BEING LOST

BEING LOST IN OUR DREAMS MAY BE AS SIMPLE AS FEELING LOST IN OUR WAKING LIFE. CERTAINLY THE SYMBOLIC VALUE OF MAZES AND LABYRINTHS IN OUR DREAMS IS ABOUT BEING LOST. WE MAY BE LOST THROUGH PHYSICAL DISORIENTATION, CONFUSION OR MISUNDERSTANDING, LOSS OR LONELINESS OR THROUGH OTHER DIFFICULTIES. THE THEME OF BEING LOST COULD ALSO POINT TO A MORE COMPLEX ISSUE, HOWEVER, AND IT IS BEST NOT TO JUMP TO QUICK AND EASY CONCLUSIONS, BUT TAKE SOME TIME TO WORK OUT THE DETAILS OF THE DREAM AND WHAT THEY MIGHT MEAN.

Mazes and labyrinths both consist of a network of pathways, but while a maze is designed to get you lost, a labyrinth has a definite goal at its heart. There may be a whole system of forked paths and dead ends but they are there to steer you towards the centre, to stop you retracing your steps and finding your way out.

A maze will often take you round in circles before spitting you out where you first began. It isn't designed to take you inward and indeed may deliberately keep you from the centre.

BEING LOST

When we dream of mazes and labyrinths, what is important is finding out why we are lost, what it is that we are turning away from. We all encounter difficulties and fears from time to time, but while some of us get on with trying to work them out, others feel unable to address them immediately and prefer to set them aside until they feel strong or clear-headed enough to do so. For the latter, this may manifest as dreams in which we are lost or misled, where we can't find our way out of a situation or to a place of safety. We struggle in the maze, held captive by our confusion. The reason we are being given the dream is not necessarily to spur us on – although that may be part of it – but rather to give us some insight into how to get out simply and easily. The dream is like a map written in code, and we can

DREAM OF BEING LOST

"I was underground, caving in a series of potholes with a friend. He had the map but it fell into a pool of deep water. We were lost and the light from our helmet torches began to fade. We were standing in a cave with many exits. We were concerned that there were underground lakes we would fall into so we felt we had to go up. Suddenly a bat flew out of nowhere and disappeared up one of the shafts. We knew which way we had to go: the bat had shown us the way.

Later on I realized that I was feeling bad about my job. I had wanted to study biology but had done accounts because it seemed a more practical career choice. I guess the bat was telling me to start again, to be true to myself. Once I did this the whole of my life seemed to improve."

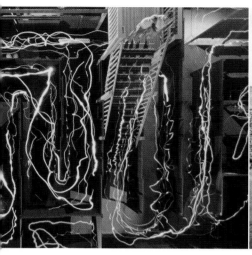

study our dream to see if we were helped through the dream maze by something or someone. This may be someone we know or a stranger; it may be some sort of angelic being or even an animal, wild or domestic.

THE CONFUSION OF CHOICE

Mazes and labyrinths often involve making a series of choices. If we make the right decisions we get to where we want to be, achieving a goal or clarity. If we make the wrong choices we remain lost, or land up where we began. It can be hard to remain clear-headed in such a situation, and if we are confused, making choices becomes a difficult process, and one in which we may easily make mistakes. The dream may well be helping us to make the choice based on intuition or on information that hasn't been accessible to our conscious mind.

The fact that we are in a maze in our dreams may even simply be warning us that some aspect of our lives is more complicated than we thought, and that we should pay attention to the complexity of the choices we have to make. In your dream, look at the nature of your decision-making process – whether it is impulsive or random, or calm and rational, based on carefully weighed up factors. Notice whether it is effective, and whether you are alone in the maze, and if not, does your companion help you or distract or mislead you? The answer to these questions may reveal the extent to which you can rely on others in your decision-making, how much trust you feel, or whether you want and are able to "go it alone".

ABOVE The symbolism of the stylized maze is a very powerful one, and one that your dream self will love to explore.
ABOVE LEFT Notice your surroundings in your dream. Are you where you want to be?
ABOVE FAR LEFT When we get our wires crossed, things get confusing. Our dreams may show us how to untangle the obstacles.

LEFT Are you lost and alone in your dream or is there someone who can lend you a helping hand? See if you can relate this to your life. Do you tend to struggle on alone because you find it hard to ask for support?

EXITS AND ENTRANCES

PHYSICALLY, AN ENTRANCE AND AN EXIT ARE SIMPLY TWO SIDES OF THE SAME OPENING, WHETHER IT IS A DOORWAY OR SOME OTHER KIND OF OPENING. ALTHOUGH THEY ARE PHYSICALLY IDENTICAL, WHAT DIFFERENTIATES ONE FROM THE OTHER IS YOUR VIEWPOINT AND WHICH WAY YOU PASS THROUGH. DOORWAYS MIGHT ALSO SYMBOLIZE A WHOLE VARIETY OF DIFFERENT THINGS IN YOUR LIFE; AN ENTRANCE OR AN EXIT MIGHT REPRESENT AN ESCAPE FROM A PROBLEM OR AN UNPLEASANT CIRCUMSTANCE, OR IT MIGHT BE A TEMPTATION TO ESCAPE FROM RESPONSIBILITY AND REALITY. WHEN YOU DREAM OF PORTALS YOUR INTERPRETATION WILL DEPEND ON THE CIRCUMSTANCES AROUND YOU.

Freud would no doubt have attributed some sexual meaning to exits and entrances, while others suggest, for instance, that doors opening outward indicate a need to express yourself more and those opening inward a need to explore some aspect of your inner being. Each of these interpretations may fit in some circumstances, depending on the context in which the door appears in the dream and on your own circumstances. But even if they do fit, it is also important to find out more about the dream and how and why the doorway features – the kind of

BELOW Every exit is also an entrance and vice versa – it depends on which way we look at it. **BELOW RIGHT** Dreams about exits and entrances may be trying to tell us something about the transitions that are going on in our waking life.

entrance, whether it is you or someone else who is opening the door, and whether you are going in or out, for instance. It may be a small doorway, a huge gateway, or a cleft in a mountainside, and you should take note of the kind of structure it is part of as this may also be significant.

TRANSITIONS

An entrance or exit marks a transition from one space to another – spaces that may be similar, such as two rooms in a house, or quite different from each other, like an interior space and a garden. This could suggest

being at some kind of threshold or making an adjustment in your life, so look at how the transition works in your dream. Perhaps you make a grand entrance to the applause of a crowd, or you have to squeeze through, or maybe you slip between one dream scene and another without really noticing how you do so. These scenarios may all say something about how comfortable you are with the transition, whether or not you look forward to it, and how easy or difficult it is.

Every time you move from one space to another you are making an entrance and an exit at the

same time, so it is worth looking at which aspect of the movement draws your attention – leaving or arriving, getting out of a place or going in. Sometimes you may be poised on the threshold itself, in a sort of limbo. How you feel about the space you are leaving behind as well as the one you are entering may also give important clues about the meaning of the transition – say, whether you have any regrets, or are relieved to be moving on. Whether or not you can retrace your steps will have a bearing on how easy it is to make your entrance or exit.

Transitions in your life may be physical ones, such as moving house, starting a new job, or going to live in a new country. But the entrances and exits in your dream can also be about emotional or spiritual thresholds, such as starting a brand new relationship or ending an existing one, or about the transition between consciousness and unconsciousness, or many others.

CLOSURE

Exits can be about achieving closure, about ending a period in your life or a way of being so that you can move on. You may need to start something afresh or begin a new venture, and it may be important for you to be able to leave behind any "baggage" you may have been carrying.

EXCLUSION

Sometimes the entrance in your dream is tantalizingly or frustratingly impassable; perhaps it's something that is perfectly visible but just beyond your reach. It may be a locked door, or a skylight up in the roof, or a barred window; if you encounter one of these, ask yourself if there are situations in your life from which you feel barred or excluded. Or perhaps you can see a way forward to something you want but are not sure how to get to it because there are obstacles in the way; if this is the case, see whether there was any

alternative route to the place you were trying to get to in your dream, or someone who could help you unlock the door or reach the skylight. These could suggest alternative ways of achieving what you are after in your waking life.

ABOVE Our dreams can show us that we have an opportunity to step out into new terrain.
ABOVE LEFT Sometimes the exits and entrances in our dreams are out of reach. We may want to go there, but it is impossible or too dangerous just now.

EXITS AND ENTRANCES DREAM

"There was a cocktail party going on in a large room that was accessed by a large door off a long corridor. There were lots of people standing around talking, smoking, eating and drinking. I kept walking in and out of this big doorway, I was the only one that was coming and going. Each time I came in I fell over, more and more drunk, and people kept turning round to look at me, but I didn't care. As soon as I went out and was standing in the corridor I was quite sober again.

For me, a cocktail party is the kind of boring, formal, old-fashioned function that older people like my parents would go to. The people at the party were all drinking, but they could handle it while I just got really drunk. But I was deliberately playing the fool each time I came in, perhaps as a way of rebelling against the older people.

I think the dream was actually about the prospect of joining my parents' business. I thought I'd come round to the idea but the dream showed that I haven't really – I actually find the business boring, and I think I'm too young to be getting into something like that! I'd rather find my own way through life, and do the kind of things my friends are doing."

BUILDINGS

LIKE US, BUILDINGS HAVE A LIFESPAN — THEY DEGENERATE, DECAY AND FALL INTO DISUSE. IN OUR DREAMS THEY COULD REPRESENT US AND WE MAY NEED TO LOOK AT WHAT POINT IN OUR OWN LIFE THE BUILDING IS TRYING TO BE. SOME DREAM INTERPRETATIONS SUGGEST THAT BUILDINGS REPRESENT THE DREAMER'S BODY, AND THIS DOES SEEM TO FIT WITH SUCH EXPRESSIONS AS "MY BODY IS A TEMPLE". BUT IF THE STRUCTURE IN YOUR DREAM ISN'T A TEMPLE BUT AN ART DECO CINEMA SHOWING OLD GANGSTER MOVIES, OR A DISUSED TIN MINE, OR HIGH-RISE CITY OFFICE BLOCKS, YOU MAY NEED TO EXPLORE MORE DEEPLY WHAT THE STRUCTURE MEANS TO YOU. IT IS ALSO POSSIBLE THAT ONLY PART OF A BUILDING IS RELEVANT.

In some cases you can take the buildings in your dreams at face value – as nothing more than a literal part of the scenery. Your unconscious has to set the dream somewhere and a building you know well may be used because it is a familiar and appropriate setting for the events of the dream. If the surroundings fit then you can probably discount them, but if the building is strange or unusual or disjointed in any way though, you need to look closer.

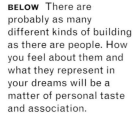

BELOW There are probably as many different kinds of building as there are people. How you feel about them and what they represent in your dreams will be a matter of personal taste and association.

TYPES OF BUILDING

The function of the building in your dream could be a big clue to its meaning. For example, churches or temples are likely to be associated with your spiritual side or your relationship to religion, while a bridge may signify that you need to cross some obstacle or forge a link between two people or things or ideas. Underground structures, such as basements, mines or cellars, may be particularly relevant if you are currently in the process of exploring and uncovering deeply rooted personal issues. And you are likely to have quite different feelings around an industrial building such as a factory or power plant from those connected with a little cottage.

Different people will also have different responses to the same setting – for instance, you may find a factory a noisy, smelly and confusing or overwhelming place to be, but for someone else its salient feature could be that it is to do with mass-production or innovation and newness, in which case it could be to do with innovation or progress in some important aspect of their life.

APPEARANCE

Particular qualities of the building may come to your attention and have specific relevance – either the materials or the style, the state of repair, or perhaps some element such as a chimney or staircase.

The clean lines and cold, reflective materials of a modern building may suggest orderliness or control in your life, forward-thinking or a detachment from your heritage, while a rustic cottage with rough wooden beams and a lived-in feel could indicate a feeling of comfort or security. Since our response to styles and materials is highly personal, however, you will need to see the building in the context of your own personal feelings and tastes.

The state of the buildings or other structures can provide another layer of significance to the basic meaning of the building. Clean and orderly or dirty, well maintained or falling apart – if you see the building as some aspect of your own being then the state of repair and cleanliness could indicate how you view yourself. A shabby or neglected building may be hinting that you need to look after yourself more, that you don't value yourself enough or suffer from low self-esteem.

The dream is an involuntary kind of poetry.

JEAN PAUL RICHTER

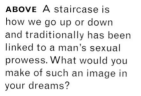

ABOVE Some buildings will take on an otherworldly quality in our dreams, as though they are trying to tell us something very deep and instinctive.

ABOVE A staircase is how we go up or down and traditionally has been linked to a man's sexual prowess. What would you make of such an image in your dreams?

STAIRCASES

It is often said that a staircase is symbolic of a man's sexual prowess, ambition or career progress. It could mean any or none of these things, but notice how important it is in your dream – as in life, it could just have a practical function and simply be a means of getting about between floors in your dream narrative. If your unconscious wants to draw your attention to your sexual prowess, it may well choose a more obvious symbol.

In any case, it is worth considering that staircases allow you access to higher places, and that you may be using the stairs as a symbol for your ability to progress or achieve greater status; conversely descending a staircase may show a loss of these things. A staircase may also transport you between different states of consciousness or the higher and lower aspects of your being. Elevators and escalators may act in the same way as staircases, and help you on your way, but bear in mind that you are taking an "easy ride" by using them.

ABOVE A tall, upright building may represent a desire to be seen. Notice how the buildings appear in your dreams – are they new or old, clean or dirty?

ABOVE Buildings get old and fall into disuse. What would a dream of a ruined building mean for you? Is there something you have been neglecting and would like to repair?
RIGHT Factory buildings can appear alien and overpowering, although they may also represent work and progress.

BELOW How we view buildings in our dreams can tell us a lot about how we see ourselves. Here a city landscape towers above an area of domestic housing.

HOMES AND DWELLINGS

OUR HOUSES AND HOMES ARE EXTREMELY IMPORTANT TO US. EVEN BEFORE WE MOVE INTO A NEW PLACE, WE OFTEN MAKE ELABORATE PLANS ABOUT HOW TO MAKE IT OURS. WE DECORATE, RE-ORGANIZE THE ROOMS AND BUILD EXTENSIONS IN AN ATTEMPT TO PUT OUR PERSONAL STAMP ON IT. OUR AIM IS TO HAVE A HOME THAT IS SAFE, WARM, AND COMFORTABLE. IN OUR DREAMS A HOUSE IS OFTEN A MARK OF THESE THINGS AND CAN SHOW US ABOUT OUR SENSE OF SELF AND HOW SECURE WE FEEL. IF A HOUSE OR OUR HOME BECOMES A SCARY, THREATENING PLACE IN OUR DREAMS, THEN THAT MAY BE HOW WE VIEW IT IN OUR WAKING LIFE AND IT COULD BE SOMETHING WE NEED TO LOOK AT MORE CLOSELY.

A SAFE HAVEN

When we are at home we feel secure and more able to cope with the difficulties in our lives and the things that we find threatening. In our lives and our dreams alike, it can be a base to return to from our forays into a potentially dangerous and unpredictable world, and for many of us, the home is the centre of our life, our heart. The houses in our dreams are often familiar to us, and an obvious line of questioning you should pursue concerns the person who lives there, what they are like and what your relationship to them is. The home you grew up in or the house of a favourite aunt or grandparent is likely to be filled with a great many memories and reminders of your childhood, and could signify a nostalgia for these times, or perhaps be bringing to your attention an issue that arose at the time you were living there or visiting often.

ATTRIBUTES

If you dream of an unfamiliar house, it is the qualities of the building that are important. It is more likely to represent some aspect of yourself – your body, your personality, or your sense of who you are. You should ask yourself what it is about this particular building that has made you represent yourself in this way.

A big, grand house may show a need to expand your horizons or capabilities, to establish yourself more solidly, or to make a bolder statement to the world about yourself; on the other hand if you find in your dream, for instance, that you live in a mansion but are stressed by the upkeep, it may indicate that you feel you have taken on something that is bigger than you can handle. Equally, a small cottage may be cosy and comfortable or cramped and mean. If the house or furnishings are shabby, ask yourself if there is something you have done that would generate such a feeling. A tidy and well-maintained house may show a healthy self-regard or clarity of mind.

ROOMS

The rooms in a house allow us to compartmentalize aspects of our lives. Different areas of our lives may be represented by the function of particular rooms – the bedroom for sleep, sex and relaxation, the dining room for nourishment, the living room for leisure and sociability. So how you feel and what you are doing in each of these rooms could be

BELOW Our dreams often have a fairytale quality to them and can surprise us. Opening the kitchen cupboard to find fluffy white clouds inside could suggest a desire to be transported from the humdrum routine of domestic life.

key to understanding how comfortable you are with these different aspects of your life.

Rooms are also said to represent your potential. If a room is familiar it signals your current or past capabilities, whereas an unfamiliar room could be showing you your unfulfilled potential; whether you are eager to explore it or back out and close the door may show how ready you are to realize that potential. Sometimes the houses in our dreams have hidden rooms or rooms that we are forbidden to enter. These may represent unexplored parts of ourselves or parts that we feel are taboo.

BUILDING A HOUSE

To dream of building a house might mean that you are interested in building greater security or turning an increase in prosperity into something concrete, though you will have to decide for yourself whether this type of interpretation seems correct. Different aspects of the building process may carry particular meanings as well. For instance, laying foundations may indicate establishing yourself, or creating a stable base for some project or aspect of your life.

Dreaming about a building project going awry could be about unforeseen problems or obstacles. Notice what building materials are being used and see what this means for you.

BELOW LEFT Most of us aspire to owning our own home. Your dreams can show you how realistic your expectations are. **MIDDLE LEFT** We all have a stylized, idyllic image of perfect living. We may visit this place in our dreams for reassurance. **BOTTOM LEFT** To dream of a stately home or a large house may mean that we need to expand our horizons and "think big".

DREAM OF A ROOM

"My mother was driving me mad. I fled upstairs, but although there are only two flights of stairs in my house in real life, I ran up three flights of stairs in my dream. At the top I found myself in a lovely attic room, full of warmth and light and nice comfy chairs. It was decorated in wonderful lush fabrics and rich colours, and there was a smell of incense in the air. This seemed to be the happiest room I had ever been in and I felt so safe and comfortable here.

This was my own space, which I created in my dream as a refuge, a place where my troubles – in the form of my mother – could not follow me, and it was a place where I felt I could really be myself."

TOOLS AND MACHINES

THE DEVELOPMENT OF TOOLS AND MACHINES IS PART OF WHAT IT MEANS TO BE HUMAN. FROM THE EARLIEST TIMES, WE HAVE DEVELOPED TOOLS TO HELP US WORK MORE EFFECTIVELY AND TO INCREASE THE RANGE OF TASKS WE ARE CAPABLE OF PERFORMING. TOOLS AND MACHINES ENABLE US TO DO A MULTITUDE OF THINGS. THEY RANGE IN SIZE AND COMPLEXITY FROM THE SIMPLE PAPERCLIP TO THE VAST AND COMPLICATED STRUCTURE OF AN OIL-RIG OR SPACESHIP. OUR QUEST FOR PROGRESS AND IMPROVEMENT MEANS THAT TECHNOLOGY, WHICH BRINGS ABOUT THE CHANGES TO OUR TOOLS, OUR MACHINES AND MANY ASPECTS OF OUR ENVIRONMENT, IS AN EVER-PRESENT PART OF OUR LIVES.

TOOLS

When we think of tools the first thing that springs to mind may be carpentry or gardening equipment, but in fact we use all sorts of objects and even employ abstract ideas to manipulate our environment or to help us do a task – so a stick becomes a tool when we use it to draw in the sand or prop open a gate, and we can use our dreams as tools for understanding those issues in our lives to which we need to pay more attention.

In your dreams look for tools being used inappropriately or ones that are malformed or malfunctioning. If the person using the tool is right and the tool fits the purpose, then you could look beyond it to the job of work that is being done. Bear in mind though, that "rightness of fit" may in fact be just what your unconscious mind is trying to demonstrate: you need to use the right tool for the job.

MACHINES

There are also complex tools that enable us to undertake bigger and more complicated tasks. Machines do not require the same effort from us as hand tools as they have their own source of energy. This gives them a more human quality – they need fuel to work just as we need food; they emit waste; and some also look vaguely human. Sometimes we even give them names and refer to them fondly as "she" or "he". Because of this affinity to machines and the fact that we use them constantly, they may appear in our dreams as symbols for our own efforts and abilities.

BELOW MIDDLE Simple tools can symbolize complex issues: what do you need to sweep away?
BELOW RIGHT Being able to assemble things in a logical way is a skill that you may need to develop.
BELOW Computers are an integral part of modern life and can appear in our dreams in unusual ways.

MACHINE DREAM

"I was inside some sort of giant machine with cogs and wheels made of brightly coloured plastic, and a lot of wires and sparking electrical connections. I couldn't work out what this machine did, or what part of it I was in. I helped make it run but I had no idea how.

I had recently become a father, and the dream confirmed for me that however wonderful our baby was, I was extremely worried about my new role, about how to cope with the baby and how to understand his needs. The clue that linked the dream to my life situation was the plastic parts which reminded me of the Lego I played with as a child."

TECHNOLOGY DREAM

"I dreamt that I was trying to get my cash card into an ATM, but the card kept bending and slipping away; the more I pushed the softer it became and the less I could insert it. I suppose if I had been a man this dream would easily have been interpreted as being about impotence, but in my case I was anxious about some exams that were looming. I was worried that when I got into the exam room my brain would go soft and everything I had studied so hard to remember would slip out of my mind at the time when I most needed it. "

MACHINES IN DREAMS

Not all machines have a human quality. Sometimes they are big and impersonal, even menacing. Machines can be immensely powerful and unyielding – they can crush us if we get in the way, they tower over us and we can feel intimidated. They may even chase us, or simply have a dark and brooding presence. These qualities may mean the machines in our dreams become symbols of intimidation, of powerful forces or inevitability in the face of our powerlessness. Not knowing how to use a machine may also make us feel disadvantaged and we may employ this scenario in a dream to represent our frustrations or limitations.

FUNCTIONS

Often it is the function of the tool or machine that is important in our dreams. A dredger, for example, easily symbolizes the process of drawing up and bringing to light the contents of the murky depths. We might just have chosen a simple bucket and spade to dig up mud, but a full-size dredger is a more captivating and obvious image. In looking at the function of the tool or machine, also consider what it is the machine is acting on – what it is uncovering or burying, neatening off, transporting, shattering or moulding. Each of these actions may relate to something that is happening to you in your waking life.

TECHNOLOGY

In our dreams, technology may represent a threat to traditional values and ways of doing things, and may bring up feelings of fear or anxiety. For technology is a powerful symbol of movement and unstoppable change. This may leave us feeling left behind, confused or alienated, and it could also be a symbol for us to slow down. Technology can also represent cool efficiency and be tremendously empowering and exciting. It makes our lives easier and enables us to do a wider range of things more quickly and with less effort. Computers, mobile phones and DVD players as well as washing machines, cars and countless other devices are all part of modern technology and can appear in our dreams.

ABOVE Large machinery can symbolize a menacing and inhuman presence in our dreams. Check to see who or what is intimidating you and revisit the dream to see if it offers a clue about how to deal with the problem.

BELOW New technology allows us to bring the past into the present. Is there anything you need to update in your life? **BELOW LEFT** A tool that doesn't work properly hinders progress. Use your dream to check what isn't working in your life.

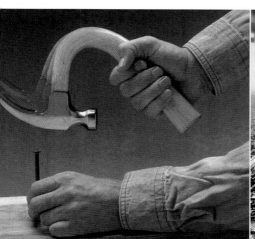

TRAVEL

In difficult times we often wish we could escape, get right away and leave our troubles behind us rather than struggle on with trying to solve them. We may dream of travel, of being on the road or flying off into the blue yonder. But travel dreams are not always escapist; they may represent our journey through life and the paths we take, or perhaps they reflect an eagerness to broaden our horizons. They are also important symbols of transition and change — our desire for some kind of change in ourselves or our circumstances, our fears around change, or our need to change.

ABOVE Travel dreams can show us where we are going in life. Notice if you are alone or with others, moving or stationary?
ABOVE RIGHT Seen from above, a complex network of roads may not look so confusing. Maybe a fresh perspective is called for?

THE JOURNEY

Because dream travels can be so varied, you will need to ask a number of questions about the nature of the journey in your dream — where you were going, the purpose of the journey, whether you were on foot or in a vehicle, travelling at speed or dawdling along. What the journey and the terrain were like and who your travelling companions were, if any, are also worth considering.

MAPS

If there was a plan or route involved in your travelling dream it is worth examining what they were like and what help they gave you. Maps can give you an overview of your journey and help you to plan a route or see where you are, but if they are unclear or misleading, don't

relate to the places you pass through, or you simply can't decipher them, this may suggest you are lacking direction in life.

DEPARTURES AND DESTINATIONS

Many a dream journey has no real starting point or end point. Instead you may simply have a

sense of being on the road to nowhere or needing to be on the move, or you may be exploring a place and seeing what it has to offer. These types of journey may have very different meanings. Not knowing where you are going can be highly significant, as it could show that you need to explore what you want out of

RIGHT Paths wind and diverge as we tread our way through life, and a dream may reflect this.

life, where you want your life journey to lead. On the other hand, it may be that getting left behind or being late may be the key issues, rather than where you are coming from or going to. If you do remember the beginning of your dream journey, it is worth looking at the starting point closely. It may represent something you are trying to run away from, or it could be a part of your past that you are ready to leave behind. The kind of departure may give a clue to which meaning is true for you.

Destinations are likely to be about goals and desires if you have chosen them, although they could equally be about situations that you are afraid of getting into if you don't seem to have control over where you are going.

TRAVELLING COMPANIONS

For the solo traveller, the journey may be a lonely one, but one in which you can be in charge,

make all the decisions and take responsibility for whatever happens along the way. If you do have travel companions, though, ask yourself what they are like, whether they are people you know or not, and how they behave on the journey. A loving, supportive companion may indicate that there is someone

you can take with you on your journey through life, while a person who hijacks your plans, dogs your footsteps, or insists on leading the way or having the best seat may be pointing to issues around people who are in some way interfering with your own plans.

People you meet along the way may help or hinder your journey, rescuing you from difficult situations or misleading you. These may be archetypal figures or may relate to actual people in your life who may be helping or obstructing your plans or goals.

LEFT Maps help us pinpoint where we are going. Is your map easy or hard to decipher?
MIDDLE LEFT Notice if your fellow travellers are good to be with or if they are annoying you.
FAR LEFT If your life feels like a long desert trek, remember that deserts also have their beauty and you can adapt to survive.

TRAVEL DREAM

"I had a dream in which travel was very prominent and obviously meant something important but I didn't know immediately what it was. I was crossing the Nevada desert in a red sports car, heading towards Las Vegas, where I was going to go gambling. Although I was alone, I could feel the presence of a blonde woman who may have just got out of the car.

I don't normally gamble in my waking life, but in relationships I can sail pretty close to the wind. I recently had a relationship with someone I was very fond of, and I now really regret messing her about. She was right to dump me. I guess I was gambling with her life and her future, and I lost. Maybe she was the woman who had just got out of my car in my dream. I think it's quite revealing that it was a red sports car as well. Although I don't own one it does symbolize the freedom and energy of youth to me."

VEHICLES

236

IF THE TRAVELS IN OUR DREAMS ARE ABOUT ESCAPING OR ABOUT OUR LIFE JOURNEY, VEHICLES ARE THE MACHINES THAT MOVE US FROM ONE PLACE TO ANOTHER, PROVIDING OUR MEANS OF ESCAPE OR PROGRESS. THE TYPE OF VEHICLE WE CHOOSE TO REPRESENT IN OUR DREAMS MAY GIVE US CLUES TO THE NATURE OF OUR JOURNEY, AND ITS STATE OF REPAIR CAN SHOW US HOW OUR JOURNEY IS PROGRESSING. DIFFERENT KINDS OF FEAR OR UNEASE WILL PROBABLY SURFACE IN YOUR DREAMS; DO YOU HAVE A FEAR OF FLYING OR A TERROR OF BEING LOST AT SEA? PERHAPS EVERYDAY MEANS OF TRANSPORT, SUCH AS BUSES OR TRAINS MAKE YOU FEEL UNEASY, PACKED FULL AS THEY ARE WITH OTHER TRAVELLERS.

MEANS AND MEDIUM OF TRANSPORT

In looking at the kind of vehicle in which we are travelling in our dreams, it is useful to consider how and where the vehicle usually travels as well as its speed and if we have control over it.

Travelling on the ground may have quite different implications to flying or going by boat, as earth, air and water have their own complex sets of symbolic meanings that also need to be considered. So road travel could indicate groundedness and practicality, while flying may suggest ideas and fancies, and water an emotional journey. Getting airborne could be an allusion to our ideas or plans taking off and coming to fruition.

We also have preferences and feelings around different means

BELOW There are many types of vehicle. The ones we choose in our dreams can say a lot about us.
BELOW RIGHT Dreams of driving a car are quite common. Are you in control or is disaster looming ahead?

of transport – for instance, catching a bus when we are used to travelling in a chauffeur-driven car may have implications of loss of status, of reliance on public services instead of self-sufficiency, of having to wait, of being part of an anonymous crowd instead of having individual attention. Depending on whether or not the journey goes smoothly, the dream may be allaying fears around these issues or confirming your worst nightmares. Meandering down a lane on a bicycle can take a long time, and you may be frustrated at the slow pace or choose to enjoy the countryside as you go; it could also give you a sense of being in control as you can decide your route as well as where you stop. Space travel, by contrast, may suggest exploration of the unknown, and as we

hurtle at an incredible speed into the vast emptiness of space, away from everything and everyone that we know and love, we may feel lonely and isolated. We may also use a space ship to represent the pinnacle of technology, change and progress.

Many people are afraid of flying or boats, so dreams of travelling in these may well be bringing to the fore some of the insecurities you may have around not being on terra firma.

CARS AND DRIVING

As they are such an integral part of our lives, cars often feature in our dreams. We attach meanings to owning or being seen in certain kinds of car, and may use these meanings to represent certain things in our dreams. So a sports car implies power and

success – material, personal and sexual – while a sedan can be associated with families and stability, an off-road vehicle with adventure and exploration, and a truck with carrying a load. The condition of the vehicle may say a lot about how we are in relation to these aspects of our lives, while whether we own it or have borrowed or stolen it could be telling us about whether we feel we deserve them.

ACCIDENTS AND BREAKDOWNS

Derailment, car crashes or sinking boats are all powerful symbols of things going wrong in our lives, especially if we are involved in the accident, and can be taken as a warning. The scale of the accident can be used as an indicator for the seriousness of the problem – so a scrape in a parking lot may be a gentle warning, but a full passenger plane exploding in mid-air over the sea could be a more urgent message. Unlike accidents, hijackings are deliberate, and may be warning you that someone wants to take over your life or is holding you to ransom.

A vehicle that breaks down may be saying that your life is running into difficulties, or that you need to call a halt to ideas of escape. If this is the case, looking at exactly how it malfunctioned could give you a more precise picture of the area of your life that has broken down. Brake failure could show that you are unable to slow down or stop; running out of power is likely to be about your lack of energy.

ABOVE Some vehicles are very complex and need great knowledge and expertise to operate.
LEFT There is a simplicity and freedom about riding a bicycle. It is low maintenance and you are self-sufficient.
BELOW Launching into outer space could be thrilling or frightening. You would have to check how it is for you.

Magic and Fantasy

Magical, mystical people, mythical beasts, heroes and demons parade through our dreams, inspired by the fictions and superstitions of our culture and brought to life by our imagination as metaphors for our hopes and desires, for the irrational terrors of our early years, and even for the tricksters and con artists we meet as we go about our daily lives. We also use them to access possibilities beyond the mundane reality of everyday life, to help us shed the conventional boundaries that keep our imagination earthbound, and give us the courage to bring the seemingly impossible within our reach.

These dreams can be tremendously challenging as we can take nothing for granted in this fantasy reality, removed from the context of the here and now, and in them we confront our fears and demons head-on. The underlying universal truths of the archetypal figures we sometimes meet allow us to get in touch with our deeper, instinctive levels of being.

FANTASTICAL DREAMS

DREAMS IN WHICH LANDSCAPES, CHARACTERS, MOTIFS AND PLOTS ARE FANTASTICAL OR SURREAL ARE AMONG THE MOST DIFFICULT TO INTERPRET AS THEY ARE NOT BASED IN OUR EVERYDAY EXPERIENCES AND WE HAVE NONE OF THE USUAL REFERENCE POINTS TO HELP US. FANTASY DREAMS CAN BE VERY UNSETTLING, SHAKING US OUT OF ROUTINE OR COMPLACENCY. THEY RETURN TO HAUNT OUR WAKING THOUGHTS AND DEMAND THAT WE STRIVE TO UNDERSTAND THEM — SWEEPING THEM UNDER THE CARPET OR IGNORING THEM SIMPLY DOESN'T WORK. THEY MAY LINGER FOR A LONG TIME AND BE QUITE HARD TO PURGE FROM OUR CONSCIOUSNESS.

FANTASY CHARACTERS

Dreams sometimes feature fantastical creatures – gentle, dreamy unicorns and ferocious dragons, seductive mermaids, fairies and elves, talking animals and a myriad others we may have created with or without the assistance of literature or legend. The creatures of our fantasies are part of our desire for things to be beyond the real world.

These creations may return us to our childhood where monsters lurked under the bed and the line between reality and fantasy was much more indistinct. They may be frightening or disturbing, forcing us to address our fears head-on, but sometimes they are wonderful, joyful creatures that show us new possibilities or have unimaginable love or wisdom. They may have exceptional powers, or take us to places that we can literally only dream of.

Creatures that we fabricate in our own minds, that are not found in myths or in the books we read as children, may have features that we take from several sources and combine into one character as a kind of catch-all for how we want to be or what we are most afraid of. It may be some idealized figure who will empower us, or a demon who threatens to destroy us.

FANTASY WORLDS

Dreams of fantasy may consist of unusual events or creatures set in surroundings that seem natural or familiar, or they may take place in weird and wonderful settings – a vast cavern that stretches upward as far as the eye can see, or the strange landscape of another planet; we may be floating in nothingness or surrounded by permeable membranes that melt away, leaving us in a new setting. In fantastical environments even the laws of nature may be different – gravity may be stronger or weaker, we may be able to do things we can't normally do, such as flying – and social structures may be incomprehensible. Great battles or forces of good and evil confronting each other directly strip away the mundane detail of our real lives, along with the rules of politics and diplomacy.

The fictitious worlds of literature are as varied as they are fantastical. Some, such as Tolkien's Middle Earth or C.S. Lewis's Narnia, may look like places we could visit, but the creatures that inhabit them and

BELOW Our dreams are very close to the hidden, magical world of the unconscious and many dreams have a fairy-tale quality about them.
BELOW RIGHT In fantasy dreams, unusual or mythical creatures are the products of a rich and fertile imagination.

key elements of the plot could only be found in fantasy. Alice in Wonderland has an explicitly surreal dream setting, although it has realistic elements alongside its talking animals, mutations, and spatial distortions. Or the infamous world of Harry Potter shows us ordinary boys and girls who are able to slip out of family life into a world where they have magical powers: people walk through walls and play games in mid-air; cars can fly and animals have special powers. Perhaps part of the reason that all these stories are so popular is that they each explore archetypal themes, such as the use of power or the struggle between good and evil.

TRANSFORMATION

Like the hybrid animals of mythology, fantastical elements may involve the coming together of objects or beings that are normally quite distinct, or the transformation of one thing into another. Material objects may take on unusual properties or space and time may be distorted. These transformations and mutations draw your attention to both the normal and the unusual properties of the objects or creatures, and you should try to reconcile both and notice what it is that is being distorted.

Fantasy dreams may represent all that we find exceptional about the world. They are our unconscious mind's way of being inventive and unconventional and can help us work through some very human issues. Fantastical or magical dreams also remind us that we are much more than logic and reasoning. We are creatures with a powerful imagination and have the ability to devise creative solutions to our problems and answers to some of the big questions about our very existence.

ABOVE Art and literature can provide a stimulus for the unconscious in its nightly dream production. Check the landscape of your dreams to see if there is anything you recognize. Is the narrative running as it should or has the story changed?

I suspect that there are more things in heaven and earth than are dreamed of, or can be dreamed of, in any philosophy.

J. B. S. HALDANE

LEFT Children are usually fascinated by magic and fantasy, perhaps because they are much closer to their instinctive feelings than most adults.
FAR LEFT The fantasy images we produce in our dreams will have a cultural emphasis. Traditionally, fairies are magical creatures who use their powers to either help or hinder us.

MYTHS AND LEGENDS

OUR DISTANT ANCESTORS TRIED TO FIND EXPLANATIONS FOR THE MANY PHENOMENA OF NATURE IN THE WORLD AROUND
THEM — THE SUN RISING, THE CHANGING SEASONS, AND CYCLES OF LIFE AND DEATH. BECAUSE THEIR KNOWLEDGE WAS
LIMITED, THEY DEVISED EXPLANATIONS BASED ON THE EXISTENCE OF SUPERHUMAN BEINGS, GODS AND GODDESSES WHO NOT
ONLY OFFERED AN EXPLANATION FOR WHY THINGS WERE THE WAY THEY WERE, BUT ALSO CREATED THE POSSIBILITY OF
INFLUENCING NATURE BY MEANS OF SACRIFICES, PRAYERS AND OFFERINGS. OTHER CREATURES PERFORMED SIMILAR ROLES —
FIRE-BREATHING DRAGONS, THE PHOENIX RISING FROM THE ASHES, GIANTS AND MERMAIDS.

LEFT Our dreams are a way of
entering the world of myths and
legends. By identifying with the
characters in our dreams we may
learn something about ourselves.

TIMELESS, UNIVERSAL TALES

In preliterate societies, the most
common way of passing on these
understandings, values and
beliefs was in memorable stories
that could be told and retold.
Their significance was easy to
understand, and the characters,
creatures and events that were
portrayed had a universal
relevance. In this way, stories
became part of the cultural
vocabulary of any society, and the
creatures of myth and legend are
deeply embedded in our psyche;
in our dreams we use them as
signposts to the qualities that
they embody, as icons.

ENTERING THE WORLD OF MYTH

In our dreams we are free to
enter mythical worlds. We can
don a mask or join a procession,
engage with the king or the fool,
the warrior priest or the god of
winter. We can even become that
character – try out its role, take
on its greatness.

These dreams put us in touch
with our instinctive and intuitive
selves – a side of us that may
need attention. They may be an
emotive plea from our
unconscious mind to dance in
the moonlight, to worship the
corn, to make a sacrifice or an
offering. But we are also fragile
beings who are subject to all
sorts of fears; myths both allay
those fears and add to them.

GODS AND GODDESSES

Mythical figures probably appear
in our dreams in much the same
way as they did to our ancestors.
In our dreams, making an
offering to calm a raging god
makes sense to us just as it did in
real life to our forebears. Our
unconscious processes have not
changed, although just as our
own personal experiences affect
how we understand any dream
element, our relationship with
these figures will be based on
how we respond to what they
typically represent to us.

We create gods and goddesses
so that we can feel safe and
protected, so that we can absolve
ourselves of responsibility for
something; but in their creation
we also unleash the terrible
aspects of such deities – death
and destruction, their capricious
nature, their awesome powers.
We create them to protect us but
we may also come to fear them,
and we learn to deal with this
dichotomy in dreams of myths.
We are shown that the qualities

and powers these supernatural beings have in abundance exist within us if we have the courage to acknowledge them.

HYBRID CREATURES

Myths and legends from around the world and through the ages are filled with creatures that are part animal and part human, or that are a mixture of two or three different creatures, and have an element of danger. Mermaids – half fish and half beautiful woman – have been blamed for many a shipwreck, as they lure sailors on to the rocks, while the sphinx, with the head of a woman and the body of a lion, is notorious for strangling travellers who cannot answer her riddles.

Minotaurs, griffins, satyrs and centaurs join the line-up of hybrid creatures from the realm of myth and legend. All have particular associations from the tales in which they feature, but they also embody qualities of the creatures they comprise. In this way, the sphinx may have qualities of femininity but also the ferocious, uncompromising strength of a lion, and by virtue of her behaviour in the Greek legend could represent any threatening and somewhat enigmatic character, particularly if associated with knowledge and learning, such as a punitive teacher. In a sense, by dreaming of a hybrid creature we are hedging our bets, or efficiently representing several qualities in a single character, trying to resolve anomalies in our lives.

PEOPLE

Not all the characters in myth and legend are fantastical. People appear throughout these tales, sometimes in elevated roles as kings and queens, other times as ordinary mortals who are caught up in greater things. Either way, they could be used to illustrate the ideals and extremes of human nature – heroism, bravery, love, power and so on. Such tales also illustrate some timeless human quandaries and problems, such as the tragedy of Oedipus, who unknowingly kills his father and marries his mother; the agony of the endless task of Sisyphus, who is obliged to push a rock up a hill, only to have it roll down as he has almost reached the brow. By working with these characters in our dreams, we work with the qualities that they embody and the battles that they fight.

ABOVE The mythical figures in our dreams usually have something very profound to convey.
ABOVE LEFT Hybrid creatures can remind us of the beast within us all.
ABOVE FAR LEFT Giant figures may assume the status of gods with the power to create or destroy life.

MYTHICAL DREAM

"In my dream I was walking through a forest. I could hear the birds singing and could feel the warmth of the sun on my skin. A soft breeze was blowing. As I walked, I came to a tiny cottage – it might sound far-fetched but it really did look like a gingerbread house, the kind you read about in fairy-tale stories. The house looked so inviting and I was tired and hot from walking, so I went up to the door and walked inside. I remember walking up a few stairs and going into a bedroom. It wasn't a room I had ever seen before. As I went in, I heard the front door downstairs click shut and the room I was in became shadowy. I started to feel afraid. There was a dark-haired man at the window and he was trying to get into the room. I tried to run away, but my legs wouldn't move. I woke up shouting.

At first it was difficult to revisit this dream or nightmare, but I decided to focus on what the man at the window represented. As I worked with the dream, to my amazement he turned into a golden-haired Apollo kind of figure, a sort of sun-god. I interpreted this to mean that I am afraid of my own power. I see it as something dark or "bad", so I try to run from it, but actually it radiates light."

ALIENS AND UFOs

WHEN FACED WITH THE UNKNOWN WE OFTEN TRY TO MAKE SENSE OF IT — IN THE FIRST INSTANCE IN TERMS OF WHAT WE ALREADY KNOW WELL, AND THEN PERHAPS IN TERMS OF CONCEPTS FROM THE REALM OF FANTASY OR SPECULATION, OF WHICH WE COULDN'T POSSIBLY HAVE ANY REAL EXPERIENCE. DREAMING OF ALIENS, SPACE SHIPS, FLYING SAUCERS AND SO ON MAY BE OUR WAY OF EXPLAINING AND VISUALIZING THE INEXPLICABLE SITUATIONS OR PHENOMENA THAT WE ARE TRYING TO UNDERSTAND AND COME TO TERMS WITH. WHEN WE HAVE TO FACE THE UNKNOWN WE TRY TO GIVE IT A FACE, A PERSONALITY. THE CREATURES FROM OUTER SPACE SERVE THIS PURPOSE WELL; THEY ARE, BY DEFINITION, ALIEN.

ALIENS

It is surprising how the aliens in our dreams are often very similar. How much this is due to us all watching the same films, and how much it is the manifestation of a new archetype that has developed in our collective unconscious, is difficult to tell. Indeed both could be true, and it is simply that the film-makers are the ones that give shape in a visual way to the archetype.

THE ALIEN WITHIN

Everything in a dream comes from within yourself – you create all of it for your own personal consumption, and there is nothing in it that is actually alien.

BELOW RIGHT Some of the most mysterious phenomena on Earth have been connected with aliens from outer space. **BELOW** When it comes to dreams of aliens and UFOs, there does seem to be some form of universal symbolism that we all understand.

If you are creating images of aliens then they represent some part of you that feels alienated or frightened of the unknown – or exhilarated by it. Some part of you is acknowledging an aspect of your life that is manifesting as alien or foreign, that has not been incorporated into your self-image, your lifestyle or your personal environment.

Aliens are often represented as scary, unpredictable creatures that seem bent on threatening our existence and invading our planet. In this way they provide an easy metaphor for situations in our own lives where we feel threatened or invaded by something or someone over

which we have little or no control. It is also significant that we have little understanding of these creatures – we cannot comprehend or anticipate their motives or intentions, and we often have no way of communicating with them. They are unknown and unknowable, and consequently we have no idea of the scale of the threat. Dreaming of aliens is often our way of working through situations that make us feel anxious – perhaps confronting head-on the source of our anxiety and allowing us to try out ways of dealing with it.

Many people feel that they do not fit into society; they feel

different from most other people they meet, and an encounter with aliens may be a positive, life-affirming experience. Being abducted by aliens may show a yearning for an alternative society where they feel they belong, or it could be an expression of belief in the existence of a society where they are valued.

SPACE TRAVEL

If aliens use UFOs as their vehicle for accessing or invading us, flying saucers, space ships and rockets might well also offer a dramatic avenue of escape for us. It may be that we actually want to break out of our limited world, and such craft offer us a way of literally reaching for the stars, exploring the unknown, having adventures not normally possible in real life. Seeing Earth receding into the distance may help us to stand back and see our world in perspective, in the context of the vastness of space.

ABOVE The concept of UFOs is fascinating. In our dreams they could represent a dramatic way of leaving the everyday world behind.
LEFT To dream the aliens are landing may mean that we should be prepared to encounter something new or strange in our lives.
BELOW When we break out in our dreams we may be trying to break out in our waking life. Spiralling weightless in the galaxy could suggest a spiritual, enlightening experience.

SPACE DREAM

"The sky was full of glowing space ships, full of smoking beings. We were firing guns and bullets at the space ships and the aliens were falling down dead everywhere, bleeping as they died. But there were more of them than I could count and they didn't all die – some were landing. Then I woke up."

This was the dream of a six-year-old child who was worried about starting in a new class at school. In his dream the aliens represented the threatening situation he was having to face and his lack of control over it.

PROPHECY

WE USUALLY FIND PROPHECY MANIFESTING IN DREAMS IN TWO DIFFERENT WAYS — FIRSTLY AS DREAMS IN WHICH WE FORESEE FUTURE EVENTS (OR FEEL THAT WE DO SO), AND SECONDLY AS DREAMS IN WHICH WE, OR OTHER CHARACTERS IN THE DREAM, ARE TRYING TO LOOK INTO THE FUTURE. WHETHER OR NOT YOU BELIEVE IT IS ACTUALLY POSSIBLE TO SEE INTO THE FUTURE, BOTH THESE KINDS OF DREAMS MIGHT SUGGEST THAT YOU FEEL A NEED TO DO SO; WHETHER IT IS THROUGH INSECURITY OR CURIOSITY IT IS WORTH ANALYSING WHY, OR WHAT IT IS YOU WANT TO FORESEE.

PROPHETIC DREAMS

There have been countless reports of people having a dream that changed their life. They saw an elevator accident, so the next day they took the stairs and the elevator plunged to the ground, killing everybody in it. Or they saw a ship sinking and cancelled their cruise holiday, although hundreds of other passengers perished. Or perhaps they may have dreamt of a car crash and saved their lives by catching the train the next day.

Perhaps we should be a little sceptical of these many urban legends. Only the success stories survive – we do not get to hear of those who took a different course of action than planned and this subsequently turned out to be the wrong thing to do. Nor do we hear of people who change their plans because of a dream and find that it made no significant difference in their lives. Dreams of prophecy are actually very rare. And yet in those cases that actually do turn out to be prophetic we are dealing with something outside of the normal, something mysterious and inexplicable. It's only when we have had a dream that came true ourselves that we can judge whether such a thing is possible. Once it has happened to us we believe, we know, we don't doubt.

It may also be that we dream how we want the future to be, and having already created the desired scenario, we find we are more able to make it happen. In this way the dream may seem prophetic, but it might be more accurate to think of it as a prompt or suggestion.

GAZING INTO THE FUTURE

Wanting to know what the future holds in store seems to be universal – no matter what society or what period in history you look at, you will find seers

---

PROPHECY DREAM

"I'm a keen tarot reader, so I'm not surprised when I find myself doing this in my dreams. In this dream I was with a female friend of mine who is single. She and I were having a glass of wine together, sitting on purple cushions. We started playing with the tarot, and she turned up the card of the Lovers. I remember thinking that I must remember to tell her, that it looked like she would meet someone special very soon.

I actually had forgotten the dream until a couple of months later, when sure enough my friend started a new relationship! Then the memory of the dream came flooding back and I told her what had happened. I think I need more practice in recalling my dreams if they are to be any use!"

and prophets, in addition to numerous tools or methods employed, often by ordinary people, to foretell events that have yet to happen.

In your dream the kind of person who is foretelling the future may be significant – is it one of the great prophets (a biblical figure, perhaps, or Nostradamus) whose predictions may hold the authority of their fame and greatness, or is it a fairground "gypsy" in fancy dress, who gazes into a crystal ball and puts on something of a performance for you, and may just be pulling the wool over your eyes? How credible they are and whether you believe in prediction is critical to how much you believe what you hear.

Some kinds of prediction rely on a kind of sixth sense, while others make use of consistent and well-established methods, such as tarot reading, palmistry, astrology or numerology, and to some extent make their projections on the basis of existing trends or patterns. Either way there may still be a leap of

faith. Much of our desire to see into the future is an expression of our desire for certainty and clarity in a world that is so uncertain and so complex that clarity is hard to find.

We turn to prophecy to help us make decisions we are faced with, or to reassure us that we

are on the right path. Dreaming of prophecy could be showing you that you need to make some choices, or clarify what the issues are before you can do so. You may fear something is going to happen, and express your anxiety by trying to find out what you are going to be faced with.

ABOVE Our desire to know what the future has in store is universal. The symbolism of tarot cards can be interpreted in a similar way to dreams.
ABOVE LEFT Whether or not we can see into the future is open to debate. To dream of gazing into a crystal ball may mean you are looking for direction.

LEFT Traditionally, virgin priestesses were attributed with the power of "second sight". If such a figure appears in your dreams pay particular attention to what she is trying to communicate – it could be very important.

MAGIC

IN ESSENCE, MAGIC IS ABOUT TWO THINGS — CHANGE AND POWER. WITH MAGIC, DRAMATIC TRANSFORMATION CAN BE BROUGHT ABOUT IN OUR LIVES, WHETHER WE ARE THE AGENTS OF CHANGE OR WHETHER SOME OTHER MAGICAL FIGURE IS ABLE TO PERFORM HIS OR HER ART ON US. WHOEVER HAS THE ABILITY TO PERFORM MAGIC HOLDS GREAT POWER, ESPECIALLY OVER THOSE ORDINARY MORTALS WHO DO NOT. WITH MAGIC WE CAN DO THINGS THAT WE ARE NOT NORMALLY ABLE TO DO, AND WE FEEL BOTH THE JOY AND THE DANGER OF HAVING THIS IMMENSE POWER. MAGIC CAN ALSO MEAN TRICKERY, HOWEVER, AND IT MIGHT BE THIS CHARACTERISTIC THAT WE ARE DREAMING OF.

ABOVE Animals often take on supernatural characteristics. If you dream of an unearthly creature you need to explore your dream fully to find out what it means. In some cultures a black cat is said to symbolize good luck.

TRANSFORMATION AND CHANGE

Dreams about magic may be a sign that we need to make changes, within ourselves or in our environment. They can be about movement or the lack of it, about being stuck and needing to make effort and expend energy in order to move on, to free ourselves from stagnation and from feeling stuck in a rut. Magic gives us an extra boost to get us to see things differently and get us moving again.

MAGIC AND POWER

In our dreams we can perhaps move objects, conjure up demons, raise a storm or calm a sea. We can kill or heal from a distance, transform people into other creatures with the wave of a wand, and become invisible.

We have probably all wished occasionally that we could do these things in our waking lives. This would give us tremendous power and perhaps it is this that we are after when we dream about magic. Sometimes it would be wonderful to wave a magic wand and make everything better, to change things that are in reality beyond our control — even to subjugate those who normally hold us in their power. We may take great delight for instance, in being able to turn a bullying boss into a tiny mouse, or an unfriendly neighbour into a puff of smoke.

Conversely, having magic performed on us, particularly if it is done against our will, or if it is done by characters who have bad intentions or who in our waking lives have authority over us, can be immensely disempowering and could be drawing our attention to a lack of power or control in our lives. A dream of losing powers that we felt we previously had can also have a similar effect.

HOPES AND FANTASIES

In a more general sense, though, dreaming of magic allows us to work out our fantasies — in our dreams nothing is impossible if we want it to come true, and we have the power to live out our hopes and desires. Dreams also prompt us to look at certain areas of our life that may be lacking in some way, and teach us what we need to do to make things happen. While in a literal way the tricks of magic in our dreams may only be possible in a dream world, their underlying truth can be carried into our daily lives and give us something to work with.

PURVEYORS OF MAGIC

In our dreams it is important to look at the nature and intentions of those who hold the magical powers — whether they are our allies or are threatening and potentially harmful characters is vital to understanding why we are dreaming of magic.

Witches and wizards, as well as magicians and sorcerers, may be sources of good or evil alike. Magicians enthral us with their sleight-of-hand performances, but such trickery may also be more than entertainment, prompting us to look at people in our lives who deceive and trick us, who are trying to pull the wool over our eyes. We need to

LEFT Witches, devils and impish creatures have traditional associations with magic. Check to see if the figures are benign or menacing and what it is they are trying to bring about in your dream.

look at how we might be living a lie, lulled into a false sense of security by our own illusions or those put out by others. In Jungian thought the archetype of the Magician is also known as the Fool, whose surface folly disguises hidden depths of wisdom. Being outside the normal order of society he can say things that no one else would dare to, and thereby shows us things we might otherwise avoid looking at.

THE TRICKS OF THE TRADE

Spells, potions and magic wands are the typical tools of witches and wizards and their presence is another indicator of magic dreams. Being "spellbound" in a dream is akin to being in the thrall of an influential person in waking life, and indeed the lesson to be learnt from such dreams could be to look at whether you are overly impressed by someone, being taken in or manipulated by them, or attracted to something in them which is not real.

If you think the dream character does seem to correspond to someone in your waking life, take note of your gut response to them, notice how trustworthy they are, and try to see beyond any surface appeal.

ABOVE The sorcerer's art lies in combining powders and potions to make spells. To dream of sorcery may mean that you need to take an inventive approach to a problem, or perhaps put things together in a unique, but powerful, way.

RIGHT A wizard is a powerful magic maker but make sure he is genuine. Is there someone in your life who has an unhealthy power over you?

ABOVE A tall pointy hat and a broomstick are a witch's standard regalia. How often do you find yourself wishing you had the power to make radical changes in your life?

THE SUPERNATURAL

THE MYSTERIOUS WORLD OF THE SUPERNATURAL IS INHABITED BY GHOSTLY FIGURES, VAMPIRES, WEREWOLVES AND A HOST OF OTHER CREATURES. MANY OF US LIKE THE COMFORT OF FAMILIARITY, AND FIND THE IDEA OF THE SUPERNATURAL DISTURBING AND TERRIFYING. BY AND LARGE WE AVOID CONTACT WITH THIS WORLD, BUT SOME SEEK IT OUT AND LINK UP WITH IT IN SÉANCES OR BY EXTRA-SENSORY PERCEPTION (ESP). DREAMS OF THE SUPERNATURAL CAN IMPLY THAT OUR PSYCHE WANTS US TO SPEND MORE TIME AND EFFORT INVESTIGATING SUCH MATTERS AS ACKNOWLEDGING OUR SHADOW SELF. ALTERNATIVELY, WE MAY NEED TO MAKE A RADICAL CHANGE OF DIRECTION IN OUR LIVES.

GHOSTS

When ghosts appear in our dreams they can represent unfinished business. Ghosts are the unsettled spirits of the dead who haven't yet found their place in the hereafter, perhaps because they still have some tie to earthly matters. As ghosts are neither fully present nor fully absent, they raise questions about uncertainty and lack of clarity, perhaps about who we are or what we are doing in our lives.

In ghostly figures we are confronted with our own mortality. They give us some sneak preview of the afterlife, without really offering any explanations. Perhaps they offer some hope as well that our existence does not terminate with our death. We can also see them as shadows of ourselves –

personifications of our own dark nature, the shadowy side of our selves that we often dare not face.

How the ghosts behave in our dream and how we respond to them is important in discovering what they mean. Some are invisible, others may be shadowy translucent figures. They may be noisy poltergeists or silent figures that only betray their presence by moving things, pointing to our lack of control over our own environment. They may interact with us, but often don't do so directly. You may feel terrified or stressed, or be comforted by their presence. They may be recognizable as strangers, deceased friends or relatives, or famous people. Your relationship to them as such will also affect what they mean in your dream – for instance the ghost may be

BELOW RIGHT Ghosts and phantoms may haunt us in our dreams and this can feel very unnerving. Try to find out what the ghostly visitation is about.
BELOW Strange unearthly figures may appear in our dreams, but these are usually the products of our dreaming psyche.

GHOSTLY DREAM

"I was sitting in a graveyard surrounded by pale, ghoulish figures. I knew they were out to devour me – it was as if I were destined to be a victim, to have my life drawn from me. There was nothing I could do as these ghastly, ghostly shapes crowded around me. But the horror that woke me wasn't them – it was the feeling of my own quiet acquiescence.

When I was thinking about this dream I realized this was exactly how I was behaving in my relationship, allowing my partner to make all the decisions, and it was burying my personality. On going back over the dream in my mind, I knew that I had to return to that graveyard and shout 'No!' and make them retreat, not just sit there and let them eat my soul."

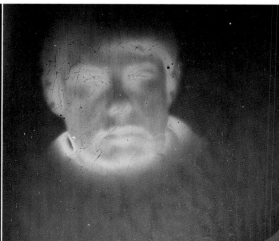

your nagging mother-in-law who is very much alive but casts a shadow over you and is forever interfering with your life.

Ghosts may be all that remain to us of people who have already died, and seeing one may provide a welcome opportunity to have contact with a loved one who has died but whose death you may not yet have come to terms with.

SUPERNATURAL PARASITES

Vampires are the infamous figures of the dead who leave the grave after dark and suck the blood of the living, drawing with it their life-force, or energy, which they need to survive, and often killing their victims in the process. These are the parasites of the supernatural world, and they share this dubious distinction with other ghostly figures such as ghouls, who prey on the dead, and the succubi and incubi, demons who take human form to suck the sexual energy out of sleeping people. In more superstitious times the Catholic Church blamed many a nocturnal

RIGHT A wolf baying at full moon is often associated with supernatural forces. Full moon is when the forces of nature are at their strongest, and traditionally has strong associations with lunacy.

sexual awakening on such apparitions, while in China ghosts are said to be "hungry".

Vampires are defeated by daylight or the simple but powerful icon of the wooden cross, showing us that even such basic forms of protection can give us an escape route from the horror. Indeed, dreams of parasitic ghosts and vampires are often about self-protection. If you dream of these creatures you should look at those aspects of your own life where you feel you are being devoured or having the life sucked out of you. Perhaps you are feeling either used or dominated by your partner, or you have an exploitative boss who makes you work long hours so that you don't have the life or energy to do the things you enjoy. More unusually you may be acting parasitically and have some kind of disturbance around

this. These dreams are our unconscious mind's way of working out such relationships, as well as making us aware that something is wrong.

BATS AND WEREWOLVES

Like vampires, werewolves and bats are nocturnal creatures that suck their victim's blood. A vampire can "shape shift" into a bat, while a werewolf is a human who becomes a vicious beast at full moon. If these creatures appear in your dreams it may be to draw attention to something going on in your life that is frightening or tricky to deal with.

BELOW LEFT Be wary of bewitching figures, as vampires in particular often appear seductive. Who is trying to suck your blood?
BELOW The spirits of the dead come to life at night. A disused building can appear very spooky.

diagnostic tool for illness, dreams as 32, 74
diary, keeping 44, 76-77
diet 164
disasters 113, 214-215
discipline 208-209
disguise techniques 41
displacement dreams 41
Divine Child, Jungian archetype 59
divorce 156, 186-187
doorways 226-227
dream groups 45
dream incubation 16-17, 18-19, 26
driving 236-237

E
Earth 124-125
eccentricity 169
EEG investigations 38
Egypt, Ancient 16-17, 34-35
elements 61
   air 125, 128-129
   earth 124-125
   fire 125, 126-127
   water 125, 130-131
emotions 130, 154-155, 166, 202, 215
empathic dreams 47
encounters in daily life 180-181
enemy figures 210-211
energy 194-195
entrances 226-227
essential oils, use of 80, 81
exercise 164
exits 226-227

F
falling 220-221

falling in love 160-161
fame 180, 189
family 174-175
fantasy 240-241, 248
   creatures 240
   lovers 178-179
   sexual 162
Far East 24-25, 34
Faraday, Ann 44
farm animals 134-135
fatness in people 117
fear 222-223
fictional literature 240-241
films 188
fire 125, 126-127
fish 137
flags 106
flowers 133
flying 48, 220-221, 236
fog 123
forms, open and closed 117
free association 41, 79, 93
free dreams 56
French, Thomas 44
Freud, Sigmund 17, 21, 40-41, 42, 44, 58, 62, 64, 66, 79, 106, 134, 162, 220
friends 176-177
Fromm, Erika 44
fruit 133
funeral 156
future 15, 46-47, 75, 212-213, 246-247

G
Gabriel, angel 35
games 143, 199, 204-205
Ganesh, Hindu god 22, 34
gardening 133
gates 16, 121
gates of horn and ivory 18

gatherings 182-183, 191
Gengis Khan, Mongol conqueror 46
Gestalt techniques 44, 78, 94
ghosts 250-151
gift-giving 185
Gilgamesh, king of Sumer 14
goals 198-199
gods and goddesses in myths 242-243
Great Father, Jungian archetype 60
Great Mother, Jungian archetype 60
Greece, Ancient 18-21
Gregory of Nyssa 26-27
grief 156-157
griffin 243
guilt 158-159

H
Hall, Calvin 44, 64
hallucination 19, 50-51
health 164
Heraclitus, Greek philosopher 20
herbs, mind-altering 19, 51
hieroglyphs 107
Hinduism 22-23, 34, 129, 170
Hippocrates, Greek doctor 19
Hitler, Adolf 46
home 230-231
   danger in 214-215
   décor
Homer, Greek poet 18
Hopi tribe 33
hospital 167
house 230
   building 231
hun 24

hybrid creatures 243
hypnogogia 50
Hypnos, Greek god 18

I
illness 166-167
Imhotep, Eygptian god 16
incubus 28
India 22-23, 34
influencing dreams 86-87
injuries 166
insanity 168
insects 135
insecurity 110
inspiration from dreams 89
interpreting dreams, ways of 74-75, 78-79
Interpretation of Dreams by Sigmund Freud 40
Inuits 33
investigating dreams, methods of 78-79
Iroquois tribe 32
irrationality 168-169
Ishtar, Babylonian goddess 15
Islam 35

J
Jesus, coming of 35
jobs 146, 202-203
journal, keeping 44, 76-77
journeys 234-235
   vehicles 236-237
Judaism 34, 35, 106, 132
Jung, Carl Gustav 20, 42-43, 44, 56, 58-59, 62, 67, 106, 249

K
Kabbalah 132
Kalahari Bushmen 31
Kali, Hindu goddess 22
Kleitman and Aserinsky 38
Koran 35
Kubla Khan, poem by Samuel Coleridge 51

L
labyrinths 224-225
landscapes 66-67, 120-121
latent content 40-41, 44
leaving home 186
legends 95, 240, 242-243
levels of dreaming 62-63

Lichtenberg, G.C. 29
Lie-tsu, Chinese Taoist
text 24
life cycle 138-139
ageing 148-149
birth 140-141
childhood 142-143
death 150-151
middle years 146-147
youth 144-145
Lincoln, Abraham, US
president 46, 212
literature, fictional 240-241
little dreams 56
Little Prince, by Antoine de
Saint-Exupery 59
logic 64-65, 168
loss 156-157, 186-187
lost, state of being 224-225
love, falling in 160-161
lovers 178-179
lucid dreaming 24, 52-53
lucky dreams 22

M
machines 232-233
madness 168-169
magic 248-249
magician 248, 249
Magritte, René 89
Mahrer, Alvin 44
Mamu, Babylonian goddess
15
manifest content 40-41, 44
maps 234
Maury, Alfred 29
mazes 224-225
McCartney, Paul 89
measurement instruments
102-103

meditation 80
Mendeleyev, Dmitri 88
Meng Shu, Chinese writings
25
mental institution 168
mermaids 243
Middle Ages 27, 28
middle years 146-147
minotaur 243
mist 123
modern approaches to dream
interpretation 44-45
Mohammed, founder of
Islam 35
monarch 106
money 206-207
Moon 15, 56
Morpheus, Greek god 18
mountains 120
Mu Jen dolls 25
music 190-191
myths 95, 242-243

N
Napoleon Bonaparte 46
nature 26, 118-137
disasters 113, 194, 214
seasons 108-109, 123
Navajo tribe 32-33
Nazis 106
nests 136
New Testament 35, 56
Night Journey of Mohammed
35
nightmares 65, 68-69
children's 71, 85
Ninsun, Babylonian goddess
14
Nordby, Vernon 44, 64
North American Indians

32-33, 56, 82, 133
nuclear power 112-113
numerology 104-105, 116

O
obsession 169
Odyssey, The by Homer 18
Oedipus, legend of 243
official dreams 56
Old Testament 34-35, 56
On the Making of Man by
Gregory of Nyassa 26
Oneirocritica by Artemidoris
21
oracle, Delphic 19
origins of the universe 108
orthodox sleep 10
Ouspensky, P.D. 63
out-of-body experiences
(OBE) 49, 71

P
Pagiboti people, Zaire 31
pain 166-167
Paracelsus, alchemist 48
paradoxical sleep 10
paralysis 165, 223
paranoia 169
parents 174
performing for an audience
188-189
Perls, Frederick (Fritz) 44, 78
Persona, Jungian archetype
58
pets 134
phasic dreams 38
philosophers, classical world
20
photography 190
planning dreams 86-87

plants 132-133
mind-altering 19, 51
Plato, Greek philosopher
20-21
p'o 24
power 106, 107, 112-113
magic 248-249
money 206-207
prayer 171
precognitive dreams 46-47
premonitions 46-47
preparations 80-81
problem solving 88-89
prophecy 19, 21, 26,
246-247
psychic dream phenomena
47
psychopathic behaviour 169
psychology see Freud, Jung
public figures 180
punishment 158, 208-209
puns 17
pursuit 222-223
pyramid 116

R
rain 122, 123
Raphael (Robert Cross Smith)
29
rapid eye movements (REM)
10, 38, 223
recall of dreams 76-77, 93
recording dreams 44, 76-77
recurring dreams 213
Egyptian ritual 17
relationships 90-95
religion 34-35, 170-171
symbols 106-107
REM (rapid eye movements)
10, 38, 223

INDEX

representational dreams 41
retirement 148-149
rivers 120, 130
roads 121
role of dreaming 10-11
romance 160-161
Rome, Ancient 18, 21
rooms 230-231
Royal Book of Dreams,
  The by Raphael 29
running from pursuers
  222-223

S
Saint-Exupéry, Antoine de 59
Salmon of Wisdom 26
satyrs 243
Savary, L.M. 45
scenery 66-67, 120-121
science 104
scientific research 38-39
screen performance 188
sea 130
seasons 108-109, 123
security 110
self as source of dreams 74
separation 186-187
serapeums 16
Serapis, Egyptian god 16
sexuality 27, 28, 42, 66, 106,
  131, 162-163, 220, 229
Shadow, Jungian archetype
  58
shaman 33, 51, 133, 135
shape 116
Shiva, Hindu god 22
short people 117
shouting 193
shrine for sleep, making
  bedroom into 80-81
sibling relationships 175

Sioux tribe 56
Sisyphus, legend of 243
skills, development of 86-87
sky axes 83
sleep patterns 10
Smith, Robert Cross
  (Raphael) 29
smoke 127
snakes 19
snow 122
space 102-103
  aliens 244-245
sphinx 17, 243
spiders 135
spirals 116
spirituality 34-35, 45,
  170-171
split personality 169
sports 204-205
square 116
stage performance 188
staircases 229
Star of David 106
Stevenson, Robert Louis 89
storms 83, 113, 122-123
strangers 180-181
streets 121
strength 110-111
success 200-201
succubus 28
Sumer 14, 15
supernatural 250-251
surrealism 240
  landscapes 66
swastika 106
symbolization dreams 41
symbols 106-107

T
tallness 116
Talmud 35

Taoism 24, 129
Tart, Charles 53
teams 200, 204-205
tears 122, 131
technology 233
teenage years 144-145, 160
telepathic dreams 47
temples 14, 15, 16, 18-19,
  80
texture 117
theatre 188
thinness in people 117
Thotmes 1V, pharaoh of
  Egypt 17
time 102-103
tonic dreams 38-39
tools
  assistance for dreaming
    82-85
  in everyday life 232-233
toys 142-143
transformation 248
travel 234-235
  companions 235
  vehicles 236-237
Treatise on Dreams by
  Hippocrates 19
Tree of Life 133
trees 26, 27, 132
triangular shape 116
trickery 248-249
Trickster, Jungian archetype
  59
TTAQ (Title, theme, affect,
  question) method 45

U
UFOs 245
Ullman, Montague 44
Uluru Australian Aboriginal
  site 31

unconscious mind 11, 40,
  62, 75
understanding dreams, ways
  of 74-75
unlucky dreams 22
Upanishads 23

V
vampires 251
Van Eeden, Frederick 52
Vedas 22-23
vegetables 133
vehicles 236-237
violence 194-195
visual arts 190
Von Leibniz, Gottfried 29

X
Xerxes, Persian leader 18

W
walls 121
war 210-211
warnings 15, 16, 21, 75,
  212-213
water 122, 125, 130-131
weakness 110-111
weather 122-123
web of life 84
weddings 184, 185
wellbeing 164
werewolves 251
wind 128-129
witches 28, 248, 249
wizards 248, 249
work 133, 146, 202-203

Y
youth 144-145, 160

Z
Zeus, Greek god 18